CW00550331

Praise for *Building the Digital Enterprise*

"The impact of digital technology on the ways technology, the enterprise, and people interact with the wider ecosystem of the economy is unprecedented. Understanding digital technology is critical to scale new outcomes and values. Mark Skilton provides excellent new mechanisms for practitioners to think digitally in order to drive new monetization in their enterprise."

—Professor Dr Ola Henfridsson, Professor of Information Systems & Management ISM, Warwick Business School WBS, University of Warwick, UK; Visiting Professor, Swedish Center for Digital Innovation, University of Gothenburg; Senior Editor of *Information Systems Research* and *Journal of Information Technology*; former Associate Editor and Senior Editor of *MIS Quarterly*

"The impact of digitization can be seen across all sectors: enabling organizations to deliver a superior customer experience through multiple channels, creating new products and services using disruptive technologies, and redefining hitherto successful business models. This represents a huge opportunity for new value growth, but also presents significant challenges in privacy, cyber security, and the need for a shift in leadership style and culture. Mark Skilton's book is an important contribution to our understanding of the evolution of business performance and industrial transformation in the digital age. The volume highlights how a variety of practitioners in business and IT are using best practice to innovate and create successful digital businesses."

—Anita Chandraker, Digital Lead, Member of PA's Management Group, PA Consulting Group

"The world economy is being transformed by digitization and developing the practice required for new digital businesses is critical for companies and markets. Mark Skilton shows how companies are dynamically building new digital solutions and sets up a way to think digitally in this new world, as well as how to put that mind-set into practice."

—Professor Dr Irene Ng, Professor of Marketing and Service Systems, Warwick Manufacturing Group WMG, University of Warwick, UK; Director, International Institute of Product and Service Innovation; ESRC/ Innovate UK Innovation Caucus Thought Leader; author of *Value & Worth: Creating New Markets in the Digital Economy*

"The march toward digitalization is forcing organizations today to seek ways to maximize new technologies at scales never seen before. In this rapidly changing business climate, Enterprise Architecture can help transform how businesses maximize their technology investments to drive higher value for customers, partners, and stakeholders. In this book, Mark Skilton provides practice examples for new digital solutions and illustrates how companies can enable architectural thinking across the enterprise."

—Allen Brown, President and Chief Executive Officer,
The Open Group, Global consortium for enabling business objectives through
International IT Standards; President, Association of
Enterprise Architects (AEA)

"The public sector is increasingly engaged in transformational change, focused on enabling the capabilities of individuals and communities as global economic, social and political forces shape society. Technology is increasingly the default means of engagement and service provision for local and central government as citizens and services become more 'connected'. Mark Skilton's book is an important contribution which illustrates the central role of digital access and delivery in contemporary public service."

—Daniel Goodwin, Advisor;
Consultant; former Local Authority Chief Executive

"The use of technology in healthcare has the potential to transform lives and outcomes not only for patients and clinicians but also the way care in the community and the wider society and its population is practiced. We see rapid advances in the use of medical technology in many life sciences and health-care fields where new innovative ways of treatment to new care models are changing how to think about the collection, analysis, diagnosis, and treatment. Mark Skilton has provided an important link with digital technology and how practitioners need to think in the uses of this technology across industries and bring this into their own field of best practice."

—Professor Dr Christopher James, Professor of Biomedical Engineering,
School of Engineering, University of Warwick, UK;
Director, Warwick Engineering in Biomedicine; Editor-in-Chief,
IET Healthcare Technology Letters

"Businesses and the economy are being driven my many forces of change as society, incomes and new regulations disrupt and change how money and markets operate. The 'digital economy' is increasingly a central issue in enabling the 'connected society' and driving new business models and practices. Mark Skilton's book provides important practitioner guidance on how to think about digital business and its economic outcomes and implications."

—Dr Alexander Roy, Economist, Strategy Manager,
Manchester Airports Group (MAG)

Digital technologies are revolutionizing the business world – challenging existing practices and enabling a new generation of business models.

Business in the Digital Economy is an accessible new series of books that tackles the business impacts of technology and the emerging digital economy. Aimed at non-technical, mid-senior executives and business managers, this series will help inform choices and guide decision-making on all major technological trends and their implications for business.

Series editors: Alan Brown and Mark Thompson

Available titles:

Predictive Analytics, Data Mining and Big Data
Steven Finlay
9781137379290

Digitizing Government
Alan Brown, Jerry Fishenden and Mark Thompson
9781137443625

Series ISBN: 9781137395245

A Guide to Constructing Monetization Models Using Digital Technologies

Building the Digital Enterprise

Mark Skilton

Professor of Practice, Warwick Business School, UK

First published 2015 by
PALGRAVE MACMILLAN

Palgrave Macmillan in the UK is an imprint of Macmillan Publishers Limited, registered in England, company number 785998, of Houndmills, Basingstoke, Hampshire RG21 6XS.

Palgrave Macmillan in the US is a division of St Martin's Press LLC, 175 Fifth Avenue, New York, NY 10010.

Palgrave Macmillan is the global academic imprint of the above companies and has companies and representatives throughout the world.

Palgrave® and Macmillan® are registered trademarks in the United States, the United Kingdom, Europe and other countries.

ISBN 978–1–137–47770–5 hardback

This book is printed on paper suitable for recycling and made from fully managed and sustained forest sources. Logging, pulping and manufacturing processes are expected to conform to the environmental regulations of the country of origin.

A catalogue record for this book is available from the British Library.

A catalog record for this book is available from the Library of Congress.

Typeset by MPS Limited, Chennai, India.

In memory of my father, who lived through many technological changes, and my mother, who is a rock of selfless love

—

Contents

PART I: The Era of Digital Ecosystems

1 Introduction – The Rise of Technological Ecosystems ⁄ 3

PART III: Digital Techniques and Practices

List of Figures and Tables

Figures

Tables

Foreword

Simon Ricketts, Group Chief Information Officer, Rolls-Royce PLC

We are living in times of unprecedented social and technological change. The tools that individuals and organizations can now access provide real opportunities to transform how our society and commerce operate. Although this is an observation that could have been made at any time in the past 30 years – by definition, technology is always about change – what is different today is the speed of change and the scale of impact. The question arises, therefore, as to how best to navigate the digital world, sifting hype from reality whilst ensuring that organizations genuinely benefit from the opportunities available.

For Boards of Management and business leaders the major challenge is always to pick the winners and to ensure that the chosen digital capabilities genuinely transform the organization. Another challenge is to manage technology from different generations until it becomes clear how to retire legacy: success depends heavily on ensuring that the "old" stops and that new processes and tools genuinely become the operating norm. The task is not helped by the propensity of the IT and consulting industry to hype bubbles of technology with claims that are often out of context and not wholly thought through. Picking the right capabilities and guaranteeing transformation requires some good habits.

Good starting questions are always, "to what extent does our current technology enable our plans and strategies?" and "to what extent are our strategies informed by an appreciation of technology that is available?" These might also be informed by observations on how well the customer or employee experience compares with competitor and peer experience. Ensuring that conclusions are based on evidence and that valuable dialogue takes place requires a clear approach to the organization of the technology function, how collaboration with the rest of the business is enabled and the process steps that ensure this.

Picking a job title for the IT leader so that it reflects current technology can be helpful but also a huge distraction. The move from Data Processing Manager to Systems Manager then to Information Technology Director and Chief Information Officer took place over some 20 years and reflected accurately the nature of the task to be managed as technology changed. Recent debates on whether the leader should be known as the CIO, CTO, or Chief Digital Officer is less helpful. This is because the choice of title is primarily about emphasis and in fact all these domains have relevance. What matters is picking one, sticking with it and, most importantly, operating a process that guarantees collaboration between the function and the rest of the business.

The critical issue is to define the portfolio of digital capability that the organization needs, getting it built and implemented whilst retiring earlier generations. DDRR is a useful aide-memoire. *Defining* the portfolio entails answering those strategic questions referred to above. *Delivering* and *running* the associated digital capability is very much about understanding the technology available and ensuring that current trends on cost effectiveness and agility are exploited. A failure to *retire* dilutes benefits and increases cost. These principles remain constant and help navigate new technology.

Whilst the term *"digital"* in the context of information technology can be seen as trendy, its prominence in just about everything one reads in this area is evidence that the subject has moved well beyond the domain of specialists. This book is an important contribution in describing how digital enterprises can work and how the various individual technologies might define the next phase of social and commercial innovation.

Preface

My father was a technical design draftsman who came from an era of pencil and paper drawings and slide rules. He had grown up in the years of World War II as an evacuee and gained an early interest in aeronautical design and flying. I remember seeing his college aerospace engineering maths books on calculus, and subscriptions to *Air Pictorial* and *Air Reserve Gazette* magazines with the many drawings of aircraft specifications and engineering cross-sections. I recall the first sight of a ramjet engine design diagram and the moment the "penny dropped" in realizing how thrust was generated by the expanding airflow heated through a constricted chamber. It enabled the engine capability by the sheer shape contours of the engine manifold design, together with the metallurgical properties in materials to support such high temperatures. The geometric shape perfectly illustrated the relationship between *form* and *function* that I found to be an invaluable lesson later in life when designing solutions. Before his career in technical design, my father had served in the Air Training Corps as part of National Service, became a trained cartographer, and was stationed in Cyprus to make maps of the Mediterranean island strategically located between southern Europe and North Africa. His early days of volunteer flying in Air Training Corps gliders had given him exposure to navigation skills that had been a trigger for his entry into the Royal Air Force where he combined his planning skills.

Looking back through the past 50 years, these three career roles of flyer, map maker, and designer have seen profound technological change. Map making back then involved using aerial photography of the terrain and scouting to locations with optical telescopes, compasses, sextants, and geometric quadrants. The creation of maps with accurate distances, elevations, and positions could take several months to transcribe into paper copies. Collected location information needed to be recorded meticulously by handwritten notes and by visiting the actual locations in person – there was no electronic transmission of this data, and visits had to be regularly repeated by trained personnel in order to update changes to the maps. Today, satellites enable geospatial-positioning navigation and digital imagery that provide real-time location information from any point on the earth. The techniques of digital image scanning and digitization enable both an object and its location data to be automated with meter and centimeter precision. For Google Street View™, for example, people drive around and collect the same information from the comfort of a car seat. Data is transmitted to huge cloud database archives for data analytics and is repurposed in websites and smartphones providing location services – transport directions that are made available via queries that take a matter of seconds. This can be done remotely in the palm of your hand using a smartphone, without having to visit the place.

Technical engineering design was another skill that involved paper drawing boards and complex human drawing skills to render paper-based schematic representation notations of orthogonal, oblique, and isometric projections. There were equally sophisticated part-numbering systems to identify the bills of materials supported by complex manual paper filing systems to coordinate many human designers and manufacturing staff activities in the design process. Specialist technical illustrators were used to create artistic interpretations and images to visualize and document the designs. Today, digital 3D computer-aided design (CAD) and simulation create physical objects that can be rendered and tested virtually, collaborating between designers, often interacting directly with customers and suppliers working remotely in different locations. Industrial robotics can enable control in warehouses and manufacturing, including materials handling with potentially minimal human contact. Computer-aided manufacturing (CAM) through to 3D printing techniques today provide the capability of the computer-aided creation of physical objects that are completely virtual, from original idea right up until the final product stage.

In transportation, planning trips abroad before the internet involved telephone calls, paper boarding tickets, and manual passport checks. If the trip involved air transport, pilot navigation in aircraft involved radio navigation using radio frequencies to determine position on earth together with printed paper maps that required skills in location coordinate reading and the use of on-board direction compasses. Today, online booking of travel plans on websites are routine. Computer software programs of machine-learning algorithms are used widely in the automation of many aspects of this, from searching for better online transport fares to on-board control systems in aircraft flight controls, or automotive vehicles enabling autopilots and self-parking assistance.

These examples show that, through the progress of time, how things get done has radically changed with the advent of new technologies. In so doing, human experience has been redesigned and has altered the potential outcomes and the practices to achieve these experiences.

This book is intended to provide an understanding of the key design ideas for architecting technology solutions using digital design principles. We seek to explore ideas of human perception, visualization, and sensing of spaces and the economic, social, and artistic value and worth in those spaces as a way to better understand how to architect and build workspaces of the future. We aim to explore these ideas in order to help make sense of the new design techniques and objectives that digital systems are introducing. Digitization challenges traditional thinking in architecture design in how we think about physical and virtual spaces. Digitization opens up new possibilities for individuals, enterprises, and the wider business world and society.

Digitization is enveloping and *entangling* everything – everyday objects, rooms, buildings, cities, vehicles, and locations. This phenomenon is creating what I call *digital ecosystems* of products and service experiences that are transforming how people, enterprises, and markets work together and compete in the new economy, the *digital economy*.

The *digital enterprise* is made up of new physical and virtual workspaces. In this book we explore real business enterprise case examples from many industries for lessons learnt in how technology workspaces are *architected*; we explore how digitization creates new business economic and social outcomes via a combination of information systems, business processes, creativity and innovation, commercial and financial engineering, and social change.

A central theme of this book is to understand what digitization of our living and working environment means – how it is changing the way we will need to think in the future in designing workplaces and the everyday objects within them.

Mark Skilton
2015

Acknowledgments

The development of this book has involved many hours of research and interviews with professional practitioners and academics in the field of business and information technology. I would like to give recognition and sincere thanks to the following people who gave their time in discussions, sharing thoughts and ideas that have helped me to craft this book. Simon Ricketts, Group CIO of Rolls-Royce; Simon Bedford, Associate Producer (Digital), Warwick Arts Centre; Geraldine Calpin, Senior Vice President and Global Head of Digital, Hilton International; Gary Lyon, Chief Innovation Officer, MasterCard Labs, MasterCard Worldwide; Matthew Hanmer, Global Product Development, Consumer Products, MasterCard Worldwide; Sybo Dijkstra, Senior Director, Philips Research, UK; Peter Latham, VP Logistics, Coca-Cola Enterprises; Mark Elkins, Head of Digital Sales and Marketing, Coca-Cola Enterprises, and Lesley Tout, Supply Chain Systems Director, Coca-Cola Enterprises; Alan Welby, Executive Director of Liverpool City Local Enterprise Partnership; Daniel Goodwin, Executive Director of Finance and Policy at the Local Government Association, and Chief Executive of St Albans City & District Council; Dr Alex Roy, Economist, New Economy, Manchester City Council; Ulf Venne, Senior Manager, Customer Engagement, DHL; Alison Crook, General Manager of Supply Chain HSS, Unipart Logistics; Professor Joe Nandhakumar, Information Systems and Management, and Assistant Dean, Warwick Business School, University of Warwick, UK; Professor Ola Henfridsson, Information Systems and Management and Head of ISM faculty, Warwick Business School, University of Warwick, UK; Vikas Vishnoi, Full-Time MBA, Warwick Business School, University of Warwick, UK; Professor Irene Ng, Marketing and Service Systems, and Director of the International Institute for Product and Service Innovation at WMG, University of Warwick, UK; Dr Susan Wakenshaw, Research Fellow, WMG; Xia Mao, Senior Research Fellow,

WMG; Allen Brown, President and CEO of The Open Group; Dr Chris Harding, Director of Interoperability, The Open Group; Jacqui Taylor, CEO of FlyingBinary; Shaon Talukder, CEO of GeoTourist; Ben Waller, Senior Researcher, ICDP; Dr Vinay Vaidya, Chief Technology Officer, KPIT; Rupert Fallows, Services Business Development, KIPT; Professor Christopher James, Director, Warwick Engineering in Biomedicine, School of Engineering, University of Warwick, UK.

Many thanks also to the Palgrave Macmillan series editors; Professor Alan W. Brown, Associate Dean, Entrepreneurship and Innovation, Surrey Business School, University of Surrey, UK; and Dr Mark Thompson, Senior Lecturer Information Systems, Cambridge Judge Business School, University of Cambridge, UK; and to Palgrave Macmillan for the opportunity to contribute to this series.

Special thanks to Simon Ricketts for his kind support and foreword; and to the chapter contributors Professor Irene Ng, Jacqui Taylor, Shaon Talukder, Simon Bedford, Dr Susan Wakenshaw, Ben Waller, and to Daniel Goodwin, who was immensely helpful. Also a big thank you to my script reviewers Dr Chris Harding, Forum Director of Interoperability at The Open Group; Philipp Kukai, PhD researcher in digital strategy at the Information Systems Group at Warwick Business School, UK, and Vikas Vishnoi, full-time MBA, Warwick Business School, UK and co-founder of Aevesto Technologies. Also a personal thanks to Vladimir Banarek for great discussions on the meaning of ecosystems; and to Penelope Gordon for her invaluable insights in product strategy monetization and metrics.

I would like to add a personal thanks to Professor Mark Taylor, Finance and Dean of Warwick Business School; Professor Andrew Lockett, Strategy & Entrepreneurship and Deputy Dean; Professor Joe Nandhakumar, Information Systems and Management, and Assistant Dean, Warwick Business School; and Professor Ola Henfridsson, Information Systems and Management and Head of ISM faculty, Warwick Business School, University of Warwick, UK, for their kind support and my endeavors at Warwick Business School.

Many thanks to all the contributors to the book and to all my colleagues and friends who have supported me over the years; it means a great deal to me. I hope this book provides some recognition for all our efforts – and to those who seek to make an original thought leadership contribution and recognize the importance of respect for professional competency-led practitioners in this important and exciting revolutionary time in technology.

Disclaimer

All company names, trade names, trademarks, trade dress designs/logos, copyright images, and products referenced in this book are the property of their respective owners. No company references in this book sponsored this book or the content thereof.

About the Author

Mark Skilton is Professor of Practice in Information Systems and Management at Warwick Business School. With over 20 years' experience in information technology in many commercial and public sector businesses, he specializes in helping companies realize their business value, covering social media networks, big data, mobility, machine to machine (M2M), internet of things (IoT), and cloud computing. He has worked with some of the top global international companies at board level to realize their vision of digital operating models across their complete technology landscapes. Mark is now Digital Leader at PA Consulting and, prior to that, was Global Director of Strategy at Capgemini. Previously, Mark was European CTO of services, outsourcing, and strategic technology consulting solutions at CSC. He has been Head of Digital business analysis at BSkyB TV and media company; led business re-engineering engagements at KPMG Consulting, and worked in transforming the business and IT of companies in over 25 countries worldwide. Since 2010 Mark has held international standards body roles in The Open Group, where he was co-chair of cloud computing and leading open platform 3.0 initiatives and standards publications. Mark is active in the ISO JC38 distributed architecture standards and in the "Hubs-of-all-things," a multidisciplinary project funded by the Research Council's UK Digital Economy Programme. Mark is also active in cyber security forums at Warwick University, Ovum Security Summits, and INFOSEC. He has spoken at the EU Commission on Digital Ecosystems Agenda and is an EU competition judge on Smart Outsourcing Innovation. Mark has an MBA, as well as a post-graduate qualification in production engineering and design management from Cambridge University and a degree in applied engineering science subjects from University of Sheffield.

Notes on Contributors

Simon Bedford

Simon Bedford is a freelance digital and theater producer, working on a range of both digital and theater projects. Most recently he was Associate Producer (Digital) at Warwick Arts Centre where he curated and produced a new strand of projects that explored creative uses of new technology. Simon previously worked at Hoipolloi theater company for eight years, becoming the company's Executive Producer/CEO in 2011. He led the company's online and social media explorations, demonstrating how they could diversify both artistic output and communication with audiences. For Hoipolloi, Simon produced award-winning theater in the UK, at the Edinburgh Festival Fringe, and on international tours across Europe and to Australia, Canada, Colombia, and the United States. From 2010 to 2013 he was an elected board member of the Independent Theatre Council.

Geraldine Calpin

Geraldine Calpin is Senior Vice President and Global Head of Digital at Hilton Worldwide, responsible for setting the strategic direction for Hilton's digital guest agenda, and maximizing commercial advantage from all direct digital channels. She joined Hilton Worldwide in 2002. During her tenure, she has been responsible for the launch of Hilton's pioneering digital check-in with room selection solution at over 4000 hotels, the introduction of its e-commerce function, and the development of its unique e-commerce and demand generation program for hotels globally. Prior to joining Hilton Worldwide, she held various roles within the travel industry, including sales, planning, operations, and marketing roles at Trusthouse Forte and Le Méridien Hotels.

Alison Crook

Alison is General Manager of Supply Chain HSS for key Unipart Logistics Industrial clients, developing best practice and waste reduction that impact both the customer experience and cost to serve. Alison has over 19 years' experience of managing complex supply chains using the principles of the Unipart Way to deliver operational excellence. Predominantly focused within the automotive industry, she has also worked within both the defense and industrial sectors. Alison joined Unipart Logistics in 1995 as a business graduate from Cardiff University, UK. Her core disciplines have been inventory and supplier management and many roles in global supply chain management. This experience includes helping to establish a global control center, and delivering industry-leading performance by combining the Unipart Way with technology to create fingertip control of a complex supply chain that allowed significant supply chain costs and service improvements to be realized.

Sybo Dijkstra

Sybo Dijkstra is Head of Philips Research UK, where programs in oral healthcare and home healthcare solutions are being conducted. Prior to joining Philips, he was responsible for managing healthcare information management research within Philips Research, driving research and innovation in advanced clinical IT solutions and clinical decision support for Philips Healthcare business. Previous responsibilities include the marketing and strategy of the Philips Healthcare Informatics business worldwide, during which period Philips made significant steps in becoming a worldwide leader in radiology and cardiology IT solutions through the introduction of new innovative products and acquisitions. Sybo has been active in Philips communications and IT businesses, holding various positions in marketing, strategy, and innovation, in which he successfully introduced advanced wireless products as well as the development and introduction of VoIP and PC-based call-processing solutions.

Daniel Goodwin

Daniel has worked in local government for over 30 years and was previously Executive Director of Finance and Policy at the Local Government Association, and Chief Executive of St Albans City & District Council. He holds a Master's in Public Administration from Warwick Business School and contributes widely on public service policy and strategy. Fostering good community health and capacity, and learning how to make sustainable long-term improvement which supports people, are at the heart of Daniel's approach. He is particularly interested in the interrelationships across the public sector and beyond, between evidence, policy, practice, and evaluation. Daniel is Senior Associate Fellow at the University of Birmingham's Institute of Local Government, contributing to thinking on local leadership and services, the wider public sector, and beyond. He is also a Fellow of the Royal Society of Arts. At present he is working on a range of consultancy projects covering futures, demand management, growth, organizational development and strategy, and operational management in both local government and health.

Christopher James

Professor James is Chair in Biomedical Engineering and is Director of Warwick Engineering in Biomedicine at the University of Warwick, UK. He has several distinguished academic and industry posts including appointed Professor of Healthcare Technology and founding director of Digital Healthcare at the University of Warwick, UK. Professor James is a biomedical engineer and his research activity centers on the development of biomedical signal and pattern-processing techniques, as well as the use of technological innovations for use in advancing healthcare and promoting wellbeing. Neural engineering forms a large part of his work, as to date his work has concentrated on the development of advanced processing techniques applied to the analysis of the electromagnetic activity of the human brain, primarily in brain–computer interfacing. He is a past chairman of several global institutes including IEEE and several other international bodies. In 2012 he was awarded the IET Sir Monty Finniston Award for Achievement for his work in the biomedical engineering field. Professor James has held editorial positions for books, journals, and publications covering medical informatics, biomedical engineering, and neural engineering. He is founding editor-in-chief of the IET journal *Healthcare Technology Letters*.

Irene Ng

Irene Ng is Professor of Marketing and Service Systems and Director of the International Institute for Product and Service Innovation at WMG, University of Warwick, UK. She is also an adjunct professor at the National University of Singapore and College Research Associate at Wolfson College, University of Cambridge, UK. Irene studied physics, applied physics, and computer programming as an undergraduate and became an entrepreneur and practitioner for 16 years before switching to an academic career. During her time in industry she occupied a number of senior positions, rising to become CEO of SA Tours and Travel group of companies (Singapore, Malaysia, China, and the UK) and founded Empress Cruise Lines, a company with an annual turnover of US$250 million, which she sold in 1996. A business economist through her doctoral training, Irene's research lies in the trans-disciplinary understanding of value and new business models. Irene is a Research Services Fellow at the Advanced Institute of Management and also the ESRC/NIHR Placement Fellow. Both an entrepreneur and an academic, Irene is passionate about the link between practice and research. She is an advisor to start-ups on new pricing and revenue models in digital businesses.

Alexander Roy

Alexander Roy is Principal Economist at Mott MacDonald, the global engineering and management consultancy. Prior to that he was Deputy Director of Research at New Economy, the economic agency and think tank for the Greater Manchester Combined Authority and its ten partner local authorities. A professional economist with over 15 years of experience in both the public and private sectors, Alex's research has had a particular focus on technology, including how the public sector can support the growth of the knowledge economy, and he has been closely involved in the rollout of digital infrastructure in many parts of the UK.

Shaon Talukder

Like a lot of UK tech enthusiasts, Shaon was the proud recipient of a BBC microcomputer from his parents and learned basic programming at the age of nine. He says: "One of my most proud achievements was being able to code with my able assistant (my sister, Moushmy, nearly four years younger than me) a 'Space Invader-style' game using a swarm of alien letter X's and defending the earth with my spaceship letter 'A' and unleashing hell by firing lots of exclamation marks at the enemy. I am not sure my sister was as impressed." Shaon was educated at Christ's College, Cambridge, and later studied pharmacy at the London School of Pharmacy, and after a period of eight years in the profession went into business with his sister. They started to acquire companies as diverse as high-end serviced apartments (Ideal Rooms) to tech, including EQ Transcriptions, which transcribes audio into text for universities, hospitals, and law firms. Their latest and most exciting venture is the augmented reality platform, GeoTourist, which transforms digital space into educational environments, using GPS and audio to describe the world around you.

Jacqui Taylor

Jacqui is CEO of FlyingBinary, a data analytics and consulting company. She has 25 years' experience of deploying technology change across the world. After implementing a banking regulatory change program with Web 3.0

tools she co-founded FlyingBinary, a web science company which changes the world with data. An appointment for the third year to the Open Data User Group as an Open Data domain expert recognized her as a web scientist of influence in the era of big data and the internet of things (IoT). An inclusion as a data innovator for a number of the smart city initiatives signals the next steps for her company and IoT. Jacqui trains advanced analysts on the science of data visualization; she is a regular speaker on cloud adoption, big data, smarter analytics, and profiting from IoT. Jacqui collaborated with data journalism thought leaders to produce her first book *Mapping the Future*, which signals the changes for the industry. Published in November 2013 by the Digital Enlightenment Forum, Jacqui has contributed a chapter to the 2014 Yearbook relating to her vision for the web and the role that open data will play.

Vinay Vaidya

Vaidya heads the Center for Research in Engineering Sciences and Technology (CREST), Phoenix, Arizona. He is also KPIT's CTO for IT engineering services. He has a PhD in Computer Vision from the University of Washington. At Boeing, he was the youngest person to receive the highest technical honor of Senior Principal Scientist, Associate Technical Fellow. Dr Vaidya serves as the vice chair of IEEE SMC Mumbai. He is an honorary adjunct in the Computer Studies faculty at the Symbiosis Institute in Pune, India. He is a member of the Research Recognition board and a PhD advisor. His outstanding achievements have earned him a position in the 2008 Marquis *Who's Who in the World* 25th anniversary edition. He has published a chapter in the Academic Press book titled *Machine Vision for Inspection and Measurement*. He has several research papers to his credit and continues to conduct research in pattern recognition and image processing, data compression, embedded systems, and security systems.

Ulf Venne

Ulf Venne is Senior Project Manager for Deutsche Post DHL, based in Cologne, Germany. Ulf is currently leading the Customer Engagement team of DHL Resilience360, a logistics risk management solution for supply chains. Before joining DHL he worked for Huawei as supply chain operations lead for Germany. In his studies he was engaged with his own web-design and IT programming company. Ulf holds a Magister Artium degree in Sinology (Chinese culture and language) and Economics from the Friedrich-Alexander-University of Erlangen-Nürnberg.

Susan Wakenshaw

Susan Wakenshaw is a research fellow with the Service Systems group. She is part of Business Innovation Group (Big) at WMG at the University of Warwick, UK. Susan has engaged in various cutting-edge interdisciplinary research projects through collaboration with academic, manufacturing, and the defense industries, such as 3D chocolate printing and new business model; SERTES; KT-Box. Currently she is working on Euro 1.2 million RCUK-funded projects: HAT and other projects such as HARRIET and a project on smart cities and smart citizens. Susan's expertise is in consumer culture theory, consumer identity projects, social theories, viable systems, technology philosophy and privacy. She studied pharmacy, management science, and marketing, and holds a PhD in marketing from the University of Lancaster. She has presented and published academic papers in international journals and conferences (such as Frontiers, QUIS, SERVSIG) in the domain of marketing and service.

Ben Waller

Ben is a senior researcher at the International Car Distribution Programme (ICDP), and is based in the UK. ICDP is an international research-based organization focused on automotive distribution, including the supply and retailing of new and used vehicles, aftersales, network structures, and operations. Through research activities, data services, education, events, and consulting, ICDP works with vehicle makers, dealers, suppliers, and related organizations to improve the quality and effectiveness of the distribution model. Ben has presented to a range of international audiences, from academic conferences to senior executives; additionally, he also authors articles for the business press and delivers executive teaching.

Alan Welby

Alan Welby is Executive Director, Key Growth Sectors, at the Liverpool City Region Local Enterprise Partnership (LEP), UK. Representing the interests of over 500 businesses, the LEP develops and promotes the Liverpool City region. Alan works closely with major companies, universities, the NHS, science parks, and local and national government to drive the development of the future economy of the region. Previously, Alan was Executive Director of Strategy at One North East, the regional development agency. His career has included senior positions in industry, higher education, local government, and the European Commission in Birmingham, London, Brussels, and Madrid.

List of Abbreviations and Acronyms

2SMP	Two-sided marketplace
ACID	Atomicity, consistency, isolation, durability
ADAS	Advanced driver assistance
AGI	Association for geographical information
AI	Artificial intelligence
AIT	Automated identification technologies
ALM	Application lifecycle management
API	Application program interface
ARPU	Average revenue per user
ATM	Automatic teller machine
ATTE	Advanced technology transformation engineering
AUM	Assets under management
B2B	Business to business
B2C	Business to consumer
BASE	Basically available, soft state, eventually consistent
BC	Business continuity
BEPS	Base erosion and profit shift
BPM	Business process management
BREEAM	Building Research Establishment Assessment Methodology

C2B	Consumer to business
C2C	Consumer to consumer
C2P	Content to purchase
CAD	Computer-aided design
CAM	Computer-aided manufacturing
CDO	Chief data officer
CDO	Chief digital officer
CEO	Chief executive officer
CGI	Computer-generated image
Churn	The rate of change of customers arriving and leaving your product or service
CIO	Chief information officer
CMB	Contact memory button
CMO	Chief marketing officer
CSO	Chief security officer
CRM	Customer relationship management
CSR	Corporate social responsibility
CVaR	Calculated value at risk
CX	Customer experience design
DDOS	Distributed denial of service (cyber attacks)
DEco	Digital-enabled ecosystem of systems
DoD	Department of Defense
DOM	Digital operating model
DOVE	Digital operating value ecosystem
DR	Disaster recovery
DSN	Deep Space Network
DSRP	Digital secure remote payments

EA	Enterprise architecture
e-citizen	The use of digital technologies to support society and citizens
e-government	The use of digital technologies to develop government administration and citizen services
e-health	Electronic-enabled health
EMV	Europay, MasterCard, and Visa
EPC	Electronic product code
ERP	Enterprise resource planning
EV	Electric vehicle
FMCG	Fast-moving consumer goods
FRS	Fire and Rescue Services
GDP	Gross domestic product
Geofencing	The ability to track and send notifications to users when in a location
GLAS	Global logistics application suite
GODI	Ghana government open-data website
GPS	Global positioning satellite
GRC	Governance, risk, and compliance
GUI	Graphical user interface
GVC	Global value chains
H2H	Human-to-human interface
H2M	Human-to-machine interface
HFT	High-frequency trading
HIPPA	Health Insurance Portability and Accountability Act
HMO	Health maintenance organization
HPC	High-performance computing
Hypercloud	A term referring to super-scale investment in data center and network infrastructure

IAN	Inter-continental global area network
IATA	International Air Transport Association
iBeacon™	A trademark for an indoor positioning system by Apple Inc.
ICDP	International car distribution program
ICT	Information and communications technology
IGPM	Institute of Governance & Public Management, Warwick Business School, UK
IMF	International Monetary Fund
IO	Input–output
IoT	Internet of things
IP	Intellectual property
IP	Internet protocol address
IPCC	Intergovernmental panel on climate change, UN
ISP	Internet service provider
IS	Information system
ISS	International Space Station
ITESs	Information technology-enabled services
IXP	Internet exchange point
LEP	Local Enterprise Partnership, UK government
LiSi	Levels of information systems interoperability
LAN	Local area network
M2H	Machine-to-human interface
M2M	Machine-to-machine interface
MAN	Municipal area network
MCX	Merchant customer exchange
MDES	MasterCard Digital Enablement Service
MES	Manufacturing execution system

Metadata	A set of data that describes and gives information about other data
m-health	Mobile-enabled health
Mi	More Independent, UK government technology strategy board initiative
ML	Machine learning
MOOC	Massive open online course
MSP	Multi-sided platform
NATO	North Atlantic Treaty Organization
NFC	Near field communication
NGO	Non-governmental organization
NHS	National Health Service, UK
NSP	Network service provider
OECD	Organisation for Economic Co-operation and Development
OEM	Original equipment manufacturer
OP3	Open Platform 3.0^{TM}, The Open Group
OWL	Web Ontology Language Semantics and Abstract Syntax
PAM	Personal ambient monitoring
PAN	Personal area network
Pareto	An economic principle of inequality of inputs and outputs, 80:20 rule
PAYG	Pay-as-you-go
PCST	Privacy, confidentiality, security, and trust
PDM	Product data management
PEC	Physical, extended, contextual
PIM	Product information management
PLC	Programmable logic controller
PLM	Product lifecycle management

PSS	Product-service system
QR	Quick response
Ramsey price	Variation of marginal cost pricing based on scarcity of products and resources
RFID	Radio frequency identification
SaaS	Software as a service
SCM	Supply chain management
SDK	Software development tool kit
SEC	US Securities and Exchange Commission
SKU	Stock-keeping unit
SmartCity	The use of digital technologies to enable citizen services in city living spaces and efficiencies
SoSi	System of systems integration
SRM	Supplier relationship management
ST	Structuration theory
STC	Spatial, temporal, contextual model
STS	Sociotechnical system
Telecare	The remote support of healthcare to patients and assisted living services
Thin provision	Demand over allocation method to optimize utilization
TIFF	Tagged image file format
TMS	Transport management system
TRM	Technology reference model
Ts & Cs	Terms and conditions
TSN	Terrestrial satellite service
TSP	Two-sided platform
UI	User interface
UN	United Nations

UNPACS	United Nations Public Administration Country Services
USEFIL	Unobtrusive Smart Environments for Independent Living
UX	User experience
V2V	Vehicle to vehicle
VaR	Value at risk
VC	Venture capitalist
VMI	Vendor-managed inventory
VNE	Value network ecosystem
VO	Virtual organization
VPN	Virtual private network
VRM	Vendor relationship management
WAN	Wide area network
WBS	Warwick Business School, University of Warwick, UK
WEF	World Economic Forum
WHO	World Health Organization, UN
XDI	Internet exchange point
WLAN	Wireless area network
WMG	Warwick Manufacturing Group, University of Warwick, UK
WTTC	World Travel and Tourism Council
ZDI	Zero-day initiative

Book Structure

This book aims to be distinctive in several ways. First, it presents a breadth of case study examples to define digital ecosystems that are now making up the digital economy on a detailed and practical level, offering a comprehensive view across many industry sectors. Second, it seeks to be a portal to the world of common methods for linking together key digital technologies to meet the goals, benefits, and challenges of building a digital enterprise in the new economy.

The scope of this book covers the development of digital technologies in their use to drive digital enterprise and the digital economy. We identify emerging foundational digital practices in 25 case studies and how these drive new social and consumer value. We then explore selected industry sector exemplar case studies of how enterprise has used digital technologies to develop successful digital business models. The book provides guidance on how digital workspaces are used for business digitization and the types of monetization mechanisms to use in order to drive value and adoption of digital products and services in the enterprise ecosystem and wider economy.

Among its most distinctive features the book provides:

- An introduction to the key concepts of digitization.
- An extensive discussion supported by case studies of digital business-model design, drawing from practitioners across many industries in the private and public sectors.
- A novel new approach for defining technologies into digital workspaces that drive payback outcomes.
- An expanding set of techniques from cross-case analysis to illustrate successful design methods for building digital enterprise and digital ecosystems in the digital economy.

These features are key because understanding what is important in the design and analysis of digital ecosystems tends to create the greatest challenges for people and organizations trying to build and grow their digital enterprise. Following the definitions to digital ecosystems and the use cases, the book has two extensive and important chapters pertaining to identifying and making sense of physical enterprise models and turning them into successful digital business models using digital workspaces. This is followed by specific techniques for how these workspaces become digital platforms that enable growth, payback, and value outcomes for consumers and providers. The purpose of this provides a connective flow between strategies to execution across digital technologies.

The book seeks to appeal to practising professional and academic audiences seeking examples of how successful digital business models have been constructed in industry. The focus of the text is on the lessons learnt, drawn from cross-case analysis and – from all these cases – from direct experience of practitioners in the field. Each chapter will seek to define an insightful set of characteristics associated with digital ecosystem solutions success.

The sequence of the chapters deliberately follows a linear flow from understanding the digital ecosystem concepts, helping to bound the scope that we explore in the book and framing the illustrative case examples in industries. We then introduce a novel way of understanding the digitization of physical workplaces into workspaces using technologies. The final chapters provide an analysis and set of lessons learnt in designing key digital workspaces using technologies that make up a digital enterprise to achieve successful payback outcome.

Part I

The Era of Digital Ecosystems

Introduction – The Rise of Technological Ecosystems

Chapter Introduction

The purpose of this book is to provide a practitioner's perspective of what it is like to develop the next generation of information technology solutions that computerize the corporate enterprise.

I hope it will also be a primer for what it means "to be digital" and the impact that has had not only on business practice but also on the expanding influence and impact of technology in the wider ecosystem of society and people's experience of everyday life.

Being digital is a *shift in mindset* that I believe is required in today's world and recognition of this fact was one of the key motivations that drove me to develop this book. The myriad of digital case studies that are an emerging reality in business today further confirmed the need to define a digital ecosystem language for practitioners – a need that has not been filled by the books and commentaries currently available. Digitization changes the physical space, time, content, meaning and use of information into a new kind of virtual space. In this book we seek to explore real practical examples and also the limits of this digitization impact, and to identify how technology-enabled solutions can construct new realities for social and economic potential.

Whether you are looking to market a new physical or digital product, or heading up a city planning organization requiring new skills and technology investment – or, as a research and development scientist, developing new medical drug treatments – you will be seeking outcomes that can be radically different in terms of how technology can be leveraged by effective investment and integration with people's daily lives. Understanding and defining effective digital architectures and infrastructures – and the act of architecting effective digital solutions – are at the core of this journey.

The pervasive technologies

The pervasive adoption of digital technologies across all industries is a global phenomenon. Materially, the internet economy, which represents online transactional data, may only represent 10% of the gross domestic product (GDP) of countries, but per annum this is growing at between 8% and 10%, far outpacing growth in traditional physical "bricks and mortar" sectors – that is, physical goods and services that are traded off-internet.[1] However, internet transactional data is only part of the wider evolution of how digital technology is being used in all manner of social and business activity today. Technology frequently enables activities in an augmented way, adding more value to, for example, telephone conversations, e-mail, searching for information or completing a document, taking a photograph, or listening to music. Between 2015 and 2025 the growth forecast of mobile and data traffic alone, and the rise of the internet of things (IoT), is projected to be tenfold. What is emerging are technological ecosystems that are infusing into the fabric of society and economies that create *network effects* that are pervasive in the digital economy. Data and online presence through websites – and increasingly mobile devices – has become highly interconnected, forming ecosystems of association and technologies. This interconnected effect has enabled value creation through what some describe as *"multi-sided platform"* business models. Groups of people, enterprises, and markets are able to meet and trade, share and collaborate through digital technologies that generate new social and business monetization models.[2]

In this chapter, we explore the definition of this clustering effect of people, products, and services using technologies and what it may mean for the future of economic and enterprise development.

This chapter covers the following topics:

- Digital economy and ecosystems
- Definition of the digital ecosystem
- Definition of vertical and horizontal digital ecosystems
- Definition of the digital enterprise
- The rise of technological ecosystems
- Introduction to digital technologies
- The state of digital technology and enterprise

The Physical Economy, Digital Economy, and the Digital Ecosystem

In order to see how these interconnections of the digital world and the physical world might work, we need to take a step back from them in order to gain a useful perspective. It is difficult to physically visualize digital impact because by its very nature this is *virtual*, not physical. It is made up of electrons and photons and held in many types of material substrates represented in computer processor units, storage memory, and networks in a microscopic and nanotechnology level that is far from the day-to-day human experience. With respect to the time frame of reference for physical human existence, we live in an economy that touches our senses and our actions through the physical objects and devices we use, and the living spaces that we inhabit. The digital economy pervades these spaces and the convergence of the digital with the physical economy is where the digital enterprise operates, with the effect that various ecosystems form across the physical and technological worlds. The term "digital ecosystems," as shown in Figure 1.1, represents the clusters of systems and human and machine associations that enable the physical and digital economies to interconnect – these are the building blocks of the digital enterprise. Multi-sided platforms may live inside a digital enterprise or connect horizontally across many enterprises. It may be a digital enterprise in its own right, such as a Google or Amazon platform. Many technologies typically inhabit the enterprise and the economy to form "digital ecosystems" that may exist in one or many platforms, representing many potential and real business models.

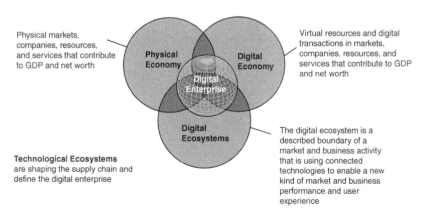

Physical markets, companies, resources, and services that contribute to GDP and net worth

Physical Economy

Digital Economy

Digital Enterprise

Virtual resources and digital transactions in markets, companies, resources, and services that contribute to GDP and net worth

Digital Ecosystems

The digital ecosystem is a described boundary of a market and business activity that is using connected technologies to enable a new kind of market and business performance and user experience

Technological Ecosystems are shaping the supply chain and define the digital enterprise

FIGURE 1.1 / Context of the physical economy, digital economy, digital ecosystems, and the digital enterprise

Economists typically refer to the physical economy, comparing two types of economic viewpoint called macroeconomics and microeconomics. The macroeconomic field is the economy as a whole, looking at changes such as national income, rates of growth, inflation, price levels, employment, and investment. The focus of microeconomics is on the decisions and factors that drive performance at the enterprise and individual level.

Macroeconomics level

At the macro level, the viewpoint is the total economic environment and the consideration is of the local, national, regional, and global economics. The economic aims here are in identifying factors that affect the overall performance, structure, and behavior across and between markets.

Typical conditions in focus are the overall market or industry-sector-level economic performance, which includes:

- What is the income and output of the industry market?
- How are consumption and consumer behavior patterns changing?
- Which trading domains and finance rules are driving growth?

Microeconomics level

At the micro level, the viewpoint is the demand and supply at the level between individual agents, including consumers, buyers, sellers, vendors, providers, and other types of enterprise in the industry. The economic aims are to identity factors that affect pricing and volume, and the availability and performance of goods and services in specific markets.

Typical considerations at the enterprise-level economic performance include:

- What is the level of enterprise operating demand and supply, bundling capabilities?
- What are the key market channel, business process, and supply chain capabilities?
- What are the requirements in capital funding, contract, intellectual property (IP), and innovation methods and capabilities?

Monetization and economics

The policy decisions, tools, and methods available to drive economic performance at the macro level and the micro level are different.

Monetization
Definition: the ability to generate financial wealth through strate-
gies and methods to convert skills, relationships, intelligence,
assets, products, and services into monetary value.

At the macroeconomic level, monetization strategy represents capabilities that generate revenue in a market: both the internal market and the external market to the enterprise. Monetization strategies are more focused on macro behaviors and scale of monopolies between participants and geographic locations.

At the microeconomic level, the monetization strategies are levers that you can pull or push inside your own company or corporation in order to generate revenue and profitability. The monetization strategies also need to consider the business environment and ecosystems that you are operating within. These strategies recognize the behaviors and influences of networks and connected spaces and the supply chain and value network inside and around the enterprise.

Differentiators and *competitiveness* of the enterprise need to consider both microeconomic and macroeconomic strategies. How an enterprise defines its uniqueness and the compelling reasons for how it differentiates its products and services to compete in the market changes with digitization. Defining sustainable pricing and market channels needs to take account of how the macro environment works in the physical markets and in online digital domains and digital markets.

The Digital Impact on Monetization Strategies

While it is important to make a distinction between the physical economy and the digital economy, the digital world can cross between macro and micro levels of economic activity because it is able to shape *both* areas of activity.

The physical economy is the physical markets, companies, resources, and services that contribute to GDP and net worth. The digital economy is the *virtual* resources and digital transactions in markets, companies, and resources that contribute to GDP and net worth. The ability to link across both the industry market and the enterprise is enabled by digital tech-nologies. Different physical and digital business models are coalescing and clustering, either by design or emerging as a result of the network effects of technologies such as broadband, mobile devices, social media, and embedded sensors.

Definition of a Digital Ecosystem

The rise of the digital ecosystem is a form of social and material object clustering of physical and virtual objects, content, services, and resources that define a *distinct and identifiable* boundary. This boundary may involve one or more segments and span vertical and/or horizontal market sectors.

In this context, the digital ecosystem "unit" is a described boundary of a market and business activity that is using connected technologies to enable a new kind of market and business performance and user experience. The digital ecosystem is defined as follows:

Physical economy
Definition: the physical markets, companies, resources, and services that contribute to GDP and net worth.

Digital economy
Definition: the virtual resources and digital transactions in markets, companies, resources, and services that contribute to GDP and net worth.

Digital ecosystem
Definition: a connected convergence of technologies in a market and business activity that enable new consumer, business, and market performance and user experience.

One important distinction in the use of the term *boundary* in this case is that it can also refer to the term *domain*. Typically, the boundary is related to a geospatial or geopolitical space that may also be described as a *dominion*. A domain is more general in defining a space of association used frequently in information systems language. To some extent it is an easier term to use and is a looser, less defined expression. Any one individual or enterprise may not control the ecosystem by definition, but the aims of the constructed digital enterprise are to establish some kind of boundary in order to build social and economic value.

Another important distinction in this definition is that the term *enterprise* is not necessarily part of the boundary that defines the ecosystem. This is an observation that was also supported by the International OECD study in January 2014 on the impact of tax collection erosion in the physical economy from the shift to new digital business models of the digital economy. The report touches on the central issue of digital business where the physical company entity may be in another sovereign country or not actually physically exist other than in cyberspace:

> *The findings are that there is no such thing as digital companies rather than digitization of the economy. There may not be therefore a solution for the digital economy but we will need to draw on features of digital economy when we revise the system.*

January 2014, OECD, Base Erosion and Profit Shift (BEPS) Report[3]

The report interestingly stated that domains are becoming an increasing economic issue, given the recognition that the country and enterprise boundaries are being changed by the digital domains.

Another implication is that the design of a digital enterprise is not a digital operating model (DOM), a business transformation approach, but a focus on the wider digital-enabled ecosystem (DEco) of systems and the organizational context. The difference is in taking assets and creating digital asset "silos" and vendor lock-in or lock-out, as opposed to treating digital strategy as a full ecosystem of potential innovation and operational possibilities.

The digital ecosystem does not necessarily exist inside one enterprise and may transcend and span many enterprises who may interact with the digital ecosystem. The collection of technologies in the digital ecosystem represents a set of architectures and technical standards that operate together, directly or separately, to support a set of user and business outcomes. Participants of that ecosystem share the terminology and protocols in order to be able to operate in that ecosystem. The degree of openness of this ecosystem may be different depending on the level of control exerted by its participants.

Digital enterprise thinking can create different architecture versions that may create incremental improvements or disruptive step change for that digital ecosystem, or create new digital ecosystems as a result.

Definition of Vertical and Horizontal Value Chains

In building the digital enterprise, a useful distinction to explore is the use of vertical and horizontal value chains in business models. In the physical world and the physical economy practitioners are often faced with the need to integrate the enterprise across the supply chain. The goal is to gain operational and market improvements or to establish growth strategies that may involve economies of scale by selling products and services vertically or horizontally across many markets. In the digital economy, vertical and horizontal value chains are radically different business models, due to the different properties of digitization that can remake and create new boundaries, connections, and capabilities for enterprise.

> *Vertical value chain*
> *Definition: the enterprise owns all or part of the end-to-end product or market-specific service. The design, creation, and delivery of the operation involves each member in the supply chain producing a different stage of the same product or service production path. The vertical value chain helps an enterprise to create efficiencies of supply and demand, managing the end-to-end quality and the cost of efficient and sustainable supply.*
>
> *Horizontal value chain*
> *Definition: the enterprise has one or more operations that can service many industry markets with the same product or service. These may be complementary or competitive commodities or specialist products or services. In mergers and acquisitions, the aim is to acquire similar operations to grow the core capabilities such as, for example: Disney merging with Pixar (film production); Exxon and Mobil (oil production, refining, and distribution); or BMW and MINI (car production).*
>
> *The horizontal value chain helps an enterprise to gain economies of scale through volume or unique access to many markets with the same demand for their product or service.*

The management structures of vertical and horizontal value chains can be quite different in managing scale and coordination across one or more enterprise entities and customer markets. Backward and forward integration refers to how the enterprise integrates with its customers at the front end and its suppliers and operations at the back end.

Monopolies may form when an enterprise gains control of the entire vertical supply chain or becomes a dominant player with large economies of scale in a horizontal market. It is worth noting that this feature can exist in digital domains as well, in the ecosystems and platforms that can create digital vertical and horizontal siloed services.

Examples of vertical value chain

Consumer electronics vertical value chain

Full vertical integration: mobile consumer electronics products have a vertically integrated path between the device and the content and the end user. The Apple corporation – managing the end-to-end product and service from design and manufacture to its own retail outlets – controls the Apple mobile value chain. The development of the Apple App Store and iTunes™ music content is controlled by Apple and managed through the Apple portal and device services.

Energy industry vertical value chain

Full vertical integration: oil industry multinationals such as ExxonMobil, Royal Dutch Shell, ConocoPhillips, and BP manage the end-to-end entire supply chain from exploration, drilling, and extraction of crude oil to the process of refining, transportation, and then distribution of fuel to company-owned retail stores.

Film media vertical value chain

Full or partial vertical integration: the big five film studios – MGM, Warner Brothers, 20th Century Fox, Paramount Pictures, and RKO – produce and distribute films. They also operate their own movie theaters. Other studios such as Universal Studios, Columbia Pictures, and United Artists produce and distribute feature films, but do not own their own theaters.

Examples of horizontal value chain

Automotive horizontal value chain

Horizontal integration: automotive engine parts and manufacturing supply to many automotive vehicle manufacturers and distributors.

Publishing horizontal value chain

The development of academic and business as well as consumer fiction and non-fiction books has moved to include audio books and e-books that are established through publishing houses and accessed via their own marketplace portals or through reseller portals and online trading marketplaces.

Retail horizontal value chain

The large consumer retail food malls and hyperstores offering a large-scale presence and "one-stop-shop" for a range of consumer goods. This is broadening to include electrical, apparel, food catering, insurance and banking, opticians, mobile reselling, and pharmacy all under one "store roof".

Horizontal integration has often been seen as acquiring market share by acquisition of providers in a product or service category in order to become a potential monopoly. This is true in some cases, but in other industry or market circumstances it is an extension of an enterprise competency across many different industries that can gain economies of scale from that expertise and focused competency. It is also not the preserve of large enterprises but a feature that both large and small companies and organizations can deploy in order to seek ways to engage many customers across a city or a region by offering a breadth of common services, rather than dealing with a multitude of choices.

Indeed, a *Harvard Business Review* blog claimed that the best companies today are horizontally integrated.[4] The argument is that information technology already enables vertical integration to connect and transact, it is then the use of social media to "flatten out the organizational structure" that can enable enterprise performance improvements related to horizontal integration. Planning for effective *product platforms* can enable a company to deliver distinctive products to the market while conserving product resources.[5] This idea is developed as a way of creating added value services by turning the product into a *platform* that can be added to and enhanced. Today the concept of a *product-service system* (PSS) is also sometimes referred to as "servicization."[6] Servicing is a transaction through which value is provided by a combination of products and services in which satisfaction of customer needs is achieved by selling the function of the product rather than the product itself, or by increasing the service component of the offer. This concept as a practitioner, is closely related to the idea of platforms and creating valuable customer experience.

Two-sided Platforms (TSPs) and Multi-sided Platforms (MSPs)

The evolution of value chains involves both vertical and horizontal value chains facilitating and enabling social and commercial trading transactions and collaboration between two or more customer and providers. But this phenomenon has also introduced the ideas of two-sided platforms and multi-sided platforms, which are created by the digital technologies that underpin many of these value chains.[7]

Two-sided platform (TSP)

Definition: a platform to provide facilitation of a customer and a provider to products or services. The service is specific to the support exchange between two communities. Examples of this include financial payment networks to bring together cardholders and retailers, retail shops bringing together shoppers and retailers, and online gaming bringing together gamers and game developers. A TSP may aim to provide specific customer services to support usage of the platform products or services such as usage and trading incentives in customer loyalty programs.

Multi-sided platform (MSP)

Definition: a platform that brings together two or more distinct but interdependent groups of customers. They facilitate a range of providers and customer interactions driven by multiple customer needs, which influence how the MSP services the customers' needs. Well-known IT industry examples of these include Facebook, eBay, Google, Amazon, and Alibaba, which all provide a high degree of constituency facilitation bringing together many different types of customer demographics and consumer behavior patterns with a variety of providers of products and services. In the case of search engines or marketplaces the MSP itself may generate information and content about the customers' online habits and available products and services from providers accessible by the MSP.

Such platforms are of value to one group of customers only if the other group of customers are present. The platform creates value by facilitating interactions between the different groups. A multi-sided platform grows in value to the extent that it attracts more users, a phenomenon known as the "network effect."[8]

It is also evident that the level of *direct* and *indirect* interaction between customers and providers can vary considerably depending on the size and scope of the enterprise and the market. Many established vertical and horizontal value chains might be candidates for digital disruption as they can be bypassed or transformed through virtual marketplaces and online directory catalog portals that can facilitate a new kind of connected exchange. There are many examples of this happening, for example in the pharmaceutical market where online medical drug services can offer alternative supply, side-stepping traditional sourcing. In the retail market, online product broker portals can bypass the traditional high street retail shop altogether through digital purchases and postal delivery direct to home. Where enterprises have invested in building integrated vertical or horizontal infrastructures of buildings, warehouses, and outlets – sometimes amounting to millions of dollars – this can be a serious challenge to business strategy.

This raises the first key question around digital enterprise and how to respond to this potential: transformation in mass "hyperconnectivity." Indeed, many industries are disrupted by new digital platforms that are changing the basis of competition, lowering competitor entry barriers, and establishing new user and customer experience that is truly game changing. In the digital world a direct physical connection is potentially enabled through a virtual medium and this connection can then establish "network effects" that can create an amplification of network connection interactions. This becomes a scaling effect that can be seen, for example, in a social network where interconnections between participants of the network multiply by the many connections possible. A level of indirect contact and intermediation is also evident in some practitioners, and distinctions can be made between MSPs and resellers: the difference being that resellers take control of the interaction between various sides, whereas an MSP enables the customers themselves to manage this collaboration. This may be as "self-service" or as a curated experience managed by the MSP, providing incentives through "gamification" or other loyalty or persuasion influences. We explore many mechanisms of this in the case studies in later chapters, as well as how digital enterprise develops its monetization mechanisms and its business model. The second key question for enterprises is where to position themselves in the value network as either a MSP managing the consumer experience and services of the MSP or as a content product or service provider to the MSP and so not in direct contact with consumers.

Examples of two-sided platforms (TSP)

Financial services two-sided platforms

The digital banking industry provides a number of direct customer online services to offer secure financial account and transaction services. The financial services payment platforms also provide a direct credit authorization service to many retail and business operations.

Citizen services two-sided platforms

The development of consumer-specific services help establish service lines for product categories. Examples of these include education-establishment services for online course development and delivery, and dedicated security checks for identity management. Other examples include online customer service support centers that use direct IP messaging to provide real-time query, sales, and technical support.

Examples of multi-sided platforms (MSP)

Healthcare MSPs

Patient care monitoring and research can use digital platforms to collect and integrate back-end medical research and front-line healthcare delivery. This is where devices worn on the medical patient are used to collect health data that is then passed through to a clinician and may be aggregated or individually passed to a medical research facility for medical study. The results of medical research can be accessed and sent to clinicians in the field faster, through transfer directly to the practices. The multi-side co-presence is in the patients, clinicians, and researchers being able to co-exist in the same space for content, time, and virtual space, enabled by the e-health translation platform.

Automotive MSPs

The connected car infotainment platform is an embedded platform in the vehicle that manages the automobile status through location-based services and content delivered remotely to the vehicle via wireless technology. The context of the services is a number of applications that provide connectivity on the move. Examples of Apple's CarPlay™ and Google infotainment – and many vehicle manufacturers branding on top of these platforms – have moved into the commercial automotive market. The multi-sided collaboration is between the car owner, the automotive manufacturers, the content providers, and the mobile device manufacturers. The convergence is in the transportation environment that offers a new kind of digital market on the move.

News and entertainment media MSPs

In the telecoms media market, the emergence of platforms that connect customers with mobile market services, media content, and services is a growing, evolving area. This type of platform creates a co-presence for customers and content providers, internet service providers (ISPs), and the telecoms network service providers (NSPs) to connect and purchase viewing content over the network.

Value Network Ecosystems

We have seen from the examples of vertical and horizontal integration and the emergence of TSPs and MSPs that organizational developments can touch many different physical and digital connections. This is the shift between a *value chain* and a *value network* brought about by the social and business connections that exist and work in different ways depending on the type of industry and the locations of customers and providers (see Figure 1.2).

Few enterprises are in reality a monopoly and a global "superpower" of the digital world in the sense that it can form and structure a complete industry. Most enterprises are collaborations between customers and their suppliers and operations to deliver a set of customer experiences that enable the company to monetize its products and services. Businesses that exist in the physical world have buildings, employees, resources, locations, and other earthly material things that represent its operating premises. Even digital businesses that are "born and live in the cloud" and that are mostly virtual organizations (VOs) still have to exist in a data center and a network, and have devices to connect to it and a physical material presence in some premise. A pure digital business with no physical materiality and that is hosted by a third party still has to contend with the connectivity and presence that it has with other digital entities such as social media, application program interface (API) connections, and content *that passes through to and from its own digital presence*. These are the value network ecosystems that describe the modern business enterprise and its environment from a digital perspective.

Practitioners are focused on how these value systems can be digitally connected between different parts of the enterprises and their wider market and business environment.

The value network ecosystems (VNEs) can be made up of one or more horizontal or vertical value chains and platforms. They are the connections to the business from the physical and digital worlds that inhabit the customer and supply chains. In the past, where the "four walls of the enterprise" represented the perimeter of the business, this physical distinction has changed in the digital enterprise. The effect is that the enterprise has moved inside out with the organizational boundary that can be across platforms and value chains

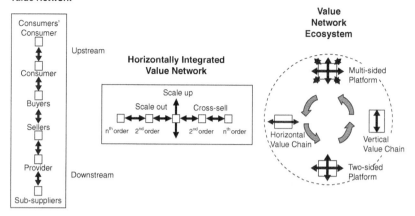

FIGURE 1.2 / **Vertical value chain, horizontal value chain, and value network ecosystem**

across an entire digital ecosystem. An enterprise can build its own or connect to third-party TSPs and MSPs to create vertical or horizontal value chains. The enterprise becomes a *value network ecosystem* that describes how it works in the physical and virtual, digital spaces.

> *Value network ecosystem*
> *Definition: a collection of value activities that may connect to many vertical or horizontal markets, customers, and providers that represent its members of the enterprise ecosystems. The value network represents the enterprise value system for creating and sharing, and creating co-benefits through its constituency of members that it connects with in its ecosystem.*

Let us look at examples of the value network ecosystem for two industries – the "smart hotel" ecosystem and the "connected car" ecosystem – to illustrate these practitioner perspectives.

"Smart hotel" digital ecosystem

In the digital world with virtual communities of customers and potential consumers, the evolution of vertical and horizontal value is a key concept for building the digital enterprise. In the example of the hotel and leisure industry, it is a great example of how physical meeting places and digital eco-systems are converging. In this sense, they are vertical and horizontal digital ecosystems that are influencing the design of the digital enterprise.

The hotel room is a "physical workplace object" that can have many "con-nected" spaces. Corporate and social events may be managed in the same premises but requiring different utilization of rooms and facilities. Customer services starting with the service desk and the concierge services through to room service, housekeeping, and build maintenance are all facets of the service enablement. Then there are the services at work in multi-sided mar-kets and devices in the rooms and from TV remote, TV entertainment, room service call, cleaning service, and in-room dining. Gymnasium and other facili-ties create extra capabilities that may all create additional value for customer experience and monetization opportunities for the hotel business chain.

The "smart hotel" will have many points of contact with the customer both physically (face to face) and virtually, via digital technology, through which to build brand loyalty and engage to build new value experience. This contact can be before, during, and after the customer's visit and can be both via the hotel and its partners. It is an ecosystem of value networks spreading across customers, hotels, its employees, and partners. Each point will, in reality, be a combination of vertical integration such as the reordering and consumption of food and beverages from suppliers to rooms, through to disposal and energy, and sustainability of these chains. The hotel will also scale horizontally across different hotel locations and regions in order to pro-vide a consistency of customer experience and efficiency of operations. The MSPs will enable customer loyalty systems as well as cross-selling to flight, food, and business services that expand the scope and potential value to the customers and the hotel. The digital enterprise for the "smart hotel" is much more than its physical room and assets. It is how each customer experience and the augmentation of grounds, foyer, rooms, and all the services around this before, during, and after the stay at the hotel, which becomes the total service.

"Connected automobile" digital ecosystem

While the hotel is an example of a connected physical space, the value network ecosystem also applies to moving objects as well. A great example of this is the connected car that is seeking to automate and enhance every aspect of the automotive vehicle lifecycle from concept design to manufacture, selling to aftermarket operating, and the direct customer driving experience. This scope is not limited to inside and outside the vehicle but also within traffic networks and other vehicle and transport ecosystems.

This mindset has connected the digitally enabled car to the logistics supply chain as a total lifecycle concept. A range of embedded technologies have been created that include advanced driver assistance (ADAS) technologies for safety and sustainable energy management. Vehicle to vehicle (V2V) provides in-transit management of other vehicles and objects relative to the vehicle and driver. Car infotainment provides remote content delivery and personalization for driver and passengers that link with mobile devices and mobile applications. Pre-planning trips or selecting and downloading movies, music, and games can all be done remotely in synchronization with the on-board car systems. Remote diagnostics, spare parts reordering, and planned maintenance can all be automated with remote downloading and monitoring of vehicle health and performance. Virtual reality car showrooms, in-car head-up display controls for line-of-sight car-driver information, through to care assist and potentially self-driving cars, are all possible today. The connected automotive ecosystem touches many associated objects and customer driving experiences both inside and outside the car. It is this extended connected system that is the digital enterprise of the future.

The vertical and horizontal value chains are being impacted by digital platforms that enable new value network ecosystems to be constructed along each point of a business operating model. Whether you are looking at how to engage your customers in your products and services, or seeking how to collect the right type of analytical data from sources in order to gain insight to better-informed decisions and judgments or user experiences, or seeking ways to build better business to business (B2B) and business to consumer (B2C) collaboration, digital technologies are reshaping how to architect these workspaces and the enterprise.

Definition of the Digital Enterprise as a Monetization Unit

We earlier suggested that the term digital enterprise did not exist in the direct sense of the physical market but that it is part of the connected manifestation of objects, networks, and connected relationships representing the digital economy. The role of the digital enterprise does, however, provide an organizational basis or framework to drive monetization and value from an economic and social perspective. It can have a legal status, though in open business models such as open source it does not necessarily exist to generate direct income for its participants. Use of digitized products and services does not necessarily involve any legal contractual relationship between the buyer and seller. These matters have created challenges in law courts over the direct and indirect responsibilities of digital enterprises, such as search engines and their indirect association with the rules of their algorithms displaying search results of third-party copyright, or the redaction of historical data in the *"right to be forgotten"* as seen in the European Commission legislation.[9] Another is the role of ISPs and their responsibilities for the use of their services indirectly by customers who themselves may not be operating within the law of their country – what responsibilities can be enforced on the ISPs and customers to comply with the law? The *net-neutrality* debate in the United States is a particularly contentious issue that relates to the telecommunications providers' huge investments in their infrastructure and the use of their networks by traffic bandwidth-hungry Over the Top (OTT) providers such as video streaming services and large social network platform operators.[10] The debate is centered around the use by some corporate customers in that consumer significant bandwidth loads may be disproportional to the perceived or otherwise overall service terms and conditions of use. Is the internet a free utility resource at the same service-availability level for all, or should telecommunications enterprises be enabled to *"throttle"* and monetize for different user demands? Some observers suggest this has happened for years in any case: for example, the availability of telecom ISP broadband services in a local area often physically defines the consumer's choice by limiting the availability of their services in the local market. An enterprise, whether it is physical or virtual, will have some legal basis in the sense of commercial undertaking but it does not preclude new forms of digital ecosystems that are social exchanges. How economics will evolve in the future will be interesting to watch as these issues become ever more central to the development of industries and economies.

At the heart of these examples is the impact of digital enterprise on industries and their associated physical and digital interconnectedness.

Digital enterprise
Definition: a form of organizational structure with a legal basis, enabled by technologies to provide physical or virtual products or services in one or more digital ecosystems. The organization physically and virtually operates monetization mechanisms that generate social and financial value and worth in one or more digital economies.

Ultimately, the goal is to collaborate and scale with demand and supply in ways that meet the constituent member's needs, which can evolve and change dynamically as communities and relations form, coalesce, and dissipate – a term referred to as *co-presence*. The value-creation process centers around how the digital enterprise enables these experiences to generate co-benefits and worth, as defined by monetary or other social value for all parties. A digital enterprise is perhaps all these things.

Chapter Summary

In this chapter we have explored the meaning of technological ecosystems and the development of the digital technology constituency. In Chapter 2 we start to unpack the meaning of digitization and to define approaches to digital workspaces.

chapter 2

From Physical Workplaces to Digital Workspaces

Chapter Introduction

In our everyday lives we seek meaning in our communications and interactions, but with little thought as to how this may work. Yet to a computational machine the act of natural language processing and "speaking" is a highly complex and difficult task. The subtle nuances of a facial expression, the tone of a human voice, and the use of body language in a hand gesture or a touch is used to convey direct yet unspoken cultural information. Will machines ever have the empathy to understand and emotionalize these same features? Will machines have the cognitive ability to understand more than direct procedural instructions and to understand the ambiguity and intonation that often accompanies natural language? These are perhaps some of the goals of cybernetic research projects today that are involved in the development of a union between the physical world and the technological world. This journey is a series of steps in the encoding of basic data into more sophisticated forms of transactions and on to complex language and representations of the physical world in virtual environments. This journey has already begun with the explosion in digital data from devices, sensors across the internet, and into the myriad of software applications.

Digital images, e-mails, video, and web pages are used to describe our lives, where we live and work, and the places we visit. The physical workplaces we inhabit are being digitized into virtual environments. A key question is how do we represent this development as the many devices and sensors collect data and move this to an infrastructure of internet networks and the myriad of software applications?

In this chapter we explore the progress of key ideas in information systems to describe the physical and virtual activities and what it means for building the digital enterprise. We examine some theories of information and then introduce ideas as to how digitization changes our perception of physical space and moments in time. These are described as *spatial* and *temporal* changes that are caused by the characteristics of digital information introduced in Chapter 1. These features facilitate the ability to change how humans and machines interact with each other and to transform their environments.

This chapter covers the following topics:

• The human–machine interface
• The semiotics ladder
• Contextualization of objects, places, and actions
• The changing space and time of our environment
• Digital capabilities and digital spaces
• Perception and space
• Aesthetics and spaces

The Human–Machine Interface

Semantics is the field of study relating to the meaning of things. The word is derived from the ancient Greek word σημαντικός (semantikos), "related to meaning, significant," from σημαίνω (semaino), "to signify, to indicate," which is from σῆμα (sema), "sign, mark, token." The plural is used in analogy with words similar to physics, which was in the neuter plural in ancient Greek and meant "things relating to nature." Semantics is often related to language semantics where the meaning of human expression through language defines how information is interpreted and communicated. Language is critical to both humans and machines, such as computers, that need to understand and communicate with each other through a common language notation. Clearly machine code language is very different to human language in which information and meaning are conveyed, interpreted, translated, and enacted in many different ways. To some extent this is one of the core issues facing digitization and human–machine boundaries that this book touches on. Indeed many machine systems involve computation and devices that are machine-to-machine interaction and do not involve any human intermediaries. This does not, of course, negate the importance of systems for human benefit: quite the opposite. I am referring to the differences in

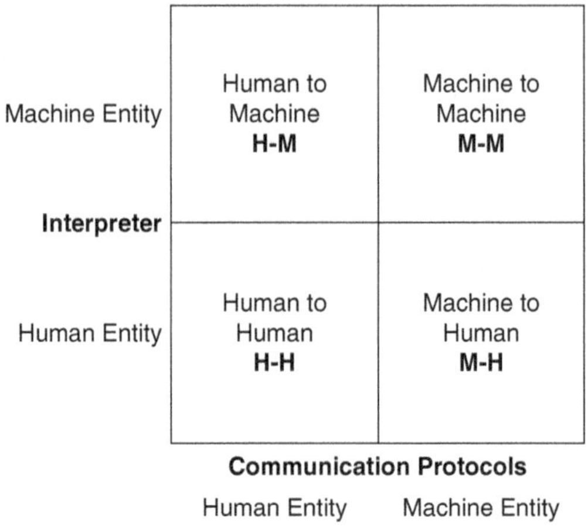

	Human Entity	Machine Entity
Machine Entity	Human to Machine **H-M**	Machine to Machine **M-M**
Interpreter		
Human Entity	Human to Human **H-H**	Machine to Human **M-H**

Communication Protocols

Human Entity   Machine Entity

FIGURE 2.1 **Human–machine boundaries**

semantic notation and communication that are a means to an end to enable human interactions and machine interfaces and integration to work. At a basic level, Figure 2.1 illustrates these interfaces.

Human-to-human communication protocols include natural language, written language, signage and visual notations, body language, olfactory language, and augmented language such as clothing and rituals. These have evolved over many thousands of years and represent the complex nuances of human behavior, societal norms, and values. The introduction of mechanization and, importantly, machinery that enabled human and information communications to be transferred over physical distances and to interpret meaning and action of human and non-human information is a profound difference.

To some extent this basic determination of machine and human interfaces is misleading in a digital ecosystem, in that there can be many-to-many relationships in the digital world. Many websites, content owners, mobile devices, connected systems, and human users represent a much more diverse and distributed environment more representative of the real-world objects, relationships and interactions of humans and machines. Millions of interactions are enabled through networks and digital technologies during every minute of the day. These collective interfaces enable a grand scale of machine-to-machine and human-to-human interaction. Understanding how these ecosystems of digital collectiveness works is a key issue in architecting both digital enterprises and in understanding and developing how economy functions in a digital way. These connections enable a kind of community intelligence that reflects a collective behavior of individuals connected in human-to-human communications through a machine interface medium such as a social network.

Both human-to-machine and machine-to-human interfaces have moved rapidly beyond the stationary handset of a telephone system or a television in the corner of a room. New visualization systems enabled by digital effects of light, image, sound, and transport can change how machines interface with humans. Mobile smartphones and, for example, embedded sensors in doors, rooms, and cars enable humans to interface with machines increasingly in the setting of body movement, room location, or environment, and with tactile and natural language options as well as touch-screen and text-type interfaces to exchange and gain information.

The Digital User Experience (UX) and Customer Experience (CX)

The connection between human and non-human technologies has been described in recent years as a kind of *digital entanglement*. In the previous section we explored context and meaning. This is important in that it impacts the user experience that is created and interpreted.

Using a holistic approach to user experience (UX) design and the customer experience (CX) we can start to explore how the human–machine boundary is changing through the process of digitization. What we see is an entanglement of human activities and digital capabilities in organizational routines that are becoming ever more empowering and transformational.[1]

Let us start first by exploring the contexts of digital entanglement. I will use the following definitions:

> *User experience (UX)*
> *Definition: the interaction of the human and a device or sensor through a user interface (UI) to affect the human-experienced outcomes. This is defined as the UX agency of the device or sensor in the context of the location and time. This agency can also apply to other forms of actors including non-living objects such as software program agents that work with the device or sensor autonomously by a machine protocol or algorithm, semi-autonomously through the control of a human.*
>
> *Customer experience (CX):*
> *Definition: the human in the context of their living environment and the human-experienced outcomes caused by the interaction with other humans and objects in that environment context location and time.*

We will see that as we explore the digitization of this space, time, and semantic meaning to create multiple contexts, then things can become radically different as the virtual world entangles with the physical objects and places.

A day in the life of living next door to a "smart photocopier"

In the room next door to my office there is a "smart photocopier" that is connected to the internet. The machine automatically detects when its ink cartridge is getting low and sends out an e-mail to reorder a new printer cartridge. Ordering online stocks is faster and convenient and as a consumable item does not need to be authorized for purchase approval or regularity checked by operators, as the embedded sensors in the photocopying machine are able to do this job. The next day the cartridge parcel arrives by recorded delivery but no one is available to collect and sign for it. I offer to sign for it in the absence of anyone else available and it is placed in my room with a note left under the door saying, "I signed for the photocopier cartridge in the absence of any human available."

The point of this anecdote is that there is a big difference between user experience and the overall customer experience. Whereas digital technology UX affects checking, ordering, and delivery of the photocopier supplies from a functional viewpoint, the end-to-end flow of different actors and organizational departments and work routines affects the overall outcome of the customer experience (CX). It may be a trivial example but it illustrates that UX and CX design is a key part to enabling the smart photocopy or smart fridge or a smart TV to automate steps in reordering, or in making suitable suggestions.

But as we will see in the digital enterprise case studies in this book, it is possible to create digital workspaces that can directly affect outcomes for individuals and an enterprise. For example, multi-modal traffic and transport arrival times can be optimized; patient healthcare delivery can be remotely supported; retail products and metropolitan services can be enabled with smart technology to assist living spaces and consumption patterns. These are increasingly linked by digital technologies that affect economic and social outcomes. Digital entanglement matters in the way that context is enabled in objects, locations, and organizational routines and procedures.

Let us start to explore digital entanglement as a way to define workspaces enabled through digital technologies. We can divide this into a social, business, and knowledge context to illustrate how this is changing physical workplaces into digital workspaces.

Social context

In the social context there can be many contemporary devices and sensors that can be immersed and connected to the social experience:

- Examples of digital workspaces can include smart rooms and building facilities that enable social gatherings with ambient lighting, humidity controls, and wireless connectivity.
- Room artifacts such as smart tabletops with interactive displays, wireless charging, and location tracking for meeting coordination and time–productivity tracking.
- Room walls and windows can become dynamic viewing boards for virtual telepresence meetings and information display communication boards.
- Wearable technology can monitor social connections and shared social experiences.
- Multiple contexts can drive customer outcomes to gain better social experience, and higher productivity of meetings and social interactions.

Business context

The presence of consumers and providers in the immediate physical location – as well as the digital connectivity to supply chains of products and services – enable new commercial, technical, and ethical models:

- Examples of digital workspaces can develop automated reordering and stock control of products and services.
- Dynamic services can be created for customers in the context of a meeting place through personalized recommendations and dynamic "menus" and promotions to assist and augment the customer experience.
- Smart point-of-sale devices and sensors can be used in fixed locations and in mobile smartphone applications to drive service efficiencies and customer loyalty programs.
- Location facilities can create immersive brand images, smart art, and dynamic displace advertising boards.
- Information about visitors and consumption habits can be collected and analyzed for improvements of productivity and targeted services.

- Employee smart badges and wearable assistant devices can help provide employee assistance and tracking.
- Multiple contexts across the business locations, outlets, and points of customer contact can drive improved customer experience outcomes. Business operations and partner collaboration can be augmented to create co-benefits and co-innovation across product and service locations.

Knowledge context

Today, mobile devices and embedded sensors present a revolution in the ability to collect and bring knowledge and insight to the location and context remotely. The knowledge context of digital entanglement has never been felt more keenly in the way that social and business behavior models have shifted with the use of digital technology:

- Examples of knowledge augmentation in context are wider and varied from mobile and tablet devices with local proximity connectivity to collect and sense their environment.
- Rooms, buildings, and whole cities can have connected space coverage from mobile and wireless infrastructure with telemetry collected on heat, light, CO_2, nitrogen, and other consumption and wastage data insights.
- Wearable technology can create wellbeing and health location and behavior incentives and monitoring, driving social value.
- Objects including automobiles, engines, buses, trains, ships, and aircraft extend the envelope of digitization to include enterprise services on the move and through local, regional, and global travel.
- Proximity between local and remote locations can span and connect social and information sharing remotely into the present context, empowering local and remote interaction, also referred to as co-presence.
- The many contexts of knowledge creates new forms of customer experience outcomes that digitization can enable.

Building digital capabilities from digital spaces

In this section we explore the ideas of information theory and concepts of contextualization. Digital technologies pervade physical locations and objects, creating new user and customer experiences.

A goal is to understand how this digital entanglement works in practical terms:

- How do the organizational routines become digitized?
- How is this scalable across multiple contexts?

- How do human activities and digital capabilities become entangled across contexts?
- How does technology become entangled into patterns of practice that we can learn and share?

The next step is to start to define how the enterprise builds these digital workspaces.

Cognitive understanding and co-presence are no longer just in the physical moments of human-to-human presence but can be created and "held in virtual space" through digital entanglement. The interpretation is not a one-way process either. The act of participating in the activity is, by definition, also to make you part of that activity.

In developing a working digital architecture of a digital enterprise we need to break down the situation into its constituent building blocks. This effect has been long considered in the notion that "understanding the building blocks is requisite to designing the wall."[2]

Semantic construction is a key concept in complex systems analysis and requirements management.[3] This book seeks to define principles from practitioners in how digital systems are constructed.

In the next section we explore how the evolution of enterprise architecture and digital technologies is changing the nature of enterprise technology design. We then explore how the concepts of contextualization are put into practical use in the design of the workspaces, and the digital content and use through the passage of time. These new digital workspaces represent the building blocks of a modern digital enterprise and the digital economy.

Definition of Digital Workspaces from an Ecosystem Perspective

If we step back and look at the bigger picture of the ecosystem, the physical world can be thought of as representing the total environment that we live in today. Yet, in the virtual sense, this has been moving through the information era to become increasingly interconnected. Telecommunications, devices, and sensors grow across the physical world and enable a kind of virtual representation of this in digital maps and shared media content from potentially anywhere on earth. The virtual work is not constrained to the geographical and physical limitations of the locations but can represent many views of "worlds," depending on what information and context are being considered.

Indeed, in the physical world there are also many types of ecosystems that might be described as systems in their own right. These ecosystems can be considered as different viewpoints of the same overall ecosystem. Examples of these include societal ecosystems that have formed over millennia in villages, towns, and cities across countries and continents. Commercial ecosystems have spawned in trading products and services in market sectors from agriculture to mining and manufacturing, and services industries have grown with populations and driven economic ecosystems for wealth creation and wellbeing.

The biosphere of natural resources

The modern exploration of ecosystems is of course not earthbound. The limits of this discussion can now include the low earth orbit International Space Station (ISS), and satellite technology and space exploration now extends to other planets – the Deep Space Network (DSN) is an example of these ambitions to reach further. The technological ecosystems are entangled across these ecosystems, enabling the potential of new digital workspaces that connect together different experiences and resources.

Definition of Digital Workspaces from a Human Perspective

The definition of physical workplaces as virtual workspaces can be based on a number of practical physical considerations. We can break this down into the immediate human space of reference in considering three types:

- **Physical spaces** that humans live and work in
- **Transit spaces** that humans travel and move between
- **Biological spaces** that represent the human body condition and living habitat

Digitization of these spaces creates new virtual workspaces that can change how the physical workplaces function and interact with the human experience.

Physical workplaces

These are the contemporary locations, streets, sidewalks, buildings, rooms, and other physical objects that are the small and larger-scale artifacts of the physical world. Consumable items such as food, money, clothes, and other temporary objects can all be seen as the things that are present in the living workspace.

Virtual physical workspaces

A virtual space of a physical location is the enablement of the physical space with digital technologies such as "smart wall" that can display content or offer touch-sensitive interactivity. Physical locations can be connected – for example in a web teleconference remote location – and can be shared as if they were in the same physical location.

Transit workplaces

Objects are also not static: cars, planes, and trains are physically moveable and as such are the same as fixed artifacts other than that they have additional properties that are "on the move."

Virtual transit workspaces

The "connected" car is an example of a transit space that may have GPS and other remote connectivity to provide information and entertainment while on the move.

Biological workplaces

The human body has many biological subsystems. The organs, together with the respiratory, nervous, muscular, skeletal, and many other elements represent the biological "systems platform." The human condition also has an emotional, intellectual, spiritual, and cultural essence of being. Biological systems can be treated as another "space" that are manifest in the real physical world. The social collectiveness of groups, communities, and organizations also represent a kind of biological living space.

Biological living systems can be taken to include more than a human-centric perspective but also the ecological environment we live in: animals, insects, plants, rivers, forests, land, sea, atmosphere, and the biosphere that encompass the planet.

Virtual biological workspaces

At the level of the human body this can be, for example, the use of implants to augment organs and monitor health such as heart pacemakers, artificial limbs, and microchip implants. Wearable technology can externally augment human wellbeing, such as fashion and lifestyle accessories seen in, for example, eyewear, wristbands, and smart clothing. Advances in organ regeneration and generic engineering suggest new frontiers of what is possible in augmented human medical condition and lifestyles.

Design of Digital Workspaces

As we have seen, digital workspaces are connected spaces in a digital ecosystem.

The physical enterprise is a commercial organization that can be constructed from physical, transitional, and human spaces – the physical objects, rooms, and buildings of the enterprise; the transport and traffic networks between the organization and its markets; the human capital and skills that represent the enterprise and its partners and customers.

There are potentially many digital workspaces that can form from the digitization of these physical, transit, and biological spaces. In this chapter we focus on six major patterns of digital workspaces in the digital enterprise (see Figure 2.2):

- Object workspace
- Room and facility workspace
- Personal workspace and business community workspace
- Travel and in-transit workspace
- Contextual-relationship workspace
- Knowledge workspace

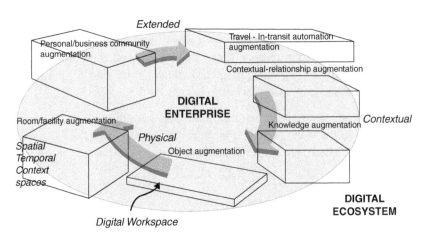

FIGURE 2.2 Definition of digital workspaces

Definitions of Digital Workspaces

Object workspace

An entity can be defined as having both content and function. Objects can be material and physical such as a chair, a cup, or a wall – or can be virtual digital objects such as music content or a digital book. Objects can be non-living or living.

Examples of physical, extended, contextual (PEC) objects located in a workspace include the physical objects in a kitchen such as a cooker, plates, forks, cups, food items, a fridge, a kettle.

Examples of spatial, temporal, contextual (STC) objects located in a workspace include the information on cooking recipes or fridge reordering that can be virtually connected to digital services. Virtual objects can be used such as 3D printing of objects to and from physical locations.

Room and facility workspace

This is the physical walls, floors, and objects within a room space – a building made up of rooms and floors. Rooms and facilities can be privately owned or public facilities such as municipal services, parks, swimming pools, and libraries. Rooms and buildings can also be virtual if connected remotely to other rooms and buildings as a connected virtual workspace, for example a simultaneous webcast of a concert/theater production or an online gaming event and viewing-audience community.

Examples of PEC room/facility workspaces include living room spaces, corridors, the building structure, the collection of buildings in a shopping mall, a set of factory complex facilities, collections of facilities that are managed as a unit.

Examples of STC room/facility workspace include visualization screens mounted on walls to display information, the air-conditioning system, and the heating control system for automated ambient environment control.

Personal workspace and business community workspace

This is the personal/private and public set of information that is connected for individuals or a collection of individuals. This may include a commercial relationship that represents a business trading community. A human body can be regarded as a collection of systems – a community, as it were, of subsystems that together function as a human body.

Examples of PEC personal and business community workspaces include a personal set of social connections; a business trading community in a supply chain network; a set of buildings and business units that represent a city community space.

Examples of STC personal and business community workspaces include wearable technology to monitor wellbeing for medical research, collecting information across a community of patients; a social network of personal friends or a marketplace of consumers and sellers.

Travel and in-transit workspace

Whereas rooms and facilities may be considered as fixed, physically non-moving assets, other assets such as vehicles and transportation network infrastructure such as roads, railways, shipping ports, and airports represent a combination of facilities and moving transit spaces. These physically moveable spaces may also be digitized and follow the human user and connectivity as they physically move from one location to another.

Examples of PEC travel and in-transit workspaces include a personal set of social connections; a business trading community in a supply chain network.

Examples of STC Travel, and in-transit workspaces include logistics package real-time tracking; connected car on-board driver assistance and infotainment system.

Contextual relationship workspace

A contextual workspace is one where the products and services are specifically tailored to the needs of the situation at that time and location. Context workspaces have a feedback loop that collects information, analyzes it, and then makes decisions and feedback to the context of the situation. Context workspaces can be passive or active in the way that the collect and feedback give a specific response to a situation: passive in not being visual or perceived by the human; active in that it involves the human user who is aware of the context action.

Examples of PEC contextual workspaces include a set of food produce displayed by category in a retail store; book sections in a physical library offering genres; a concierge service at a hotel reception desk; an information service center in a city center.

Examples of STC contextual workspaces include an online book recommendation service; a GPS satellite navigation planner using real-time road traffic adjustments; a body health feedback sensor providing real-time alerts on movement or exercise; an automated alarm system for intruder alert, which may notify the authorities automatically through geolocation monitoring and alerts; an interactive art display that has touch sensors to activate different displays.

Knowledge workspace

This is the information about an object, place, or person that provides awareness and insight into the condition and nature of the objects and locations.

Examples of PEC knowledge workspaces include information manuals on the use of TV devices for channel and services selection setup; a set of photographs about a location stored on a digital map service register of attendees for a concert music event; an engineering design schematic drawing.

Examples of STC knowledge workspaces include a digital brand with associated products and social media activity about the brand; a set of shared wiki pages for collaborative knowledge sharing and employee development; a set of open-source code downloads and coding development by a crowdsourced community; a set of recommendations and ratings online about a restaurant and its service.

In summary

Together these workspaces represent a combination of many different types of digitization experiences to be found across industries and markets. The digital enterprise is a construction of these workspaces, building out of the connected systems and physical locations into ways that create new value networks.

The digital workspace is seeing an explosion of technologies that are connected and immersed into these workspaces. The illustrations given here are just some of the technologies that are available today in these domains. But, as we have seen earlier in this book, the number of objects, devices, and connections are projected to grow to huge numbers. This is the digital ecosystem of 25 billion objects and beyond.

Digital Workspaces as Digital Platforms

Let's take a building, for example, which can have chairs, tables, and other objects placed in rooms. The building may be part of a set of buildings, walkways, roads, and municipal facilities such as street lighting, traffic management, and community services that together may represent a village, town, or city. Inside the building there can be objects that themselves can connect to other objects in the same building or virtually to other objects in other buildings to create a virtual workspace across physical buildings. The buildings and the wider location and resources could connect with other cities and location services as a wider ecosystem of communities and collaborations.

These can be considered as areas that digital workspaces can connect and build together into a set of physical and virtual services. In building our digital enterprise we describe this as constructing digital workspaces that together represent the operation of the enterprise.

In our earlier discussion on horizontal and vertical integration of a supply chain we saw that the physical enterprise may be connected in ways that cut across markets and other enterprises. In the same way, digital workspaces may be used to establish horizontal and vertical supply chain networks in a virtual connection between customers, suppliers, and other enterprises (see Figure 2.3).

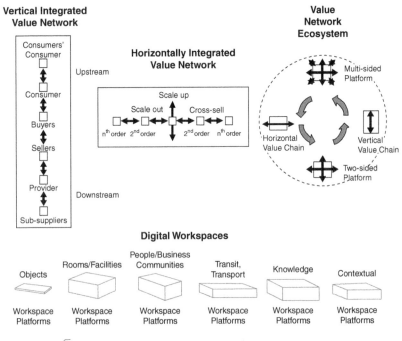

FIGURE 2.3 Digital workspaces and value networks

FIGURE 2.4 / Digital workspaces as platforms

The physical ecosystem of social, commercial, and environmental can also be connected virtually in what we saw as a digital ecosystem. Physical and digital products and services can be traded and collaborated in marketplaces. In the digital economy we saw that two-sided marketplaces (2SMP) and multi-sided marketplace platforms (MSPs) could form to enable many customers and suppliers to come together to conduct e-commerce. These are *digital platforms* that can be developed to enable digital enterprises to work both inside and outside the organization in the physical and digital economy (see Figure 2.4).

Value network ecosystems are built using these digital platforms. Digital workspaces can be thought of as digital platforms that support activities in the enterprise and the wider ecosystem.

Digital workspaces can be used to define how the digital enterprise is built by connecting physical spaces in the enterprise and the wider ecosystem. It supports market-making activities through the creation of digital business models that work by using these workspaces to connect physical and virtual objects, locations, and transport between locations.

This is the "big idea" of digitization and how digital ecosystems and the digital economy will work in the future. Digital workspaces move beyond the idea of user experience (UX) and customer experience (CX) into considering how digital workspaces are constructed so that users, customers, and the enterprise work as a digital business.

Digital workspaces are digital platforms that support a multilayered set of capabilities that are specific to each enterprise. Tables 2.1–2.6 list some examples of digital technologies that can be used to construct these digital workspaces. In the next chapters we look at real case studies of how organizations have used digital technologies to build their digital enterprise.

TABLE 2.1   Digital knowledge platform examples

Digital Workspace Platform	Examples of Digital Technologies Enabling this Digital Workspace
Knowledge augmentation Knowledge Platforms	• Crowd knowledge – example: Wikipedia • Real-time metrics dashboard visualization • Multi-device data synchronization • Augmented communication library – context of past activity and associations • Personal data profile, lookup bio image search, and knowledge access • Co-innovation • 2D and 3D design visualization • Location information support, e.g. nearest stock, person, assistance

TABLE 2.2   Digital contextual augmentation platform examples

Digital Workspace Platform	Examples of Digital Technologies Enabling this Digital Workspace
Contextual relationship augmentation Contextual Platforms	• Automated identity recognition • Location/local knowledge access • Ideation, co-creation • Preference-based communication routing automation • Location information support, e.g. nearest stock, person, assistance • Integrated work and user/device • Knowledge augmentation "did you know…?"

TABLE 2.3   Digital transit platform examples

Digital Workspace Platform	Examples of Digital Technologies Enabling this Digital Workspace
Travel - In-transit automation Travel-Transit Platforms	• Travel platforms • Package transit tracking, transport management platforms • Workflow management • Transport event feeds • Real-time performance management • Smart connected transport scheduling • Intelligent vehicle sensors • Inter-network seamless identity management • Real-time sourcing/supply chain integration • Inter-network integration, e.g. wireless and Bluetooth

TABLE 2.4 Digital personal/business community platform examples

Digital Workspace Platform	Examples of Digital Technologies Enabling this Digital Workspace
Personal/Business Community Personal Platform Community Platform	• Personal platforms • Community platforms, e.g. smart city energy grid • Community information grids • Real-time office/location activity • Voice commands • Physical projection to multi-user eye synchronization auto zoom/in and out of location • Real-time voice language translation • Real-time living space and ambient living • Smart room – object environment integration • Inter-network automated transfer • Information personalization – own viewpoint • Bio signature scanning • Furniture space sharing • Smart energy management • Integrated real-time diary–work scheduler • Real-time multi-party work orchestration • Crowdsource – ideation

TABLE 2.5 Digital room/facility platform examples

Digital Workspace Platform	Examples of Digital Technologies Enabling this Digital Workspace
Room/Facility augmentation Room/Facility Platforms	• Room platforms • Facility platforms • Wall, surface gesture integration • Transparent surface projection • Virtual whiteboard • Object physical virtual animation • Solar energy, home grid • Wide angle group projection, social interaction • Spatial augmentation, virtual room • Virtual location collaboration • 3D movement sensor • 3D stereoscopic measurement and digitization • Object-to-surface projection – interconnectivity; virtual model adjustment, input • Automatic proximity on/off sensing – body/location/lighting/touch • Room-embedded physical sensors • Office surfaces information augmentation

TABLE 2.6   **Digital object platform examples**

Digital Workspace Platform	Examples of Digital Technologies Enabling this Digital Workspace
Object augmentation Object Platforms	• Wearables, devices • Appliance/spare component specification augmentation • Low carbon materials • Integrated object classification and semantic awareness search • Multipurpose device – dynamic use applications in context • Flexible substrate displays on physical objects, e.g. electronic paper, smart cup • Physical/virtual object integration • Tablet/work device to virtual projection device integration • Accelerometer sensors • Physical object bio-sensing example: cup • Multi-form factor modality support • Life sciences integration • Transport/item identity specification tags • Movement three-axis gyroscope sensors • Conduction battery charging • Product cluster information • Contact memory buttons (CMB) • Near-field communication (NFC), quick response (QR), and radio frequency identification (RFID) tags

The Next Technological Era

The development of digital workspaces is part of a continuing evolution of technology over the past decades. The earlier ideas of technology and internet network-centric connectivity created a human-centric technology vision. Information could pass between the "four walls" of the organization to external entities and social networks.

But within a mere decade or less, this era is now long past. Instead we have an explosion of digital data and connectivity with mobile devices and sensors that are ushering in a new technological era of immersive connected spaces. The early innocence of the information economy has given way to a new reality on the horizon that promises new forms of digital intelligence. The human is no longer the center of the digital universe. Devices, sensors, and smart machines play a role in creating a multiplicity of physical and digital experiences for which we are only just starting to see the possibilities. Our challenge is that we make these systems what they are and must direct their development for the benefit of society, and social and economic sustainability.

Chapter Summary

In this chapter we considered some of the basic academic foundations of modern information theory in its construction of semantic meaning and the contextual use of information from simple to complex meaning. The journey of the practitioner in the real world evolves as the technologies available to develop new software and hardware capabilities constantly change. This will continually challenge the practitioner and the research theorist to keep up with the rate of change and make sense of the new opportunities and potential threats that these may bring.

The next chapter explores the reality of the digital enterprise today through case study examples as we pass on this journey into the next technological era. We look at what it means to define a digital enterprise and how the use of digital workspaces can help describe the potential practitioners and lessons needed for successful architecture of the digital enterprise.

Part II

Digital Enterprise in the Digital Economy

chapter 3

The Business Impact of Digital Technologies

Chapter Introduction

The scale of digitization is a pervasive story across all industries in the developed and developing world (Figure 3.1). Digital information through devices and networks span local, regional, and global economies. As technology adoption spreads, information become digitized, and products and service barriers are transformed.

As a practitioner having worked in many of these industries, it is interesting to see the extent to which technology has evolved in companies and markets to exploit the data and connections to consumers and providers. Digital ecosystems have formed from these connections to enable the enterprise to join with the consumer and suppliers in ways that can have a potential transforming effect for all.

Foundation digital practices – changing business models

In the previous chapters we developed the narrative of digitization, examining the different viewpoints and perspectives of digital technologies that are changing the solutions landscape.

In this chapter we start to explore how businesses are using digital technologies to change their enterprise organization and the way they work. We describe these as *foundational*, as they represent key examples of common digital-technology practices that can be found across many industries.

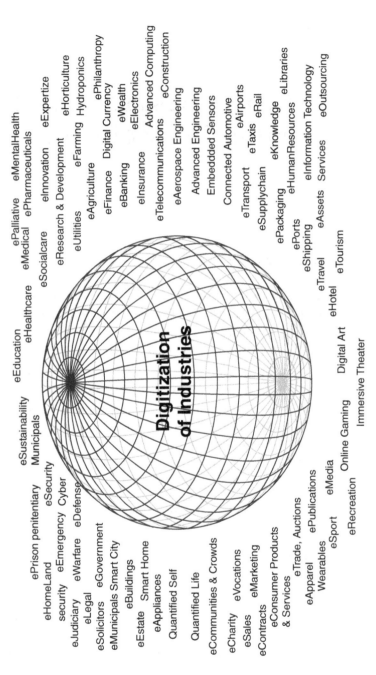

FIGURE 3.1 The digitization of industries

Each case study in this chapter will illustrate the use of digital technologies from an example industry to demonstrate the key principles to build digital enterprise practice.

Case Studies of Common Digital Solutions

In this chapter we explore 25 common foundational digital practices that could be considered as common foundations that are cross-cutting all industries. Table 3.1 lists these case studies and their common foundational digital practice.

A schematic diagram of the common digital practices (Figure 3.2) follows Table 3.1 as an illustration of how these may be thought of as part of shaping the wider digital economy of connected services and industries.

TABLE 3.1 Foundation digital practices

	Example Industry Sector	Common Foundation Digital Platforms	Example Foundation Digital Practice
1	Government-funded innovation	Establishing a digital enterprise platform for a city	Digital living spaces and the "internet of things" platform
2	Consumer home products industry	Establishing a digital platform for a home	Smart home
3	Consumer energy industry	Establishing a digital platform for energy efficiency	Smart energy
4	Metropolitan industry	Establishing a digital platform for city services	Smart city
5	Consumer electronics industry	Establishing a digital platform for retail trading	Smart retail
6	Global package logistics industry	Establishing a digital platform for logistics management	Supply chain logistics and e-commerce
7	Consumer goods industry	Establishing a digital platform for corporate social responsibility (CSR)	Corporate social responsibility
8	Automotive industry	Establishing a digital platform for multi-channel marketing	Multi-channel marketing
9	Fast-moving consumer foods industry	Establishing a digital platform for social marketing	Crowdsourced marketing

Continued

Table 3.1   *Continued*

	Example Industry Sector	Common Foundation Digital Platforms	Example Foundation Digital Practice
10	Software gaming industry	Establishing a digital platform for media delivery infrastructure	Hybrid cloud orchestration
11	Hospitality industry	Establishing a digital platform for hospitality engagement	Mobile guest services
12	Sportswear industry	Establishing a digital platform for lifestyle	Wearables and gamification
13	Financial services consumer industry	Establishing a digital platform for financial payments	Embedded digital payments
14	Healthcare services industry	Establishing a digital platform for patient care	Augmented patient care sensor feedback
15	Agriculture industry	Establishing a digital platform for geospatial safety	Geospatial mobile services – citizen safety
16	Emergency assurance industry	Establishing a digital platform for disaster management	Disaster recovery
17	Open government	Establishing a digital platform for citizen data services	Open data
18	Healthcare travel industry	Establishing a digital platform for health services	e-medical data access exchange for connected care
19	Medical research industry	Establishing a digital platform for medical care	Translation research "bench to bedside"
20	Security services industry	Establishing a digital platform for social monitoring	Social media emergency management
21	Consumer products industry	Establishing a digital platform for crowd innovation	Open innovation crowdsourcing, crowdfunding
22	Automotive design industry	Establishing a digital platform for vehicle automation	Smart electric cars
23	Aerospace engineering industry	Establishing a digital platform for product-service maintenance	Smart maintenance
24	Financial investment services industry	Establishing a digital platform for analytics machine learning	Machine learning and data analytics
25	Security defense industry	Establish a digital platform for cyber threat management	Cyber defense

Digital Enterprice — Common Digital Workspace Practices

Shaping the Digital Economy

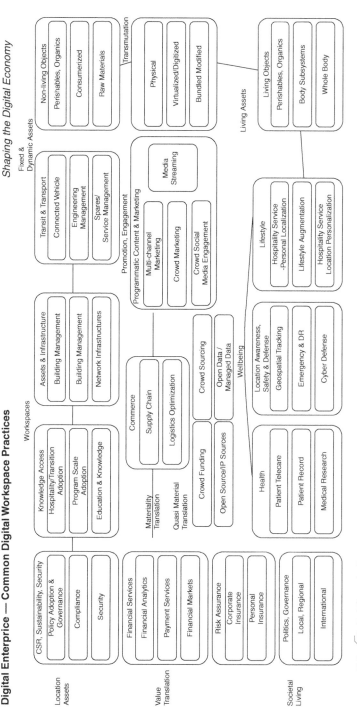

FIGURE 3.2 Digital foundations

1. Government-funded Innovation – Digital Living Spaces and the Internet of Things Platform

Case study – ELLIOT project, experimental living lab, practitioner concept of digital living spaces

The ELLIOT (Experiential Living Lab Internet of Things) project is a European Union Commission FP7 initiative started in 2010 and completed in June 2013 to explore the use of internet of things (IoT) technologies in living spaces. The consortium of digital media and marketing-channel technologies from Italy, and academic institutions from Germany and the UK, aimed to develop pilots in the following industry scenarios listed below:[1]

- **E-services for life and health** at the San Raffaele Hospital, Italy.
- **Design and use of intelligent product applications** in an IoT environment in Germany, addressing safety and security issues in intra-logistics.
- **Green services** in France, where a flow of environmental data is collected from various **mobile** ("citizen mobile sensors," "city green electric vehicles," and green watches) and **fixed** sensors (city devices, sensors on inhabitants' balconies).
- **The remote assistance for cardio-patients** case in Bulgaria, based on an intelligent IoT platform to provide medical services to patients remotely from a medical center.
- **The energy efficiency scenario** in Slovakia, aimed at implementing the energy efficiency, goal-driven, intelligent application of a smart office.
- **The retail-use case** in Hungary, to operate an intelligent shopping environment, where user-friendly customer experience is achieved using IoT technologies – RFID, barcode, NFC – on personal information terminals.

The project aims to develop an *"internet of things (IOT) experiential platform"* where users/citizens are directly involved in co-creating, exploring, and experimenting with new ideas, concepts, and technological artifacts related to IoT applications and services. ELLIOT studied the potential impact of IoT and the future internet in the context of the open-user-centered innovation paradigm and of the living lab approach.

2. Consumer Home Products Industry – Smart Home

Case study – Bosch HomeConnect[TM], practitioner concept of smart home

BSH Bosch und Siemens Hausgeräte GmbH, (or Bosch and Siemens Household Appliances, BSH) is the largest manufacturer of home appliances in Europe and one of the leading companies in the sector worldwide. The group is a joint venture set up between Robert Bosch GmbH and Siemens

AG, with reported annual sales of €9.8 billion in 2012 and which operates 42 factories in 13 countries in Europe, the USA, Latin America, and Asia.

The BSH product range covers a wide spectrum. It includes large home appliances for cooking, dishwashing, and laundry in the washing and drying product category; refrigeration and freezing; as well as a multitude of small appliances, such as fully automatic espresso machines, floor care, and hot-water appliances in the consumer products categories.[2]

Our living rooms have become a potential area for digital technology to support the augmentation of the human living experience and to generate savings in energy, wastage, and space management. Many home appliances have the potential for connectivity to allow remote access and control using embedded software, sensors, and actuators to manage the use of these devices.

BSH developed a unifying platform called HomeConnect™ designed to connect all your home appliances, regardless of the brand. Outside the core needs of flexibility, usability, and efficiency, customers revealed through BSH research that connectivity was high on the list of desired features, allowing remote control and service functions.[3]

Homeconnect™ is based on widely adopted technologies: a smartphone and a Wi-Fi router are all that is needed to use the free Home Connect app to operate connected household appliances. Users register online with a valid e-mail address, and data is exchanged between the app and the connected household appliances using the Homeconnect™ protocol. Only the most necessary data is stored on the dedicated Homeconnect™ server – and it is stored anonymously.

The aim is to establish a single mobile application that can support a simplified lifestyle to manage and improve the efficiency of home appliances. With an estimated 90% of home appliances coming from different brands, interoperability is important in order to simplify control over the many different appliances and potentially different services. Currently there is no set standard for appliance connectivity, but the aim would be to have Homeconnect™ work with other domestic control systems, so that in the future it could be integrated into a larger home control service.

3. Consumer Energy Industry – Smart Energy

Case study – Google Nest thermostat, practitioner concept of smart energy

Google Nest thermostat is the result of a $3.2 billion acquisition of a home automation company by Google in January 2014. The Nest device is more than just an automated heat and water boiler-sensor, it also operates as a smoke and CO detector,[4] and forms the basis of a smart home platform that many industry commentators at the time saw coming with the Google acquisition.[5]

A key principle in smart metering is to give consumers feedback of the actual consumption patterns in order to improve energy efficiency. Studies in consumption behavior suggest that 20–30% of heating and energy that people pay for is wasted.[6]

The Google Nest works on the principle of ascertaining when you are out of the house or office, and adjusting your heat settings accordingly. Although most customers will be looking to use the device for their homes, this piece of kit could be ideal when looking to keep costs down in the office, particularly during holiday periods or weekends. Perhaps more crucially, the Nest connects to the internet via your smartphone app and sends you handy usage reports. It can then make recommendations as to how you can save money on your home energy bills.

By linking the home sensors of heating and water to mobile apps control, and an internet connection to a cloud platform, Google can establish a home services platform that can integrate and expand living space services potentially into a wide range of appliances and consumption services.

The initial concept around *smart metering* in home commercial management centered around the use of smart meters to detect energy utility consumption in heating, lighting, combustion, water consumption, and air-conditioning units. The scope of *smart energy* encompasses the wider perspective of smart grid; smart renewable energy sources such as solar, wind, and tidal sources; and smart reclamation and wastage management through recycling energy and waste.

4. Metropolitan Industry – Smart City

Case study – Amsterdam Smart City (ASC), practitioner concept of smart city

In 2011 the city of Amsterdam established an initiative called "Amsterdam Smart City (ASC)," an "urban living lab" to potentially test and demonstrate innovative products and services. It is a partnership between business, authorities, research institutions, and the people of Amsterdam.[7]

ASC was initiated by the Amsterdam Economic Board, the City of Amsterdam, Liander, and KPN. It has grown into a broad platform, with more than 70 partners that are involved in a variety of projects focusing on energy transition and open connectivity. ASC is all about the total sum of testing innovative products and services, understanding the behavior of the residents and users of the Amsterdam metropolitan area, and sustainable economic investments. Using a collective approach by bringing partners together and setting up local projects, ASC makes it possible to test new initiatives.

The term "smart city" is defined as incorporating five themes: living, working, mobility, public facilities, and open data. There are a range of projects focusing on energy transition and open connectivity. A wide range of digital technologies are being developed to demonstrate proof of concept and to help with implementation in various city locations. Examples of these projects to test new initiatives for the smart city include:

- 3D printing canal house where partners collaborate to develop 3D printing services.
- Amsterdam free Wi-Fi offered on Amsterdam IJburg harbor connected on KPN's consumer fiber.
- Apps for Amsterdam is a crowdsourcing of open data contest in the municipality of Amsterdam to submit mobile apps covering one of six themes including safety, mobility, vacancy, energy, tourism, and culture. The aim is to stimulate "open data."
- WEGO car sharing is a sustainable platform to allow neighbors and friends to safely rent their cars to each other.
- Watt for Watt campaign to develop residents' awareness of how they use energy, with the aim of keeping energy costs at an affordable level.
- Digital Road Authority – incident management to enable emergency services to arrive on the scene as fast as possible.
- The Digital Road Authority – air-quality monitoring to reduce CO_2 and nitrogen emissions by guiding directly to an unloading zone.
- The Digital Road Authority – providing inhabitants with personalized travel advice.
- Public swimming pools which reduce energy usage in the operation and heating of the pool facilities.
- Smart sports parks focused on energy efficiency, smart lighting, biodiversity, and shared resources.
- Smart parking which allows you to book your parking spot in advance in private or public spaces. It enables drivers to spend less time looking for parking and thus reduces CO_2 emissions.

- Smarting living showroom in IKEA to provide various products that support energy saving, and water and waste management.
- Smart-energy electric boat providing a "Vehicle2Grid" application in a boat in Amsterdam.
- Smart citizen kit measuring the humidity, noise levels, temperature, CO, NO_2, and light intensity of the neighborhood.
- Serious gaming design to enable and encourage playful bottom-up participation of residents in creating a smarter city.
- Municipal buildings' monitoring of energy consumption.
- "OrangeGas" managing sustainable fuel pumps at petrol stations.
- Health-Lab collaboration between companies, government, care, and research institutes to stimulate ICT and care developments.
- Flexible street lighting that has a switching system for public lighting, maximizing market mechanisms through the use of a smart grid system.
- IRIS project to establish legal frameworks that offer the best opportunities to develop sustainable energy provision.
- City-zen project innovations to develop one of the largest smart energy labs in Europe.

5. Consumer Electronics Industry – Smart Retail

Case study – METRO Group future store, practitioner concept of smart retail

Metro AG, otherwise known as Metro Group, is a German global diversified retail, wholesale/cash-and-carry group based in Düsseldorf. It has the largest market share in its home market, and is one of the most globalized retail and wholesale corporations. It is the fifth-largest retailer in the world measured by revenues (after Walmart, Carrefour, Tesco, and Kroger).[8]

Metro Group established an initiative of 75 partner companies to develop innovative technology solutions relating to the Future Retail Store Initiative founded in 2002 by the international information technology companies Intel and SAP.[9]

The Metro Group explored two major areas for smart retail:

- The use of mobile shopping to develop technologies to support consumer retail.
- How radio frequency identification (RFID) technology could be used to enhance the retail experience from the logistics supply chain to the shopping store experience.

VMI

A combination of logistics tracking and stock awareness at the retail outlet enables the concept of vendor-managed inventory (VMI) to be automated, enabling improved stock tracking and replenishment planning by the supplier to the retail store.

VMI assists in stock management, throughput efficiencies of stock movement, and transport management optimization such as fuel and emissions reductions, as well as meeting closer demand profiles of the retail outlets.

Mobile shopping

The initiative developed mobile shopping services for consumers in the stores to assist in their shopping experience. The application for iPhones and Android devices shows users the location of the hypermarkets and keeps them informed about promotions.

RFID

The initiative explored the practical use of RFID functionality. RFID data can be transmitted by radio signal; the heart of RFID is the transponder, a tiny computer chip with an antenna. Consumer goods and retail companies use special labels on individual products and in the RFID tag a number is stored, the so-called electronic product code (EPC). It helps to identify items and shipping units clearly. The EPC refers to authorized users via special software that includes information such as manufacturer, date of shipment, and weight. The information is stored in a database.

6. Global Package Logistics Industry – Supply Chain Logistics Integration and e-Commerce

Case study – UPS logistics cloud and e-commerce, practitioner concept of e-supply chain logistics integration and e-commerce

United Parcel Service (UPS), headquartered in North America, is the largest shipment and logistics company in the world. UPS delivers more than 15 million packages per day to more than 6.1 million customers in more than 220 countries and territories around the world.[10]

In a 2011 report into the impact of parcel/package distribution, the UPS enterprise activity has an overall economic impact contributing 5.5% of North American GDP and overall 2% of global GDP. With such astonishing reach it is not surprising that the use of information technology is central to providing the critical infrastructure to enable around-the-clock package logistics.[11]

Dave Barnes, chief information officer at UPS, spoke at the ConnectShip Technology Conference in Tulsa, Oklahoma, about the power of technology to drive logistics. He said: "In the UPS logistics cloud, customers don't have to waste precious resources on creating their own global network. They tap into ours."

E-commerce has been a key driver in creating a huge business for the package delivery industry. According to shipment-tracking software developer ShipMatrix Inc., in 2014 UPS delivered about 42% of e-commerce goods, down from the company's estimate of 55% in 1999.

The rise of online cloud competitors such as Amazon have also grown and enabled rapid expansion of packaging services that compete with UPS and other major package distribution players. UPS appointed a new chief executive officer (CEO) in June 2014, David Abney, who said that the rise of e-commerce "has challenged some of our traditional ways of doing business," changing how the Atlanta-based company dispatches drivers, loads trucks, and earns money. From now on, he says, "UPS must slash its costs on e-commerce shipments at a faster rate than the continuing decline in average revenue. Next year, UPS will start charging by the size of ground shipments rather than weight alone, effectively raising prices."

The imperative of cost-effective and efficient package supply chain has never been more important. In recent years the market has seen the development of free shipping being offered by many retail companies. This has driven fierce competition and the power of large cloud marketplace companies such as Amazon.com "squeezing" delivery companies.[12]

UPS logistics involves a wide variety of packages and mixed modes of transport – land, sea, and air – together with an organizational operation that spans the globe. The technology strategy stated back in 2011 included a "logistics cloud" that connected the supply chain operations across all parts of the extended organization. The enterprise strategy focused on the following areas:

Mobility

The cost of mobile devices falling enabled widespread remote collection through handheld devices. UPS developed delivery information acquisition devices (DIAD). The statement in their public announcement by Dave Barnes, their chief information officer (CIO), says: "Anytime, anywhere isn't limited to the United States either. Customers can also use their smartphones to create shipping labels in Germany, the UK, Italy, Canada, and France. We expect the international expansion to continue on all mobile devices. Our strategy is to give customers accessibility to vital applications in the real world – in real time."

Scalable business platform

The UPS global logistics network adjusts to support businesses regardless of size, supply chain complexity, industry, volume, or season. Any business can plug into the network and use as much or as little of it as needed. The technology makes it possible, and the cloud makes it easy.

For example, ConnectShip is a scalable platform that grows with customers over time. Its patented architecture makes it possible for developers to create solutions that meet a company's short-term needs, while paving the way for long-term innovation.

Telematics

Telematics integrates with GPS and tells us exactly where each vehicle is in real time – or whether the driver is moving without a safety belt. Such technologies improve safety and fuel efficiency, and lower our carbon footprint.

Paperless order-to-pay process

The UPS paperless invoice system automates the customs process so that a package can be cleared before it even arrives at its destination. Electronic forms are available right away, so customs officials can start processing the shipment while it is still in transit. Customers then have a traceable, electronic record of everything, which can be archived.

Global import and export management

UPS import control is a technology enhancement that puts control over inbound logistics and costs in the hands of the importer rather than the exporter.

Global visibility management

UPS Progistics is a patented technology developed by ConnectShip to enable corporate-wide visibility into transportation management. The system adds visibility, reporting to the transport management system (TMS) aggregated from many individual TMSs in local regions around the globe into a common visibility interface.

7. Consumer Goods Industry – Corporate Social Responsibility

Case study – Marks & Spencer "Plan A," practitioner concept of corporate social responsibility and digital technologies

Marks & Spencer (M&S) is a major UK retailer specializing in the selling of clothing, home products, and quality food products with an annual reported turnover of £10.3 billion in 2014.[13]

M&S launched an initiative called "Plan A" in 2007, a corporate sustainability initiative with a vision to "help protect the planet – by sourcing responsibly, reducing waste and helping communities."[14] Plan A sets out 100 commitments to achieve in five years. A newly introduced "Plan A 2020" consists of 100 new, revised, and existing commitments, with the ultimate goal of becoming the world's most sustainable major retailer. Through Plan A, M&S are working with suppliers and employees to inspire customers, be in touch with the communities they depend on to succeed, innovate to improve things for the better, and act with integrity.

The company operates across a global supply chain network, and as such has to consider the sustainability strategy in this network context. For the first time in 2012 M&S reported it had achieved carbon neutrality for all M&S-operated and joint venture retail operations across the world, by reducing emissions, sourcing renewable electricity, buying, and retiring carbon offsets.

One of the company's key approaches is to design "sustainable stores." An example case study is M&S Cheshire Oaks in Ellesmere Port, the largest retail store that M&S has ever built and one of the largest sustainable retail stores in the world. Designed to be the most carbon-efficient premier store, it takes a holistic approach into key sustainability factors such as water, carbon, biodiversity, the community, materials, and zero waste to landfill. It is the third in a series of sustainable stores, following Ecclesall Road in Sheffield and Stratford City in London. It achieved a BREEAM "excellent" rating, which is the leading and most widely used assessment method.

BREEAM (Building Research Establishment Assessment Methodology) was established in 1990 and is the longest established in the world for the design and assessment methodology of sustainable buildings. It provides a holistic approach to measuring and improving all types of new and existing buildings. These include scientifically based criteria covering a range of issues in categories that evaluate energy and water use, health and wellbeing, pollution, transport, materials, waste, ecology, and management processes. Buildings are rated and certified on a scale of "Pass," "Good," "Very Good," "Excellent," and "Outstanding." By setting sustainability benchmarks and targets that continue to stay ahead of regulatory requirements, this encourages the use of innovative means of achieving sustainability targets.

8. Automotive Industry – Multi-channel Marketing

Case study – Volvo automotive marketing, practitioner
concept of multi-channel marketing

Volvo Group is a Swedish multinational manufacturing company with principal activity in the production, distribution, and sale of trucks, buses, and construction equipment; and in supplies of marine and industrial drive systems and financial services.[15]

Volvo Cars is an affiliated but separate company involved in the manufacture and marketing of sport utility vehicles, station wagons, sedans, compact executive sedans, and coupes. With approximately 2300 local dealers from around 100 national sales companies worldwide, Volvo Cars' largest markets are the United States, Sweden, China, Germany, the United Kingdom, and Belgium. In 2011, Volvo Cars recorded global sales of 449,255 cars – an increase of 20.3% compared with 2010.[16]

Volvo Cars used social media to drive customer engagement across multimedia channels using the Salesforce.com marketing cloud, an international software as a service (SaaS) solution. The use of the marketing technology supported the company brand strategy "Designed around You."[17]

Volvo realized the need to establish a different engagement with their customers and potential consumers with the increasing role of social media networks. The use of traditional customer relationship management (CRM) was evolving into a more social experience that had an impact in building a dialog and relationship with customers who were increasingly tech savvy in mobile and website use.

A comparison of traditional customer relationship management and what has been described as "Social CRM" is an interesting example of how social media networks have changed aspects in social engagement of individuals and communities of consumers and buyers with sellers. These two definitions illustrate this change:

Traditional customer relationship management (CRM)

Definition: The use of sales- and marketing-centric technologies including e-mail, customer surveys and feedback, customer analytics, and sales force automation. Sales engagement is through relationships between sales and product outlets; marketing sensing is through advertising campaigns and promotional management.

Social CRM

Definition: The integration of the sales engagement process to social networking sites to connect and build social communities. This is a different kind of engagement that utilizes blogs, podcasts, user-generated content, and social rating feedback. Digital technologies using behavior analytics, web and mobile applications for user experience (UX) design and gamification stimulate social selling and social innovation. The marketing and sales process generates a co-created customer experience (CX).

In Volvo, the transition to a Social CRM approach was to develop a social marketing strategy and upgrade of existing Volvo product and brand websites to link to social media sites such as Facebook, Twitter, and others. The aim was to engage existing and potential new audiences using a cloud-hosted marketing platform to integrate the customer and product experience across multiple customer touchpoints.

9. Fast-moving Consumer Foods Industry – Crowdsourced Marketing

Case study – McDonald's crowdmarketing, practitioner concept of crowdmarketing

The McDonald's Corporation is the world's largest chain of hamburger fast-food restaurants, serving around 68 million customers daily in 119 countries across 35,000 outlets. A McDonald's restaurant is operated by either a franchisee, an affiliate, or the corporation itself. McDonald's Corporation revenues come from the rent, royalties, and fees paid by the franchisees, as well as sales in company-operated restaurants.[18]

McDonald's used social media and crowdsourcing to generate new product ideas and consumer engagement through social strategies. In the London 2012 Olympics, McDonald's was reported to have attracted 20,000 submissions for its user-generated content campaign to support its Olympic activity since the start of the Games.[19] The company extended this approach to spending £10 million on its biggest Olympic activation campaign to date with activity celebrating the "personal stories" of the people working at the Games as it eyed a long-term legacy of being known as the "people's restaurant."[20]

The marketing strategy for McDonald's UK is to associate with the co-branding benefits of the Olympic Games. These includes messages such as "skill, determination, and hard work" in respect to the athletes competing in the Games, but used instead to focus on those playing their part in the Games "away from the glare of the stadium lights," whilst also positioning the McDonald's sponsorship of "Games Makers."

The digital marketing activity focused on gathering social media activity to support the co-branding. These included gathering together tweets, videos, and posts to create user-generated content about the Games, which many observers have described as the "first digital Olympics."

10. Software Gaming Industry – Hybrid Cloud

Case study – SEGA rapid cloud testing, practitioner concept of hybrid cloud orchestration

The SEGA Corporation (株式会社セガ Kabushiki gaisha SEGA), is a Japanese multinational video game developer, publisher, and hardware development company headquartered in Tokyo, Japan, with multiple offices around the world. SEGA's current business focus in 2015 includes providing software as a third-party developer. SEGA, along with their many software studios, are known for multimillion-selling game franchises including Sonic the Hedgehog, Virtua Fighter, Phantasy Star, Yakuza, and Total War.[21]

SEGA Europe, the European distribution arm of the corporation and maker of popular games such as Sonic the Hedgehog and Super Monkey Ball, needed to develop rapid testing of software development in order to increase the speed of delivery of games to the consumer market.[22]

The success of SEGA's business relies heavily on its ability to build and develop games quickly, efficiently, and cost-effectively. Customer satisfaction and loyalty depends heavily on game quality, so effective testing is hugely important. SEGA states that the testing process is one of the most time-consuming aspects of designing a new game, with the need to share large volumes of uncompiled code with up to 1000 different testers across the globe. Traditionally, once game builds get toward their final stages, the size of the files involved can be enormous, and difficult to share. In the past, SEGA had relied on transporting files via courier within country boundaries, and via overnight file transfer for international instances, but this was slow, carried an inherent security risk, and dramatically increased overall testing times. One of SEGA's priorities was to find a better way to manage large data files across geographic distances, but without losing control of where the game builds are located, or which version each testing office was using – and without compromising on security.

The demand for development and testing of software games varied considerably across any given year, requiring a variable information systems environment that was "elastic" and could expand and then contract as demand for resources increased or decreased. Also, there is a need to move the software games to market to launch and deliver the product. This means that the service needs to be not only "on-demand" but also flexible to be developed and tested in a secure private collaborative environment, but then delivered into a public platform where customer "gamers" could purchase the product or use pay-as-you-go and play online in a public-hosted cloud service.

The solution approach to developing a rapid software development and test service was to consider using cloud-computing technology that could respond both elastically and support an end-to-end delivery-to-consumer service.

SEGA had already successfully virtualized around 80% of its on-premises infrastructure with VMware, a virtualization management software specialist. SEGA further developed their initial virtualization into a hybrid cloud environment working with VMware and Colt, their cloud implementation partner who hosted and operated Colt's public cloud.

After initiating a proof of concept with VMware and its cloud service provider partner Colt, SEGA created a hybrid cloud solution that enabled it to flex capacity off-premise to Colt's public cloud when required, increasing its business agility. SEGA also wanted to make use of Colt's international footprint of data centers in order to avoid latency issues and improve the speed at which it could provide services to its customers.

SEGA distributes the codes to the majority of UK game testers, leveraging high bandwidth between all of its UK sites. For the game-testing studios around

Europe and the rest of the world, SEGA provides an external cloud version of the same service, hosted on the Colt Virtual Cloud Director (VCD) platform. SEGA uses the vCenter Orchestrator tool to help automate much of its best practices into the system, freeing up administration times and allowing the team to provide more value-added services.

11. Hospitality Industry – Mobile Guest Services

Case study – Hilton International mobile guest services, practitioner concept of hospitality mobile services

Hilton International, a renowned global hotel business, has used mobile app technology to create a new service that runs on a guest's smartphone to support digital check-in, selection of rooms, and customization of services through to check-out – all on a cell phone.

Hilton International have developed web-based floor plans online across 650,000 guest rooms at more than 4000 properties worldwide. It has announced that by 2016 hotel guests will be able to use their smartphone as their room key in the majority of hotel rooms.[23]

The development of hospitality service is key in the hotelier and tourism industry, which supports many kinds of guests from casual holiday visitors to corporate business residents. Hilton announced a new service called Hilton Straight-to-room™, which enables the use of a cell phone as a remote key. In their guest market research they found that 84% would like the option to quickly check in and to go to their room on arrival. This gives business travelers more options than waiting to check in to get their room key, or having to go to the restaurant or bar area.

This is enabled by digital technologies from smartphones to near field communication (NFC) to connect and open doors with embedded sensor technology with secure connectivity. The hotel digitization of rooms and facilities enables a new level of guest and partner services to provide more personalized guest experience in the context of the visit, and to offer support to inbound and onward journey planning – as well as loyalty and brand development.

Hilton has begun by piloting a smartphone app at ten US properties in early 2015. Also in early 2015, Hilton's HHonors™ mobile room-key app will be enabled at all US properties of Conrad Hotels & Resorts. In 2016, Hilton plans to deploy the technology across 11 brands globally, including DoubleTree, Hampton Inn, Embassy Suites, and Waldorf Astoria.[24]

12. Sportswear Industry – Wearables and Gamification

Case study – Nike+ gamification system, practitioner concept of wearables and gamification

Nike Inc. is a US multinational corporation that is engaged in the design, development, manufacturing, and worldwide marketing and selling of footwear, apparel, equipment, accessories, and services. It is one of the world's largest suppliers of athletic shoes and apparel and a major manufacturer of sports equipment, with revenue in excess of US$24.1 billion in its fiscal year 2012.[25]

Gamification is the use of human feedback to stimulate behaviors based on targeting stimulation and influence. Typically, gamification has an element of social group visibility to drive feedback and behavior from a community and a "scoring" system to rate the level of feedback preference. The "Like" button is probably the most well-known example of gamification where the number of "likes" can indicate a crowd preference for a product or service, creating a trending activity in a social network or marketplace store. Gamification can create feedback mechanisms that drive different outcomes depending on what personal goals and outcomes are served by the product or service.

Gamification as a behavior influence mechanism can be used for almost any system of activity that can be changed by human response. In fact, bias behavior can be introduced by most systems that have a feedback mechanism that can influence a group. Nike used the Nike+ wearable band to collect information and to integrate this with a gamification platform to drive better customer value and performance outcomes.[26]

Commentators correctly observed that Nike used effective gamification to help customers using their products to perform better at activities that they want to do, by providing a framework that gives immediate feedback about how they are tracking against their goals, and a sense of motivation (encouragement or pain) to help them go the extra distance to achieve those goals. What's the catch? People have to want to play.

13. Financial Services Consumer Industry – Embedded Digital Payments

Case study – MasterCard MasterPass™, practitioner concept of embedded payments

MasterCard, a world-leading payment services company, have developed a digital payment service called MasterPass™. MasterPass is a digital service that allows consumers to use any payment card or enabled device to discover enhanced shopping experiences that are as simple as a click, tap, or touch online, in-store or anywhere.[27]

MasterPass™ is an evolution of the PayPass™ wallet services by MasterCard that supports the development of cashless payment and is an evolution in the financial services industry. It enables customers to use their digital wallet to make payments via a mobile device through contactless technology or online website.

Digital wallets and digital payments have evolved from physical credit cards and debit cards. These represent new ways for payment to be processed digitally between consumers and merchants in physical locations or online through websites or on mobile smartphones or tablets, for example.

The issuers such as MasterCard and the banks use these systems to enable faster and higher levels of convenience and customer service experience. It also enables new contextual customer services to be developed in order to offer higher levels of customer personalization by, for example, offering payment services embedded in websites for easier processing, or suggesting purchases to support customer choice, and faster ordering such as restaurant menu selection and payment.

The MasterPass suite of services includes:

- MasterPass checkout services: to provide merchants with a consistent way to accept electronic payments regardless of where the consumer may be. For in-store scenarios, either at the register or in the aisle, MasterPass will support the use of NFC, QR codes, tags, and mobile devices used at points of sale. For online purchases, MasterPass provides shoppers with a simple checkout process by eliminating the need to enter detailed shipping and card information with every purchase.
- MasterPass-connected wallets: to enable banks, merchants, and partners to offer their own wallets. Consumers can securely store card information, address books, and more in a secure cloud, hosted by an entity they trust. The wallet is open, which means that in addition to MasterCard cards, consumers can use other branded credit, debit, and prepaid cards.
- MasterPass value-added services: to enrich the shopping experience before, during, and after checkout. These will include information such as account balances and real-time alerts, loyalty programs, as well as offers and experiences.

14. Healthcare Industry – Augmented Patient Sensor Feedback

Case study – TELUS home health monitoring (HHM), patient and consumer health platforms

Patients with chronic conditions such as congestive heart failure (CHF), chronic obstructive pulmonary disease (COPD), diabetes, asthma, hypertension, and some other health issues can benefit from an HHM program leveraging remote patient monitoring technology that typically lasts from three to six months.[28]

Once the patient is referred to the program by a healthcare professional in the hospital or at a primary care facility, they are introduced to a clinical care team that will track and adjust the execution of the care plan as well as provide support and guidance for the patient.

Benefits include increased patient satisfaction and overall quality of care. Increased patient satisfaction and overall quality of care can be found with the use of HHM, because of closer interaction with health professionals and reduced anxiety, as well as fewer emergency-room visits and hospital stays.

Patients also value remaining at home for their care, as opposed to being in a hospital. Patients get access to a mobile tablet or a personal computer that can be used from their home. Healthcare professionals get the benefit of capturing health data that can be shared with healthcare providers with a centralized view of all patients on the HHM program.

15. Agriculture Industry – Geospatial Mobile Services – Citizen Safety

Case study – Canadian Prairie Tech Enterprises farming safety, practitioner concept of geospatial mobile tracking

A Canadian group of rural farmers from Saskatchewan formed a company, Prairie Tech Enterprises, to develop a unique safety device that will improve farmyard safety for their children and other farm families. This was done in collaboration with an RFID technology firm in Markham, Ontario, who did all of the technology development and engineering work on the product. A plastics company in Saskatoon, Saskatchewan, is making the cases for the product.

The Whereabouts™ safety device has two components, a receiver in the cab of the vehicle or farm equipment, and a sender in an RFID-coded wristband. Each child will be equipped with a wristband that sends a signal to the receiver and alerts the driver of the vehicle that the child is nearby. The receiver gives off both a visual signal with flashing lights and an audible alarm when someone wearing the sender gets within 100 feet of the vehicle or farm equipment.

The aim is to develop cost-effective improvements to safety and to reduce risk on farms. The service can work for farm animals, children, employees, and contractors to monitor their geolocation and provide geofencing alerts when moving into harm's way of nearby farm machinery, or in defining perimeter fencing for safety boundaries.[29]

16. Emergency Assurance Industry – Disaster Recovery

Case study – Excelerate command and control, West Midlands Fire and Rescue Services (FRS) disaster recovery, practitioner concept of disaster recovery

Many natural disasters such as fire, flooding, earthquakes, tornadoes, and tsunamis often impact the local buildings and telecommunications infrastructure, preventing normal activity and use of communications technology – and affecting communities and the public in general. An integrated information and communications strategy for disaster management is critical in coordinating response and outcomes of different emergency services, fire brigades, civil protection, health services, blue light forces, and non-governmental organizations (NGOs).[30]

West Yorkshire FRS developed a satellite-enabled command and control system to improve incident management and establish a fully resilient solution.[31] The solution was the result of a fundamental review of command support facilities that also considered the lessons learned from recent major incidents in the UK such as the incident at the Buncefield oil storage depot in 2005, the 7/7 bombings in London in 2005, and the severe floods across parts of Britain in 2007. The outcomes of the review led to the development of a concept of operations: how they wanted their new vehicle and systems to be used.

The system uses satellite-based broadband and wireless video-enabled mobile command unit in the field of operation, and a fully satellite-enabled command room. The Excelerate company technology enables the command room to support West Midlands FRS commanders with the ability to view sector and incident imagery directly in the command room via the command units.

17. Open Government – Open Data

Case study – government open data interchange, practitioner concept of open data

This is government data made available free to anyone to use: data produced or commissioned by government or government-controlled entities and that is open, as defined in the open definition – that is, it can be freely used, reused, and redistributed by anyone. It provides the ability to transfer and acquire products and services across multiple country borders, providing secure, regulation-compliant information to citizens and businesses via open APIs.

The aim of open data is based on the concepts of a well-functioning, democratic society – that citizens need to know what their government is doing. Open data can be described as helping in releasing social and commercial value, promoting participatory government, enabling cost efficiencies of public federal budgets, supporting democratic use of data by citizens, optimization of common citizen services, creating value of open data insight, and cost efficiencies of public federal budgets.

Examples of open data services include:

- Land availability services
- Academic publication open access
- Scientific research shared access
- Sustainability
- Wildlife endangered species
- Art search access
- Library cross-search service
- Weather data
- Government spending and tax
- Open source computer coding with open source licences
- Open knowledge around citizen and local services
- Open content such as sharing writing, prose, photos, and videos in a freely available way.

Several national governments have created websites to distribute a portion of the data they collect. It is a concept for a collaborative project in municipal government to create and organize culture for open data or open government data. A list of over 200 local, regional, and national open data catalogs is available on the open source datacatalogs.org project, which aims to be a comprehensive list of data catalogs from around the world.

The use of open data in government is growing; large examples of this include 132,445 data sets in the US government open data portal. Prominent examples include:[32]

- The US government's open data portal[33]
- The European Commission's open data portal: open-data.europa.eu[34]
- Ghana's open data initiative: the government open data website, GODI, launched in February 2012[35]
- Canada's open data portal: Open Government Canada[36]
- The Japanese government's open data website, launched in December 2013[37]

Metadata

The definition of data standards for sharing information to support common definitions and interoperability is key to open data initiatives. An example is the beta version of the data.uk.gov portal, which offers open data providers and publishers with a quick and easy way of creating and publishing metadata compliant with the UK Location Information Infrastructure and UK INSPIRE standards.[38]

The UK government open data can use a variety of formats including: GEMINI 2.2, ESRI, MEDIN, and Dublin Core. For example, the GEMINI metadata standard for creation of UK location application profile-compliant open data, using GEMINI specification and discovery metadata for geospatial data sources.[39]

18. Healthcare Industry – e-Medical Data Access Exchange for Connected Care

Case study – Maccabi Healthcare Services connected care, practitioner concept of managed medical data access

Maccabi Healthcare Services is the second-largest health maintenance organization (HMO) in Israel, with over 25% of the domestic market share.[40]

Maccabi has pioneered connected care by developing "thinking digitally" and putting in place the coordination needed between health providers to manage all the required patient care activities.

The Israeli government has made significant progress in the computerization of health records for citizens and linking this with HMOs. By establishing digital patient records at the heart of the national system, this enables digital health services to be computerized off the back of these core data records. This enables many new digital process scenarios to be envisioned and implemented; citizens own their digital medical data and can access this through digital services provided by HMOs, GPs, and hospital services.[41]

Closed-loop connected care

Examples of digital care include blood tests that can be done in a lab and recorded against a patient's digital record. The results are then transmitted from the lab to the patient's GP practice so that they can view this with the patient. The patient can then use a smartphone app to look at their patient record and also view their test results. Further automation can be achieved through the blood test lab using an automated conveyor system that performs the tests and records the results digitally.

A range of digital-connected care services are possible, including:[42]

- Patient digital record details of location and health status
- Patient GP visits diagnosis and treatments
- Prescriptions and purchases at Maccabi pharmacies and 700 private pharmacies
- Automated diagnostic procedures and results
- Medical visits
- Hospitalization
- Community care and therapy

19. Medical Research Industry – Translation Research "Bench and Bedside"

Case study – U-BIOPRED medical data collection, practitioner concept of medical big-data research assistance

U-BIOPRED (Unbiased BIOmarkers in PREDiction of respiratory disease outcomes) is a system that supported digitization of data collected from research bench-side to the patients on the bed as personalized care. It is a research project using information and samples from adults and children to learn more about different types of asthma to ensure better diagnosis and treatment for each person. The project is collecting a rich set of study participant characterization data: clinical, patient reported outcomes, imaging, and "omics" (proteomics, lipidomics, trancriptomics, breathomics, physiomics, genomics) with a plan to integrate the data into a sub-phenotyping "handprint of severe asthma."[43]

Clinical researchers conduct disease research, which is referred to as benchside, while treating the patients on the bedside. Their study of molecular diagnostics involves studying the genomic and proteomic expression patterns in order to distinguish between the normal, pre-disease, and post-disease tissue or blood samples at the molecular level.

Molecular diagnostics involves processing of large amounts of data. Such data is collected, analyzed, and stored for each patient. The clinical researchers combine the data belonging to multiple cancer patients and derive the expression patterns of interest. This analysis process involves selecting cohorts of patients based on their clinical and/or measured molecular characteristics and running different kinds of statistical analysis algorithms on this data.

Bio-informaticians and bio-statisticians help these clinical researchers in data analysis. Initially they may take the data sets and conduct data analysis. Over a period of time, this research will evolve into algorithms that can be reused on the fly when the clinical researchers want to process data.

Ultimately, the clinicians will be interested in the easiest ways to apply the results of their analysis and research (at bench) to the patient (at the bedside). The suggested treatments from such a platform will be patient-specific, enabling personalized treatment with minimum side effects.[44]

20. Security Services Industry – Social Media Emergency Management

Case study – Twitter use in emergency management, practitioner concept of social media behavior and use in emergency management

The ubiquitous rise of personal smartphones and the use of social media websites such as Facebook, Twitter, Snapchat, Vine, Google+, YouTube, and many others enables the potential to monitor and track crowd social behavior in real time. Many individuals, from community online crowds to formal organizations, are using information from social channels and mobility to tackle incidents such as terrorist attacks, natural disasters, evacuation, and response.[45]

Specific government embassies may be interested in identifying their citizens and transporting them back to their countries. This may involve devices that can identify citizens based on fingerprints, or based on real-time photo identification. Systems connected through the internet, systems that operate in low bandwidth connectivity, or even no connectivity are used. Such agencies may require travelers to register in advance the data captured at airports when traveling out of the country, so that their data is handy in emergencies.

Affected individuals and their families need communication through the networks during such incidents. Fast recognition and regular updates of status data to the subscribing families will help. This could include capturing photos and videos of affected parties using cell phones and making them available to the subscribing families. Data analytics could be used to identify the people from photographs and video footage, based on the photos given by the families. The computation can all be happening on cloud-based high-performance computing processors.

Recent research posted in December 2012 by Panos Panagiotopoulos of the London School of Economics, UK, has shown observations that Twitter is a significant part of emergency prevention, response, and recovery for many local authorities. During unexpected events, councils are likely to tweet extensively and include hashtags such as #snow, #alert, #gritters, #police, or #weather.

During the UK riots of 2011, research also showed a peak of activity on social media from public authorities, media, and citizens who used them to make sense of the situation and intervene. The analysis showed that local authorities used Twitter in order to reduce the immediate effects of the riots and support community recovery. The research also showed that the level of Twitter activity was not always related to the extent of local disturbance. In areas where the riots were extensive, Twitter was not used and vice versa.

21. Consumer Products – Open Innovation Crowdsourcing

Case study – P&G open innovation and crowd funding, practitioner concept of crowdsourcing and crowdfunding

Procter & Gamble (P&G) a global consumer products brand enterprise, has been an early leader in the use of open innovation crowdsourcing to drive corporate innovation and product development.

The definition of open innovation by P&G is the practice of tapping externally developed intellectual property to accelerate internal innovation and sharing internally developed assets and know-how to help others outside the company.

P&G saw the value of establishing the power of co-creating through thinking differently with open innovation, and established executive-led targets of over 50% new innovation through open innovation methods.

Open innovation at P&G works both ways – inbound and outbound – and encompasses everything from trademarks to packaging, marketing models to engineering, and business services to design. It's so much more than technology.

Historically, P&G relied on internal capabilities and those of a network of trusted suppliers to invent, develop, and deliver new products and services to the market. They did not actively seek to connect with potential external partners. Similarly, the P&G products, technologies, and know-how they developed were used almost solely for the manufacture and sale of P&G's own products. Beyond this, they seldom licensed them to other companies.

P&G developed and launched their Connect + Develop (C+D) program as the co-creation crowdsourcing platform.[46] The digital collaboration platform was a key part, helping deliver the P&G open innovation strategy. The idea of partnering externally to accelerate innovation was applied across the company and around the world in all their work and with all their brands. Crowdsourcing enabled many ideas to be sourced, collated, reviewed, and shared for social interaction, and further development created the power of network effects of combining internal and external ideas through crowdsourcing.

In addition to ideation and open innovation development, P&G also looked at crowdfunding as a way to enlarge their exposure to early stage technologies that could match P&G's innovation needs. P&G for example established a partnership with CircleUp Crowdfunding to bring together start-ups for funding who are searching for new entrepreneurial enterprises. The partnership enabled P&G to gain access to a network of new companies and technologies that had already been through a vetting process. CircleUp also enabled new innovative ways to manage investment liquidity to assist in accelerating ideas into product reality.[47]

22. Automotive Power Industry – Smart Electric Cars

Case study – ChargePoint electric charging network, practitioner concept of electric car ecosystem

The electric vehicles (EV) initiative aims to extend conventional cars through the implementation of the EV ecosystem, enabling interactions between different actors ranging from designers and manufacturers to drivers and services providers. An open web-based system provides real-time control of the smart car data stream, enabling personal, relevant, and timely services from different perspectives.

ChargePoint is the world's largest and most open EV charging network with over 19,200 public level 2 and fast-charging spots. ChargePoint is growing rapidly, as of 2015 adding over 500 new charging ports every month.[48]

Electric charging network coverage

ChargePoint's mission is to help people make the switch to EVs and to provide an open charging network so that they can plug in wherever they go. ChargePoint is focused on providing a seamless charging experience for drivers, partners, and station owners. With ChargePoint, you can plug in wherever you go. It has also developed digital technologies to provide real-time data to drivers on the web, on a mobile app, and in car navigation units.

ChargePoint's website states that every seven seconds a driver connects to a ChargePoint station and, by initiating over 7.1 million charging sessions, ChargePoint drivers have saved over 6.2 million gallons of gasoline, avoided 46.2 million pounds of greenhouse gas emissions, and driven over 149 million gas-free miles.

23. Aerospace Engineering Industry – Smart Maintenance

Case study – Boeing integrated engine maintenance, practitioner concept of smart maintenance

Boeing's integrated solutions system optimizes maintenance efficiency by using radio frequency identification (RFID) and contact memory button (CMB) to store point-of-use lifecycle data about a part, component, or section of the airplane. This enables automation of engine maintenance by placing data on the engine to support maintenance management during emergency repairs, rotables replacements, and various other planned maintenance tasks.[49]

Working exclusively with Fujitsu and a major US airline, Boeing has developed, tested, and validated the airline industry's first comprehensive RFID and CMB technology for commercial airplanes. This system can significantly reduce an airline's operating costs by eliminating untimely, labor-intensive maintenance while providing easy access to maintenance histories.

Boeing's RFID integrated solutions system employs unique tools such as RFID and CMB to automatically identify, track, and manage critical airplane parts.

It is a comprehensive solution for a series of integrated technologies and maintenance process improvements that can help airlines improve their overall maintenance efficiency and performance.

RFID integrated solutions combines RFID tags and CMBs installed as *embedded technology* on parts and components throughout an airplane. RFID is an automated identification technology that uses radio frequency waves to transfer data between a reader and items that have RFID devices, or tags, affixed. The tags contain a microchip and antenna, and operate at internationally recognized standard frequencies. The RFID tag is similar to a barcode but offers significant advantages. The RFID tag stores data and offers enhanced data collection, the ability to read without a direct view of the RFID label, a dynamic read/ write capability, simultaneous reading and identification of multiple tags, and tolerance of harsh environments. CMBs are another form of automated identification technologies (AIT) used in this offering; there is significantly more information in a CMB, which is easily accessed by direct contact.

By providing a comprehensive, turnkey solution, RFID integrated solutions eliminates the need and long lead time for operators themselves to retrofit their fleets with automated identification technology.

24. Financial Services Industry – Machine Learning and Data Analytics

Case study – StatPro data aggregator services, practitioner concept of financial services machine learning and data analytics

The financial markets that conduct online digital trading of trillions of transactions every day represent a significant industry adopter of data management to model and optimize the decisions made on investment returns. A financial portfolio represents the scope and value of funds invested for a financial asset manager and the investment organizations responsible for trading, which is termed 'assets under management' (AUM).

StatPro have developed an advanced financial portfolio analytics dashboard that provides a portfolio analysis hosted by cloud computing. The goal of the software is to increase client financial investment trade sales, enhancing the client customer experience while meeting industry standards and regulations to reduce overall transaction and administration costs of portfolio funds.[50] The key digital technologies include the use of big data analytical algorithms for advances, statistical analysis of the financial markets, and investment portfolio performance.

The StatPro platform provides data visualization that assists human asset managers to analyze the financial analytics for assisted decision making. The StatPro machine algorithms are the result of encoding knowledge from extensive mathematical and financial expertise and methodologies for sophisticated risk measurement products.

The cloud-hosted platform enables remote access and self-service features for asset managers. The big data analysis collects data and performance computations for the financial portfolio analyses. Some examples of the decision-assistance algorithms include historical data simulations of value at risk (VaR) to calculated value at risk (CvaR) expected shortfall, and expected upside and diversification grade for all portfolio sectors and constituents. StatPro can also store the history of your portfolio's ex-ante VaR, generating a trend line of VaR at selected confidence intervals.

The risk dashboard can provide an expanding library of risk scenarios (stress tests) that can be applied to the portfolio, gauging both cash and percentage impact on market value. Each scenario can then be looked at in more detail, showing the impact on a segment and individual security level.

Overall the use of machine learning and big data enables the rapid assessment of risk limits and fund asset management decision support.

25. Security Defense Industry – Cyber Defense

Case study – TippingPoint, Zero Day Initiative (ZDI), practitioner concept of cyber defense

The rise of cyber attacks represents a modern-day phenomena in the use of digital technology, from nefarious activities by organized crime to the basic challenges of maintaining privacy and avoidance of theft of personal or corporate and national government data. Such theft of digital data is described as a *data breach* in those organizations or persons affected by the cyber attack.

The Verizon 2014 report of data breaches states that while 2013 may be remembered as the "year of the retailer breach," a more comprehensive assessment of the InfoSec risk environment shows that 2014 was a year of transition from geopolitical attacks to large-scale attacks on payment-card systems. Of the 63,437 security incidents reported by the survey from 50 contributing global organizations representing 95 counties, a majority 74% of security incidents were in the public sector industry. Of the 1367 confirmed data breaches recorded, the top three were 34% in the financial industry; 13% in the public sector; and 11% in the retail sector.[51]

The report provides an analysis of the types of attack patterns of cyber data breaches and the impact of speed of attacks, from when they are perpetrated to the time they are discovered by the victim. Cyber attacks typically seek out and exploit vulnerabilities in the software and hardware of information technology. They can also use physical access such as unauthorized entry to buildings, loose password governance, and security policies that can leave data and systems open to unauthorized access, copying, deletion, or malicious disruption.

The term "Zero Day Attacks" refers to an attack that exploits a previously unknown vulnerability in a computer application or operating system, one that developers have not had time to address and patch. It is called a "zero day" because the programmer has had zero days to fix the flaw, as a patch is not available. Once a patch is available, it is no longer a "zero day" exploit. People who find vulnerabilities may often sell this on to companies and government authorities, who may use this for prevention of cyber warfare.[52]

The Zero Day Initiative (ZDI) founded by TippingPoint was created because the ecosystem of potential sources of cyber threats in general is becoming more complex and sophisticated, requiring continuous awareness and up-to-date technical security research knowledge concerning as-yet-undisclosed vulnerabilities. The founders of ZDI believe that one effective way to capture this data is by establishing a best-of-breed research clearing house and community.[53]

TippingPoint provides intrusion prevention systems to deliver in-depth application, infrastructure, and performance protection for corporate enterprises, government agencies, service providers, and academic institutions.

The ZDI community aims primarily to:

- Ensure responsible disclosure of vulnerabilities, giving affected vendors the opportunity to issue solutions/patches to end users.
- Give advance notice to other security vendors – customers may receive quicker and more effective protection responses from those vendors.

The existence of the ZDI community helps make the general internet and technology community safer for computer users as well as promoting professional practitioner recognition for participating security researchers, and a channel for TippingPoint to provide customers with zero-day protection.

Chapter Summary

Digital technologies are the devices and platforms that underpin the many example digital industries shown in the case studies in this chapter. From a perspective of vertical and horizontal value ecosystems, there are some clear examples of how digitization has enabled integration across industries.

Part III

Digital Techniques and Practices

4

Techniques for Building Effective Digital Business Models

Chapter Introduction

In the previous chapter we explored a wide range of industry case studies in the use of digital technologies for enterprise outcome performance. While to some extent this is still in its infancy in some of the industries discussed, others are already outliers leading a new digital enterprise that is reimaging their business. The combination of selected technologies is already full steam ahead, however, in the sense that we are already past the early stages of evaluation. Today, many mobile devices, applications, and social content are "out there" being developed in the marketplace in real time.

In this chapter we observe through practical case study how digital technologies have been used in practice to create new digital business. We will use digital workspaces to describe and visualize how these technologies have been combined to enable a new digital business model to emerge. We look at selected industry sectors and specific companies from the perspective of their digital enterprise journey, including perspectives from experienced practitioners working at the forefront of the drive to lead and innovate with new digital technologies. The examples in this chapter are lessons learned in how practitioners have used concepts applied to digital technologies to build a digital enterprise.

The chapter concludes by drawing together the various digital business models into a summary catalog of common digital workspaces across all the cases explored. These offer guidance for practitioners seeking examples for building a digital enterprise.

Case Studies of Digital Business Models

In this chapter we examine the selected examples of digital business models and their digital workspaces set out in Table 4.1. A diagram (Figure 4.1) is provided after Table 4.1 to illustrate the visualization concepts used in the case studies set out in this chapter.

TABLE 4.1   Digital business model case studies

	Example Digital Business Model	Digital Business Model	Example Digital Workspaces
1	Digital retail business model	Establishing an integrated digital retail-to-supply-chain enterprise	Digital shop Digital supply chain Digital marketing
2	Digital financial services business model	Establishing a digital financial services enterprise	Digital wallet Digital payments Digital financial services
3	Digital advanced engineering business model	Establishing a software-managed product-engineering enterprise	Digital product management Digital car automation Digital application lifecycles
4	Digital hospitality business model	Establishing an integrated digital hospitality enterprise	Digital guest experience Digital hotel service delivery Digital hotel
5	Digital government and cities business model	Establishing an integrated digital municipal infrastructure and services	Digital economic cluster Digital value of life Digital society and clustering Digital cities
6	Digital logistics business model	Establishing an integrated digital logistics infrastructure and operations performance enterprise	Digital logistics control Digital performance management Digital operations
7	Digital healthcare business model	Establishing an integrated digital healthcare and patient care enterprise	Digital mobile monitoring Digital responsive care in the community Digital medical translation research

Digital workspace model notation of a digital enterprise

The case studies in this chapter will depict how digital workspaces are used and combined to span the digital enterprise. Figure 4.1 illustrates this concept.

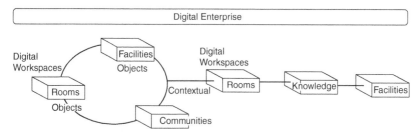

Digital Enterprise

Digital Workspaces

Facilities Objects

Digital Workspaces

Rooms

Contextual Rooms

Knowledge

Facilities

Objects

Communities

FIGURE 4.1 **Example digital workspaces notation concept for a digital enterprise**

1. Digital Retail Business Model – Enabling Digital Consumer Retail

Introduction

The growth of fast-moving consumer goods (FMCG) industries is a feature of the modern world, with consumer products and services in every part of our daily lives. Whether we are purchasing a train ticket, buying a soda, picking up prescription medicine from a pharmacy, or buying food in a retail outlet, these experiences are increasingly part of the "on-the-go" lifestyle.

Economists describe this as the rise of "consumerism" that has been enabled by the development of modern manufacturing and packaging processes, supported by sophisticated sourcing and distribution logistics. This is nothing less than a transformation in society since the mid-1960s that has seen the supply chain adapt and grow to meet consumer buying habits and led to the rise of large supermarkets and malls and an increasingly diverse range of goods and services.

Yet the physical logistics and mass product availability is now rapidly changing and expanding to include online business and social networking models driven by emerging digital technologies. The term "e-commerce" that describes this online sales and electronic purchasing activity has spread from the basic online websites into a whole revolution of digital marketplaces and electronic trading that now span complete supply chains from end to end. In the food and drink categories in retail, the opportunities are seen in the use of online technologies to improve consumers' desire for convenience and to drive higher product logistics efficiencies. With online services such as "click and collect," "delivery slots," and "third-party delivery locations" such as "drop and pickup zones," consumers are expected to increasingly use e-commerce services in the coming years ahead.

A report in June 2014 by the Kantar Marketing survey organization forecasts that e-commerce will account for 5.2% of global FMCG sales by 2016 – up from 3.7% in 2014.[1] At first sight this seems a small fraction of the total market, accounting for US$53 billion of global FMCG sales by 2016. However, this is an increase of $17 billion (47%) on the current $36 billion. These trends are seen in many recent surveys across several countries and trade regions, all pointing toward a rapid growth of online retail purchasing.

Conversely, the rise of digital purchases has also created a myriad of consumer choice and the emergence of the phenomena of *cart abandonment* is also on the rise, when shoppers fail to complete online purchases they put into their digital shopping basket. Recent studies confirm that this is becoming more prevalent and yet a BI Intelligence report suggests that 63% of abandonment online shopping could be recoverable with good online retail practices.[2]

The growth of online e-commerce is significant in some subsegments such as consumer products for fashion, gardening, health, and lifestyle, which are see-ing double-digit growth of online e-commerce purchases. The IMRG Capgemini e-Retail Sales Index forecast shows a 17% increase overall, up from 12% from previous year 2012, representing £91 billion spent online globally in 2013.[3]

Professional industry digital-marketing practitioners see this as a wider trend in social media and multi-channel that sees digital as the way of owning the relationship between the shopper and the brand and total experience. Digital is an accelerator to business and is the new order of business capabilities. The digital shop and digital marketing are enabling new ways that involve both the *non-digital world* of physical locations as well as the online virtual engagement through brand advertising that understands how it works in the *digital world*.

The influence and effectiveness works all along the supply chain that repre-sents the value network of the retail enterprise. Digital technologies can help optimize and expand into a new digital retail that embraces new capabilities from open innovation, crowdsourcing, and crowdfunding to drive new capa-bilities and exciting new ways to create customer experience and vendor partner engagement. This is beyond the simpler view of vendor relationships management that is a tactical digital fix. It requires a deeper professional prac-titioner perspective of how generative value works using digital platforms, networks, devices, content, and services in the real world of the digital enter-prise. Success in this is critical to driving the digital economy of the future.

At the core of all this is the need to understand shoppers' behavior and to meet their needs through relevant content and brands.

Toward the digital retail future

How the fast-moving consumer retail enterprise is responding to the online growth opportunities and challenges is today being fought out in the growth of physical and digital business channels. The old days of large superstores and malls, where physical presence is king, may be giving way to a range of smaller store options and volume discounters. The growth of online retail stores, both from the direct retailers and new "cloud marketplace" entrants, have started to support the changing browsing and buying habits of consumers. The new consumer generation is increasingly comfortable with mobile digital technology and services that can be both physical and online. Their needs still largely remain the same but the diversity of choice enabled by near-instant online information is driving new behaviors linked to lifestyles and social feedback.

Table 4.2 illustrates some of these outcomes from the delivery side and the consumer side with the FMCG market.

TABLE 4.2   **Examples of retail and logistics operational customer and consumer desires, needs, and outcomes**

Enterprise Operational Customer Outcomes	Consumer Outcomes

• Brand awareness
  o Lifestyle
  o Consumer choice
  o Spontaneous purchase
• Delivering right product to market
  o Product portfolio mix
  o Stock-keeping unit (SKU) packaging
  o Pricing and bundles
• Changing consumer tastes
  o For example, sugar reduction
• Sustainability
  o CO_2 reduction, reusable materials, waste reduction
• Corporate social responsibility
  o Support for societal needs and events
• Supply chain efficiency
  o On-time delivery
  o Planned maintenance, workforce skills, automation
• Partner network collaboration
  o Outlets, kiosks, vending machines
  o Partner revenue performance
	• "I want a product that fits my lifestyle."
	  o Personal lifestyle demographic match. For example "Social friends, my sports, fun time."
	• "I want to choose a product packaging that fits my lifestyle."
	  o For example, "Small bottle container for sports or utility bags."
	• "I want products that meet my values."
	• "I want a product that is sustainable."
	• "I want environmentally friendly products."
	• "I want products when and where I want to purchase and consume."

From the consumer side, the choices to purchase consumer retail products are driven by many behavioral and contextual criteria that may be both circumstantial in the place they live and their own personal values and preferences. In a highly competitive market where there are many products for consumers to choose from, the role of brand awareness is vital to get the message across to support and influence them. This is, firstly, to be aware of the product, and secondly, to match the appeal of the product brand to the target audience so that they are likely to want a product that meets their needs. Thirdly, having gained the attention of the consumer, to assist in the selection and purchasing experience by providing conveniency and efficiency for the consumer, which may include providing the right price and time spent so that the consumer perceives the experience as rewarding and enjoyable. The final part – actually consuming the product – can also create an experience, from the physical taste or feel, and so on, of the product to the association in the ease-of-use and aesthetics of the packaging, through to the disposal and potential follow-up with incentives to repeat purchase more product and the consumer recommending the product to friends.

Producing the great consumer experience

All aspects of the product journey – from the supply chain to support customers through to the sales and marketing and engagement with the end consumer – involve working with people. These include retail employees, partners, operators, engineers, sales staff working in the field, store outlet managers and their staff who buy and manage retail product stock, and the end retail experience. It also involves the consumers who themselves may be, or may influence, the direct purchaser of the product – either for themselves or for others in, for example, a family shopping basket. Each person's *"touchpoint"* in these location roles represents an opportunity to influence and incentivize the outcomes of the brand experience on the product journey, from thinking to buying and consuming the product.

From the customer operation and logistics perspective, it means understanding how to optimize the different physical locations, rooms, and facilities where the consumer product is manufactured, stored, and displayed (such as shelf space in a store, fridge, or vending machine), ready and available in time for the consumer to pick and purchase.

Figure 4.2 provides a conceptual view across the domains of workspaces that may inhabit the world of FMCG supply chain operations.

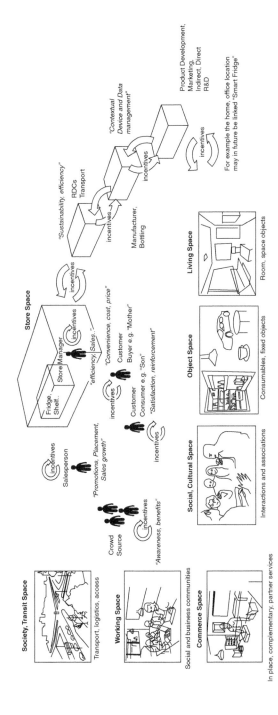

FIGURE 4.2 The evolving marketplace and supply chain

Yet with the introduction of digital technologies such as smartphones and smart home appliances – for example, smart fridges, pantry spaces, or connected internet TVs – the vision of the supply chain and the consumer is to potentially become much more interconnected (Figure 4.2).

At each location, in each context of the customer and consumer and their relationship with products, there are opportunities to influence and incentivize a great consumer experience with the brand. The taste, packaging, location display, ease of purchase, and many other factors come into play in creating and distributing the messaging in the brand content.

Building brand equity through digital social listening and engagement

Digital marketing is able to build the physical and digital brand of the retailer and their products and services in new ways. It is about social listening and engagement to enable the creation and distribution of brand content that consumers want to listen to and will be influenced positively by. This is about creating "stories" that relate to the brand in a way that will engage the consumer to convert into a sale. Understanding how these *stories* work needs to align with the direct sales and consumer engagement channels in a multichannel approach. This can be described as direct sales and wholesale, and then different market segment channels. For example, the "Consumer Home" channel could align to retailers who are then selling on to end consumers in their store outlets. The "Convenience" channel could align to smaller distributors and through wholesale to smaller outlets.

Digital is key to owning the relationship with the shopper. Digital is an accelerator in the FMCG business, in which availability and speed of supply to demand is critical where consumers are concerned. The "digital shop and digital marketing" is enabling new ways that involve both the *non-digital world* of physical locations as well as online virtual engagement through brand advertising that understands how it works in the *digital world*. Recent 2014 FMCG studies have shown that almost 50% of in-store sales are somehow influences – a purchase could start online and end up offline, or vice versa. Many retailers experiment with digital shopper marketing via online media and, for example, with social networks such as Facebook, and have built up experience that recognizes the need for different profiles of online shopper – and to tailor business plans for online that work in a multi-channel way. These studies explode the myth that the online world will cannibalize sales in the physical world.[4]

Gamification

Another area being exploited by retailers in FMCG is the trend in *gamification*, a concept for applying game design in order to engage and motivate people to achieve their goals.[5] Many retailers have seen the benefits of using cell phone apps rather than cardboard in-store displays as the method for getting promotional offers directly into the hands of the potential consumer. In one campaign, for example, a "point to win" game app used on a cell phone in Tesco One-Stop convenience stores had average personal usage playing over three times compared to a consumer not involved in mobile gaming.[6] At the core of all these methods, there is the need to understand the shoppers' behavior and to meet their needs through relevant content and brands.

There are several digital marketing strategies that are clearly seeing traction and operational performance for the consumer and the enterprise as a whole, as shown in Figure 4.3.

Digital shop

Digital technology can be used to influence the consumer upstream in the *touchpoints* to encourage them to buy the product "pre, during, and post"

FIGURE 4.3 Digital marketing capability strategy examples

shopping experience. Brand marketing to the physical consumer who is physically "in the store" is very different to an online shopper who is in a digital "store" or may not even be on a website directly related to the product.

In the store location it is possible to target consumers to specific purchases using digital technologies. For example, the use of proximity sensors such as iBeacon[TM] from Apple, to direct messages and advertising to consumer smart mobile devices while they are in-store, providing incentives such as voucher-cloud[TM], a website digital platform that can be used to offer discount codes and vouchers.[7]

In the online world the development of the "digital shop" and marketing experience involves what can be described as "loyalty-relationship marketing." This was originally called "customer relationship marketing," but that was not pointing toward ways to use customer information directly in the moment of the relationship experience. This created a "treadmill of promotions" that were not targeted at individual customer and consumer needs. The new focus is "data-driven marketing" that seeks ways to collect and use shopper data that creates much more compelling and relevant tailored promotions. This not only better supports what the end consumer wants but also makes improved use of data up and down the supply chain for better supply chain efficiencies. There are lots of opportunities where you can do this to create a better consumer experience and better business outcomes.

Content to purchase (C2P)

A second area where digital can have a major impact is the lifecycle of the consumer product before, during, and after the purchasing experience. Influencing the consumer at all touchpoints is about digitizing every part of the point-of-sale lifecycle in what can be described as "content to purchase" (C2P) (see Figure 4.4). Another name for this is "context-based marketing" or "programmatic marketing" where digital content is automated to optimize the search, purchasing, and usage along each touchpoint of a customer experience.

For example, product information on barcodes with LCD screens in the store can display information to consumers while they are in the purchasing decision process in-store. But this information is *out of context* if it is not situated next to the shopper. *Context-based* marketing is where the use of digital content can change the *promotion message* dynamically by product line while the consumer is thinking about, or in near proximity to, the product or purchasing experience. The overall effect is to create opportunities to offer a faster consumer experience and drive "convert to sale" moments.

Content to Purchase (C2P)

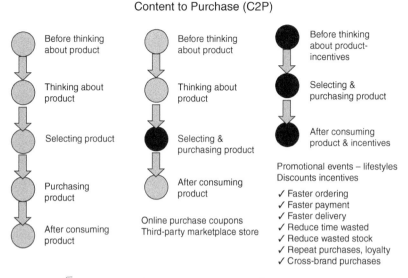

FIGURE 4.4 Content to purchase (C2P) FMCG example

Location-based services

A third area of digital opportunity is in the way that the actual locations of the enterprise's operation, its employees', assets', and partners' performance can be better optimized. For example, a sales force can be supported in their visits to retail outlets by remotely using digital information to better assist information and decisions during visits. With so many outlet locations to visit, the frequency of visits can have a direct impact on the business to influence sales outcomes.

Another location-based technique is in the optimizing of, for example, well-displayed product chillers that could have smart display boards that change their advertising dynamically. For example, changes in the weather could alter the advertising for different products, depending on hot or cold weather conditions – cold drinks in the summer; tea and coffee beverages in the winter. An ideal is to make this "live advertising" change for each individual consumer's personal preferences. There have been instances in garage forecourts, for example, of using face recognition of drivers to target in-store and gasoline advertising. While this has an attraction for retailers, the issue of personal privacy is also raised in being "followed" in this manner. On the other hand, it is well known that Facebook, Amazon, Google, and other online media sites use personalization of online advertising based on "cookies" and personal preferences in order to target adverts to individuals visiting their websites.

This can be taken even further by retailers, for example, offering their franchise network partners services that help them to run their businesses and indirectly sell more retailer product. A public example of digital location services is the "Coca-Cola – PRO avec vous" program in France that provides a service to small- to medium-size business partners. With the title "Being independent does not mean working alone," the "PRO with you" by Coca-Cola acts as a partner "to accompany you in your daily business."[8] The service provides a mobile app for Android or iPhone that enables remote support to help increase sales of drinks and also provides an incentives scheme where partners collect points to convert into exclusive amenities and services.[9]

The use of remote digital support services can help stores get advice 24/7 on products and promotions, help create better interactive questionnaires and customer services, and overall electronically enable outlets to run their business better. For example, franchise outlet partners can create their own "happy hour" promotions and drive better outcomes. It is an omni-channel approach to customer service.

New disruptive digital business models

Digitization is more than just "business as usual." It is also a way to explore and define new business models. There are many examples of digital disrupting and creating new retail business models, including the use of *crowdsourcing* to test pricing and display promotions in stores. This can provide feedback and improve ideas for how to enhance the consumer experience. We have found that maximizing effective use of big data intelligence needs very good data analysis skills so you can start to see how you can use digital to link to the digital market and connect up the whole digital enterprise.

It is about how to create really engaging user experience. Technology is moving very fast and everything is possible, such as augmented reality, for example, and there are often first-mover advantages in the ecosystem of the market. Business model innovation is how you create "influence at a distance" to enable revenue streams. It is about the total business model and how you are digitizing your business. [10]

The connected retail supply chain

While marketing and sales functions have been heavily influenced by digital technologies, the other major side of the business we explore in this case study, the logistics and supply chain, has also seen changes.

The role of logistics is at the heart of the business strategy and capabilities of any FMCG enterprise. It enables the execution and delivery of the product and the service experience to the consumer and its partner ecosystem. This often involves many operations both inside the span of organizational control of a retail FMCG enterprise as well as integration with partners in planning, transport, and services up and down the supply chain network.

The coordination and management of this operation requires *standardization* of processes to enable effective *communication*, *engagement*, and *high-performance productivity* and efficiency throughout the production and logistics cycle. These core operations enable supply chain planning to be connected to the product and to the partners and outlets. *Vendor-managed inventory* and *digitized product content* with own digital embedded content, or third-party content and tagging, provide advantage capabilities when combined with digital technologies.

Digitization may be viewed in the supply chain on one level as a way to help build partnerships between countries, sites, and employees in the use of information technology. Digital technologies can enable and empower a focus on a "customer first" philosophy across markets, exchanging data with customers and supporting vendor-managed inventory (VMI), which is today routine practice in many retail FMCG enterprises. This can be done at different levels of the supply chain plan (Figure 4.5), from aggregate region and stock category, down to the specific store level details such as store location, time of day and night, and individual in-store location.

With digital this can go even potentially more fine-grained down to specific customer groups and preferences and individual product stock-keeping units (SKUs). This enables the organization and the employees to collaborate better to help drive this.

Communications

Various tools can be used to enhance communications at and between sites, the field operations, and in office administration locations. Examples of these include the use of digital signage to develop ways to engage the workforce in many locations. This can also support corporate communications to sites and offices, including the canteens and manufacturing sites. Another example is the use of tablets and smartphone devices to allow people to access content for employee "self-service" at kiosks and hotspots in the workplace. Digital technologies can also help in technical practices, as in for example plant maintenance operators who can use tablets for access to mobile engineering

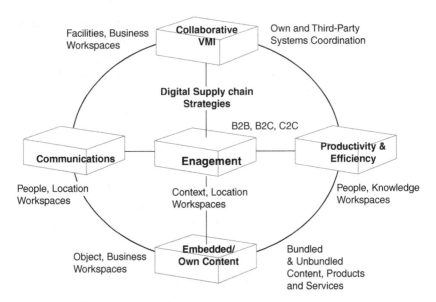

FIGURE 4.5 Digital supply chain capability strategies

and maintenance specifications. In staff training and development, the use of smartphones across all sites to team leaders and staff can help drive employee programs in skills development.

Engagement

Digital technologies are also supporting collaboration inside and outside with partners and with the management of our operational assets in the supply chain. Technology can enable staff workforce engagement, enabled by virtual webinars and workplace collaboration, to build engagement in offices, the management teams, and on site locations and with suppliers. In the case of physical assets such as fridge coolers, for example, RFID tags can be used to track the cooler geographic store locations in order to keep an inventory and status of these assets.

Productivity and efficiency

In the FMCG business, the speed and throughput of products and services is critical. The end-to-end performance of the supply chain matters in how productivity can be boosted to drive even greater efficiencies and effectiveness. Digital technologies and "big data" in particular can help in many ways, examples of this include areas in the engineering maintenance of production machines through to the logistics of operational data management:

- *Machine data* is an area that enables engineering quality and reliability of plant equipment to be optimized. The mass of data that is available today from machine sensors creates opportunities for pattern recognition to detect and take preventative maintenance throughout the operation.
- *Procurement and spend analytics* is another area that can take advantage of the many internal and external sources of information on the products and materials in the logistic chain for optimization of cost of goods sold.
- *Logistics and transportation* can also use technology to connect transport management systems with third-party haulers to enable tracking vehicles, direct driver cabin communications, and the setup of "automatic retailer alerts" for delivery on-time schedule management.

Vendor-managed inventory (VMI) digital booster

Being able to simultaneously meet the retailer and consumer needs and outcomes requires a combination of strategies that can work across the supply chain operation to address the different customer markets and consumers both physically and online. Logistics today include ways to integrate with outlets better through methods such as VMI supply chain operations techniques. It is possible to use technology to enhance VMI by providing alert systems that provide logistics tracking of vehicles between outlets and delivery availability. By setting systems-generated alerts in the store and online it is possible to monitor customer needs and purchasing activities directly as they happen in the store so that deliveries can be planned. These features are part of the connected supply chain that enables retailers to achieve operational outcomes that support customer outlets to deliver the product to the consumers.

Embedded and own content

Digital content in the form of QR codes, EPC barcodes, and RFID tags can be used to embed content physically into products in the retail store. These are commonplace in most retail operations but represent an emerging area for the digitization of object workspaces that can drive additional retail services. For example, smartphones can use NFC connectivity to scan retail store adverts and displays in order to gain information about products and services. It is about creating a connection with the consumer and the store and services that are not static non-contextual visits, but engage with the brand and the customers to create an uplifting value service experience.

Leadership in the fast-moving consumer "connected enterprise"

In this case study we have seen retail FMCG digital capabilities driving new experiences and value for consumers, with the combined use of strategic excellence in marketing and logistics and the use of digital technologies.

This demonstrates that each stage of the supply chain is a potential moment to influence either the customer or the operations and partners to deliver product and service excellence. By using digital techniques with the product and operational practice, it is possible to engage directly with the social spaces and lifestyles of consumers.

The "retail store" experience and its physical spaces have effectively "moved" to the contextual spaces of the social gatherings, rooms, and objects that it serves. The digital enterprise is a very different mindset and the supply chain business model is an excellent example of this transition for practitioners in business and information technology.

The future of retail FMCG performance will involve more than just commercial profit and shareholder value: it will need to embrace new trends in sustainable low-carbon product sourcing, lifestyle, and consumer-led choice. These strategies will be heavily influenced by digital and will impact supply chain efficiencies; new retail business models; and managers, employees, and consumers.

2. Digital Financial Services Business Model – Innovation of Digital Financial Service

Introduction

The financial services market is a critical sector providing the economic services for processing monetary transactions that represent the flow of funds and investments that drive the modern economy. The World Bank describes the development of an economy's financial markets as closely related to its overall development. Well-functioning financial systems provide good and easily accessible information. That lowers transaction costs, which in turn improves resource allocation and boosts economic growth.[11] This idea is central to understanding the past decades of financial services development and how it has become intertwined into the fabric of society and its wellbeing.

The key financial services players in this segment include institutions and organizational entities such as the commercial banks and investment banks, foreign exchange services, credit and debit cards and payment companies, and insurance and various investment fund management services. Several intermediary providers also exist, providing advice and service mediation such as discount brokers in buying and selling shares, and the management of investment funds and sources of venture capital.

The industry has been driven by deregulation to stimulate economic access to capital in both the consumer commerce markets and in the investment and stock-trading institutions. Legislation in the 1990s removed barriers in the market prohibiting one institution from acting as any combination of investment, commercial bank, or insurance company. This opened up new opportunities for the financial institutions to develop a range of innovative consumer and enterprise services, as well as enabling start-up companies to enter with alternative financial services models such as mobile and crowdfunding.

The International Monetary Fund (IMF) has described competition in the financial sector as being seen as necessary to open up economic development by driving more access to financial services, while encouraging innovation and growth in the financial sector as a whole.[12]

To enable these many forms of financial services, the industry is underpinned by a range of business and technology networks that span private and public telecommunications and managed data centers. Financial institutions have seen huge investments in these systems to connect the financial staff, traders, and services with their end customers through the screens and scanners enabling access and trading of financial services. As a result, these infrastructures have enabled a host of new forms of payment mechanisms and the rise of m-commerce and, latterly, contactless and digital wallets to enable an increasingly personalized, friction-free, and convenient experience (Figure 4.6).

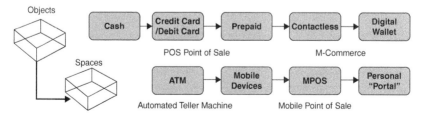

FIGURE 4.6 The emergence of physical to digital payment systems capabilities

The growth in ubiquitous automatic teller machines (ATMs) have enabled services once traditionally found inside banks and building societies to be accessed remotely, providing access to physical cash as well as financial account information and many transaction services.

The movement from physical cash to electronic payments has also enabled consumer freedom in both obtaining credit and the convenience of payment. For example, handheld card-reader machines used in retail outlets have been around for years, connected to payment networks managed by merchant card providers.

In particular, the growth of consumer credit and retail banking since the 1980s has seen a rapid adoption of new methods of electronic payments that has revolutionized the early concepts of secure electronic payments.

The evolution of physical and virtual financial services

To explore how key digital technology innovations in financial services are changing the industry – and its impact on many others – we need to examine how financial institutions have responded to the change in their role and transformation of financial processes.

One of the major trends facing the financial services industry, and others such as insurance, has been the significant shift in how other industry sectors have used digital technology to either substitute or cannibalize financial services into their own business model. Online retail payments, mobile apps that provide online banking to customers seeking alternative loans, peer-to-peer crowdfunders, and the emerging new digital currencies such as Bitcoin are altering the role and definition of financial services.

In response the financial services are seeking ways to become part of the financial payment and services ecosystems that are moving into the work-spaces of shops, transport, and enterprise organizations, their products and services (see Figure 4.7).

This phenomenon is also changing how financial services are perceived and used by the customer through the use of smartphones that can access as a "personal payment and digital wallet." Increasingly the internet of things (IoT) is now expanding this to a point where potentially any object can be a "point of sale."

To enable these digital financial services connections, many standards have evolved for contact and contactless authentication, and a range of payment

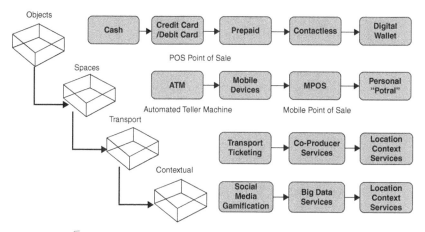

FIGURE 4.7 Evolution of physical and digital financial services capabilities

mechanisms now exist in the industry. Examples that are in wide use include the following:

- **Contact cards standards** – supports what is described as "IC credit" and "chip and pin" using the Europay, MasterCard, and Visa (EMV) tokenization mechanisms for payment processing.
- **Card-not-present transactions standards** – for e-commerce transactions over the telephone and internet. Examples include the MasterCard Chip Authentication Program (CAP) and via dynamic password authentication (DPA).
- **Contactless standards** – including PayPass from MasterCard, payWave from Visa, and ExpressPay from American Express. These support a limited range of transactions, typically US$30 to $100 from any mobile device, card, or fob key to a compatible payment device using NFC radio frequencies.
- **Online money transfers** – including PayPal, Google Wallet, WePay, 2Checkout, Stripe, Braintree, ClickBank, and many others that offer web and mobile gateway services between merchants and banks and payment issuers. Many of these include added-value services for individuals and businesses.
- **Mobile payment apps and internet integration** – an example is QkR developed by MasterCard that works through a cell phone with payments charged to an associated credit card, not through NFC in the mobile device, but the mobile internet connection wirelessly, or 3G/4G technology.

- **Mobile payment apps and contactless integration** – Google Wallet is a partnership between MasterCard and Google, an Android application that enables the mobile device to send credit/debit card information directly to a PayPass-enabled payment terminal.
- **Embedded mobile authentication** – Apple Pay is an example of using mobile device technology biometic identity authentication and NFC to integrate with payment providers such as MasterCard and the iPhone 6 Apple Pay implementation.
- **Other contactless standards** – QR codes are printed code symbols. Some industry standards are such as the Merchant Customer Exchange (MCX) run by merchant consortiums including Walmart, BestBuy, Sears, and others. The code image is scanned by a camera that can be linked to a mobile app that can in turn link to a payment service such as registered store loyalty cards, registered credit and debit cards, or a bank account. RFID identity tags are another type of physical tag that is used in contactless credit and debit cards.

The development of common mechanisms is important in establishing the digital ecosystem has common standards for secure and trusted exchange of commerce.[13] Often, in the case of new technology, the real and perceived risk has to be managed: in the case of digital wallets or contactless payment services, limits may be put on transaction value and volume in order to limit the impact if the card is compromised.[14] But this technology and the use of secure and trusted services will increase the rate of adoption and help drive new innovation in financial services.

Authentication and trust

This concept of *authentication* services is central to the original financial services industry role in providing consumer credit and secure, trusted services to provide cardholder verification of their identity and availability of funds for electronic payments. This premise is founded on the ability to validate transactions between trading parties in a secure and reliable, trusted manner.

The issue of trust in financial transactions is vital to the management of legal and effective commercial and economic progress. The traditional model of payment service to enable issuers providing card services to consumers and businesses who transact with merchants and bank acquirers has be to secure and viable. New "digital currencies" and mobile commerce has to be able to support these communities as well. For practitioners, financial fraud and theft of financial cash and assets is part of a landscape that requires robust and managed financial services and regulation to counter illegal activities.

The issue of trusted transactions and fraud are important issues in the industry. Recently the Payment Card Industry (PCI) Security Standards Council has set new rules for merchants and financial institutions. The new rules take effect from October 2015, meaning that stakeholders already adopting the EMV standard will be protected from fraud liability, but other retailers may need to upgrade their point of sale in order to avoid being liable.[15]

Financial regulation is part of the necessity to drive controls that protect consumers and industry conduct. This is also needed in order to balance the deregulation in the industry such as the Gramm–Leach–Bliley Act (GLBA) in the United States, sometimes referred to as the Financial Services Modernization Act of 1999.[16] These policies seek to drive more competition and innovation, creating the entry of new financial business models to the financial services market.

Yet the financial service industry, often stereotyped as a laggard to new business change, is facing an unprecedented time with the explosion of digital commerce and new, disruptive digital models driving new devices and consumer behavior. In particular, the new forms of digital currency and payment systems are entering the lexicon of industry services, and the use of mobile commerce is opening up the boundary of what it means to be a financial services provider.

Digital convergence everywhere

The new phenomenon of digitization in the financial industry is a huge opportunity for digital convergence. The world of physical financial payments and transactions is rapidly converging with virtual financial payments and services that are integrated with the customer and enterprise context.

With the use of software combined with embedded sensors in mobile devices, such as NFC and biometrics, this can extend into web pages and physical objects such as ticket machines, airport check-in, and many others. This is the contextualization of services that enables payment services to be personalized and relevant, and increasingly drives the embedded integration of digital technologies into the social and commercial activities of every day.

Making financial services markets work

This involves understanding the overall role that finance plays in an enterprise; the share price and the consumer decision process for payments of high- and low-value items are directly impacted by the effectiveness of spending and payment services. The emergence of the "digital wallet" is a new product innovation at MasterCard that can act as a digital "personal portal" to hold not just a person's credit, debit, and other account details, but also can provide contextualized preferences of their buying behavior and preferences in, for example, restaurants and other outlets and locations.

These innovations are adding huge value to consumers and partners, but you must have the ability to also offer resolution and arbitration when things need correction. Trust is, of course, critical in financial services. In dispute management you have to be able to trace back through the path of the transaction. You need this in order to make the currency work in a virtual sense.

Speed of adoption and the "value of time is money"

The rate of adoption of the shift from physical cash to cashless and the digital wallet will be driven by making the mobile commerce services convenient and easy to use. This can be illustrated in the example of a visit to a restaurant and how this can change with digital technologies.

Various studies have shown that on average a person takes, for example, 12 minutes waiting time to pay for their meal. The issue is that time has a value and that time is money in the literal sense of missing opportunities to serve customers better with higher satisfaction, loyalty, and revenue potential. It is all about maximizing the value of time and avoiding lost opportunity costs.

In the restaurant case we can use digital payments to reduce waiting times, but this can be expanded to include pre-ordering on a cell phone and, after the meal visit, in added-value services to encourage repeat visits and recommendations to friends to also visit the restaurant. Digitization and the role of financial services becomes embedded in the enterprise processes to help optimize the customer experience and the financial performance (see Figure 4.8).

Digital strategies for financial services

What is clearly emerging is the change in physical and virtual systems to enable financial services. This can be summarized in two areas: physical and virtual location context.

Restaurant order & payment

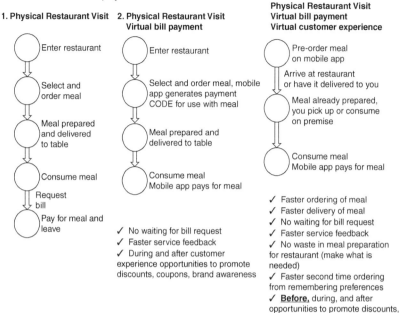

1. Physical Restaurant Visit

Enter restaurant

Select and order meal

Meal prepared and delivered to table

Consume meal

Request bill

Pay for meal and leave

2. Physical Restaurant Visit
Virtual bill payment

Enter restaurant

Select and order meal, mobile app generates payment CODE for use with meal

Meal prepared and delivered to table

Consume meal
Mobile app pays for meal

✓ No waiting for bill request
✓ Faster service feedback
✓ During and after customer experience opportunities to promote discounts, coupons, brand awareness

3. Virtual order
Physical Restaurant Visit
Virtual bill payment
Virtual customer experience

Pre-order meal on mobile app

Arrive at restaurant or have it delivered to you

Meal already prepared, you pick up or consume on premise

Consume meal
Mobile app pays for meal

✓ Faster ordering of meal
✓ Faster delivery of meal
✓ No waiting for bill request
✓ Faster service feedback
✓ No waste in meal preparation for restaurant (make what is needed)
✓ Faster second time ordering from remembering preferences
✓ **Before,** during, and after opportunities to promote discounts, coupons, brand awareness

FIGURE 4.8 The move to integrated context payments

Physical location payments

Many new digital platforms are fast evolving to take avantage of mobile, cloud computing, big data, and ubiquitous telecomminications networks. Figure 4.9 illustrates some of these major trends. Mobile platforms and mobile aplications can act as digital wallets sorting physical cards and through contactless technologies make physical payments. New security identity systems such as fingerpint biometrics are adding new forms of identity authentication.

Virtual location payments

Virtual location payments systems that do not require the physical presence of the customer enable digital e-commerce and many other added-value services for websites, cell phones, and smartphones. This area is seeing new digital platforms emerging, providing financial services multi-sided market-places that are integrating into online stores such as those we see in Amazon, Facebook, and many others.

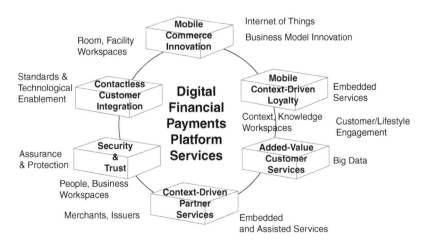

FIGURE 4.9 Digital platform services capabilities examples in financial services

Many start-ups and small- to medium-size enterprises are able to use virtual payment services to integrate with their business. Other start-ups have used these technologies to provide their own financial services and enter existing and new markets as disruptive incumbent providers. The example of Stripe, an online payments processor, provides individuals and businesses with a method to accept payments over the internet. Developers can embed Stripe's API on their website to accept payments, instead of getting a merchant account. Stripe charges fees for the service and a per successful transaction charge, but overall costs to customers are less than traditional card providers due to no set-up fees, monthly fees, minimum charges, validation fees, card storage fees, or charges for failed payments. Stripe has a seven-day waiting period for transactions to be completed so that it can profile the businesses involved and detect fraud. As of 2014 the Stripe service was available in 14 countries and being rolled out to many areas.[17]

Embedded contextual finance and digital enterprise services

The future for financial services will involve many digital strategies that make financial data and information a strategic competitive advantage for the providers as well as the enterprises and end customers they serve (Figure 4.9).

The importance of digital platforms supported by robust trusted digital payment standards and secure data management will be a defined change for the industry.

MasterCard, for example, have developed their MasterCard Digital Enablement Service (MDES) that is a platform to enable any connected device to transform into a commerce device able to make and receive payments.[18] Announced in September 2014, this is one such example of how the role of financial services payments have evolved into contextual embedded services. The MDES system works on the Apple iPhone 6, iPhone plus, and Apple Watch to enable secure payments to take place for contactless and in-app payments. All MasterCard transactions made through Apple Pay are ready to use industry-standard EMV-level security,[19] and are protected using standards-based payment tokens. EMV is an example of a financial industry consortium standard for secure payments. Tokens are card numbers that mobile devices use in place of the card number printed on the plastic. MDES validates and manages the authorization, supporting contactless payments and digital secure remote payments (DSRP). DSRP is a transaction method where a consumer is able to make in-app purchases using a token. Contactless payments leverage NFC technology for point-of-sale transactions, while DSRP delivers EMV-like transaction for in-app payments.

While virtual currencies are still in their infancy with respect to challenging banks,[20] regulations to protect consumers and manage fraud will over time see the shift from physical to cash to virtual finance in all areas of the financial industry and beyond.

3. Digital Advanced Engineering Business Model – Advanced Product Lifecycle

Introduction

If we consider the history of the invention of the petrochemical combustion engine, it has passed through many epochs of manual, steam power, gasoline, and electric-driven propulsion designs. With each product "version" the skills have needed to evolve to enable the realization of the technology from the idea to the real world. If we look back only as far as the mid-1980s the conceptual design through to manufacture predominantly involved mechanical engineering design and physical machining and assembly techniques. Computer-aided design (CAD) had begun to appear and was starting to define and influence product design. Robotics for materials movement, and computer-aided machining and assembly was rapidly becoming a feature of the modern production plant's shop floor. Computing was also not just limited to the components and product creation but had also started to embark on becoming part of the total automotive vehicle itself. In the early days, apart from the analog in-car radio and the electric motor-powered aerial on the external chassis of the vehicle, little else other than the introduction of an electronic ignition and speedometer was commonplace. There was very little electronics involved in the automated control of the engine or other drive components or the overall management of the driving capabilities. Fast-forward in time to 2015 and the integrated engine power unit and the complete automotive assembly and car-driver experience is dominated by computerized systems and sub-subsystems that aim to optimize fuel consumption and reduce emissions with significant cost-efficiencies of production, through to operating cost savings and an enhanced driver performance. Product features that are now commonplace in most commercial automotive vehicles include:

- On-board integrated satellite navigation.
- Braking and suspension assistance.
- Electronic engine start, electric steering, and engine performance management.
- Journey and fuel emissions planning and management.
- Engine energy reclamation in hybrid and electric cars.
- Remote electric motors for mirror and seat adjustments and air conditioning based on driver preferences.
- Bluetooth connectivity for wireless cell phone synchronization.
- Automated car diagnostics and drive alert systems such as tire, fuel, and other systems status.
- Automated car diagnostics for car maintenance assistance.
- On-board integrated cell phone for hands-free communication.
- Internet connectivity for in-car infotainment that works with mobile apps to download and synchronize music, videos, and other personal data such as meetings, e-mail, and route planning.

This is a continuous cycle of product innovation that brings the idea to market and enables new product capabilities. In the case of the automotive sector we can often see future technology advances in the higher-end specification of luxury-brand automobiles. New enhancements are now emerging in the "driver assisted" technologies that include crash prevention and speed detection. Others include features such as vehicle-to-vehicle (V2V) collision detection and in-car driver travel-planning route services and driving conditions assistance. These new product capabilities have sometimes been described as aspects of the emerging "connected car" that embraces an expectation of semi and fully self-driving cars in the near future. These innovations will include both enhancements to existing vehicles as well as "disruptive technology" that will potentially redefine how vehicles and drivers will interact and work together in the future. This scope will reimagine the transport industry and will include shifts toward a bigger picture of integrated traffic management and vehicle systems to reduce congestion, optimize energy consumption, and meet emission targets.

Embedded systems and the internet of things

In this case study we explore the use of embedded software in machines as a way of enabling new kinds of product capabilities. The term *embedded software* refers to software code that is written and hosted physically inside products and other objects not typically involved in computing. Embedded software is also something referred to as *firmware*, which is often related to specialist software and hardware that are specific to animating and enhanced control capabilities from complex engineering machines to everyday objects such as TVs, fridges, doors, windows, lights, heating, and many other examples. This type of digitization can also be seen as part of a technological journey in the way that the general rise of computing has become embedded and integrated into everyday devices and objects that assist humans and drive new commercial value and performance. Embedded software is today a key feature in many industries from aerospace jet engines and aircraft auto-pilot to machine-learning algorithms in financial market trading. These "smart" software systems are exploiting the data collected from sensors and systems to aid in real-time automation control to advanced analytics computation.

The "internet of things" (IoT) is a term that is starting to popularize the movement of embedded sensors and software in objects and can be described as the network of physical objects accessed through the internet. These objects contain embedded technology to interact with internal states or the external environment. In other words, when objects can sense and communicate, it changes how and where decisions are made, and who makes them.[21] From a practitioner point of view, this is a journey of how sensors and, more broadly, digital technology, is evolving to connect products and services with enterprise systems and the customers and providers of these products and services.

Developing a new product and software engineering journey

KPIT Technologies (formerly KPIT Cummins) is an international software services provider specializing in product engineering and IT skills to use advanced machine-embedded technologies to transform services to business and engineering.[22] Rupert Fallows, the services business development expert at KPIT, describes it as "a unique capability that is about doing something different in the way products can be enhanced by growing from a linear to a non-linear model of thinking." KPIT have developed this approach in the emergence of embedded sensors in automotive systems. This means that instead of the traditional basic journey planning for fuel consumption of a vehicle, a more sophisticated use of embedded technology can be used to fine tune and assist the total car operation, achieving much higher performance. An example is the KPIT ReVolo[TM] technology that works as a plug-in that can be installed into an automotive vehicle to convert it into a hybrid vehicle, a parallel hybrid solution that transforms vehicles into hybrid vehicles. The system is a platform to integrate and manage the car battery, electric motor, and motor control operations automatically with embedded software management. Improved performance outcomes include an additional 30% emission reduction, 25% travel cost reduction, and 35% fuel efficiency improvement.[23]

Vinay Vaidya, chief technology officer at KPIT, describes the difference as being in the way that the system's technology is working with the existing hardware objects such as the motor unit, battery, and mechanical chassis to optimize the total driving performance. Vinay explained, "We can collect data using the 'cloud' to learn how the car is performing and to analyze this data. We found that we could create mathematical consumption models to see how we could improve fuel mileage efficiency. From this it is possible to analyze usage patterns to identify driver behavior for example. This could include the driver 'not charging the battery fully' to other factors that may affect the total performance of the vehicle. With this ability to collect a lot of data it is possible to analyze and provide very useful feedback messages to the driver to correct and advise activity and behavior." Vinay explains that this was a unique value case in using embedded technology to help improve efficiency and the driver experience: "We can solve problems before the customer says it's a problem!"

Advanced lifecycle engineering and product systems

The embedded technology integration with the vehicle enables the whole lifecycle of the driving experience to potentially be optimized. The benefits of embedded software technology can help both the driver and owner of the vehicle as well as the provider and suppliers who sell and service the vehicle, including warranty and maintenance. Table 4.3 provides illustrations of the range of outcomes from the customer and the enterprise perspectives.

TABLE 4.3   Machine learning performance and customer outcome examples

Machine-embedded Enterprise Outcomes	Customer Driver/Owner Outcomes
• Rapid data collection and aggregation • High-performance computing analytics • Customer behavior analysis and advice • Validation of warranty claims and actual versus planned and abnormal use • Improve speed of engineering information collection, search, and communication • Improve semantic matching of product specifications, sourcing, and design	• Reduce emissions • Increase fuel efficiency • Reduce travel costs • Safer driving experience • Enhanced product/object functionality • Enhanced partner services – total lifecycle experience • Enhance actual performance data feedback to improve vehicle design • Reduce costs and time to develop new car designs

Software-defined products and services

In exploring the impact of embedded machine technology on the human experience, I was introduced to the Tesla Motors example of "smart suspension system."[24] Tesla, a renowned manufacturer of premium electric cars, in September 2014 released a "software 6.0" update in what they described as an "over-the-air" update, announcing its release to their customer owners on their website: "updates aren't just for squashing bugs, but adding features" to the car.[25] This technology enables a remote connection between the Tesla company services and the on-board systems embedded in the vehicle. This particular software update would, among a list of things, provide enhancements to allow the vehicle and driver to respond better to the road conditions. This in itself may not be remarkable at first sight, with the rapid increase in computer technology to manage car systems, but it is remarkable for the way in which the approach to design management has changed – providing new product functions *after* the original product had been sold and left the factory. To illustrate this point, consider the situation where the driver traveling on a road hits a pothole in the contours of the road and has to swerve to accommodate the road-surface conditions. The on-board air suspension system can "remember" the elevation of road conditions by use of its motion sensors and satellite navigation positional information. The next time the driver take this route, the air suspension system adjusts the height of the car automatically, based on this past information, and in so doing, optimizes this aspect of the driver experience. What is remarkable is that this was a software upgrade that was provided to the on-board vehicle control system remotely, *after* the original car had left the factory, been purchased, and was in use by the customer. In the case of the Tesla software 6.0 upgrade example, it is seen as another way to generate a more personalized owner-ship experience and help make the car "smarter" about owners' individual preferences. This capability also has other benefits such as assisted-driver hill starts and energy savings from improved aerodynamics and road handling. By being able to deliver software upgrades remotely, Tesla can enhance both the convenience for the consumer in not having to return the car to the dealer to perform the upgrade, but also build a closer product–service relationship with its customer base. The Tesla software 6.0 update includes a range of new features including:[26]

- Traffic-based navigation providing directions and trip-commuting route options.
- Commute advice with pop-up alerts on the in-car 17-inch viewing screen on possible delays or other traffic and journey information.
- Provides an in-car view of daily personal schedules that can include locations and event timings, which in turn can be used to plan the journey.
- Enabling location-based air-suspension settings, making use of the model air-suspension to control vehicle height adjustments.
- Allows the car owner to name their model in order to personalize the car mobile app and screen information.
- Ability to start the car using the driver's cell phone, a useful feature if the key fob is not available or has been lost.

This example illustrates a powerful new pattern of digital technologies that enable products and services to be dynamically adjusted and improved through the "embedded" content and software platforms that now make up part of the product. The act of the embedded software and its sensors working together can be described as "machine learning" to improve the response to conditions and create new recommendations or automated actions. This enables a "smart feedback loop" that senses, analyzes, and then responds back to the conditions based on a set of the rules that may be pre-set or "learned."

Vehicle-embedded object-engineering optimization strategies

As a practitioner, the ability to collect data, filter out non-essential or anomalous information, and create purposeful feedback loops in the engineering and operational agency of objects is a powerful capability. The collection of actual usage data of vehicles can develop new sources of data insight that can work across the lifecycle of the product before, during, and after its use by the customer. Benefits can be enabled not just for customers but also to enable practitioners working in the provider organizations – in this case the car manufacturers and their supply chain partners – to better serve and detect product usage and performance potentially in real time.

Vinay Vaidya at KPIT illustrates the potential with the example of the ability to collect a lot of data on the warranty period of vehicles and its usage: "There are a lot of claims in warranty but we can validate if these are actually valid. With big data analytics we can analyze data usage patterns and can produce models to predict the expected level of warranty payment liabilities. This is useful business intelligence information for budgeting in the next quarter, when providers are seeking to manage the warranty cost levels."

Vinay explains that this is the diagnostic side of machine automation. The basic process is the ability to collect large data sets and to create models to predict expected outcomes and to compare this with the actual usage patterns (see Figure 4.10).

He further comments that: "The KPIT ReVolo™ technology is an automated data collection and analytics service that can be used in warranty, for example to aid the human input and decision making in checking the data quality and reliability." The use of dynamic platform integration with the components and sensors of the vehicle, and the planning and analytics systems, clearly enables optimization of the driver and driving experience as well as the overall lifecycle of planned and expected usage patterns for providers.

Vinay explains how this integration can help the wider implications of business organizational performance: "In the case of an Indian bus company we were able to collect data from the bus using an intelligence taskforce system … We can capture data about the bus's location, the bus's unique identity number, and integrate this with a number of usage data collections during the time that the bus is in service. This information can become part of the 'Bus Planning System' that can be provided potentially to bus operators, police or route planners, for example, to help analyze and improve the overall bus service or resolve specific operational issues such as passenger disturbances."

Enabling high-value closed-circuit "managed services"

The use of a dynamic platform that integrates the driver, the vehicle, and the providers can support the provision of "managed services" to all these entities and enterprise activities. In the case study example, the ReVolo™ platform can be used to collect and provide hosted data by KPIT and offered back to client operators of the vehicle such as the bus operator or the drivers themselves to enable data analysis and services. It is also possible to have a ReVolo™ mobile application that can be used by the driver to visualize the current status of the vehicle information such as fuel efficiency or traffic conditions ahead.

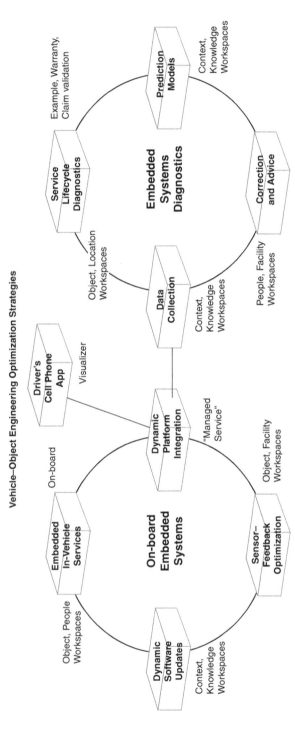

FIGURE 4.10 Vehicle-embedded object-engineering optimization strategies capabilities

Data analysis scaling in real time – the speed of processing performance strategies

The use of embedded technologies also touches on the frontier of what is possible in the speed and response of automated systems to real-life situations. In the case of a vehicle that may be able to travel at high speed, the engine and components work at several thousand revolutions per minute (RPM) and the speed at which data and events may occur is in the order of seconds and subsecond events. The key issue is that the speed of the computing has to be able to operate at the same speed as these real-time, real-world physical events and object movements. In discussion with Vinay Vaidya and Rupert Fallows at KPIT, these are unique challenges in the field of machine learning (ML) where the computational speed of automatic systems may, for example, have to process multiple simultaneous systems such as controlling driving, steering, or braking speed. The success or failure of these systems to act in time can have a vital and potentially catastrophic impact on, for example, a "vehicle lane departure control system." KPIT conducts research and development that includes high-performance computing (HPC) where the multi-core CPU design of embedded software is at the forefront of finding innovative answers that Vinay describes as "processor scaling" to meet "data analysis scaling."

Vinay illustrates this by describing a situation where an on-board computer processor is receiving data from a sensor about the road position of the car. If a car traveling at high speed is steered out of the driving lane then this may have a life-threatening impact with an oncoming car, with potentially catastrophic results. The challenge is to have an on-board computer processor that can work fast enough to collect the sensor data, process the machine learning algorithms for the situation, and then take appropriate automated action. These situations may happen in matters of seconds, which need equally fast automated systems. Vinay explains that it is not just the time that a single process spends in computing data from one sensor, but also being able to process and prioritize many different competing sensor-software data systems in the same time frame. Vinay continues: "For example, there is a scanner in the front of the car which is running software to detect lane position and automatically sense when the vehicle moves out of lane, providing a 'lane departure warning alert.' But there is also another software and sensor on board the vehicle to detect pedestrians who may be near the vehicle. So you have a situation where two competing sensor-data conflicts need to process. One is about the pedestrians and the other the lane position. In a situation where a car may move out of a lane and detect a pedestrian, this takes a lot of time to process (by the on-board computer) – then we have a performance issue."

If a single CPU processor, for example, takes up to four minutes to complete the computation cycle, this is clearly too slow for a real-time physical event that could happen in seconds. Hence, the use of multi-core processors and other multi-threading high-performance processing techniques to optimize utilization of all the cores is a critical step. Put a different way, in another case this illustrates the progress by KPIT and their research into self-driving cars and vision-camera sensing systems. If a system needs to process 40 frames of visual images per second to "see" what is ahead, but the computing power is only able to process for example 10 frames, then this reduces the response time and the "visual accuracy" by as many magnitudes. In the case of self-drive cars, the ability to *post-process* the image requires cameras on the vehicle. With falling costs of CPUs and other sensors making automation cost-effective, the challenge is now more in the software engineering to enable these to work in real time. A low-cost scientific camera with 400 frames per second and 1.5 megapixel resolution can cost less than US$350 and is capable of many applications. The cost-effective prices of such technology, together with stereo vision using two cameras, and computer vision techniques, requires advanced software engineering of the embedded systems in order to react in time to manage the situations such as lane departures and to protect pedestrians and drivers.

Sensor – machine-learning optimization

This is a unique and new problem that will face practitioners in the internet of things (IoT) world, where processors try to make predictions and move actuators to respond to real physical events. As Vinay at KPIT explains: "With all these potential sensors and controls necessary for automation, the creation of a viable product engineering system needs to be designed to meet realistic outcomes. The battery on the car, for example, clearly has to do a lot of work!"

This can be seen as a kind of second-order level of multi-sensor and platform-processing problem that can be solved by faster multi-core processors, software design, and looking at how sensors are connected to the software control systems. Vinay explains: "We need to consider how self-learning of the information from the vehicle can be used to do diagnostics and prognostics. We can use the technology to try to optimize the sensors and to reduce the sensor data noise so that we can process just the essential information. For example, we can detect the temperature at a particular speed in the vehicle. In collecting this data we can then use this (through analytical models) to predict the temperature and location inside the vehicle cabin. This type of feedback can be very valuable to original equipment manufacturers and their car design engineers, for example, to help improve the engineering, materials, and aerodynamics or ergonomics of the car and, in so doing, reducing time to market and reducing costs to do the development."

Using embedded software to enhance the supply chain

While the development of embedded machine-learning and sensor services are the domains of the on-board vehicle systems and diagnostics, the customer service and logistics planning are the preserve of the enterprise supply chain. The information controlling the actual product performance in the vehicle can also prove very useful when integrating this data with product management and the enterprise planning systems. In particular, enterprise resource planning (ERP) is a popular software platform through which to manage the business planning and functional administration of the organization. ERP software can, for example, run financial ledgers, sales and purchase order management, materials and stock management, and many other features (Figure 4.11).

Today, these types of software are often delivered as "software as a service" (SaaS) and are hosted in a cloud-computing environment that enables additional functions of elastic scalability and on-demand services for the business and IT users. ERP can integrate and extend its functionality to other types of

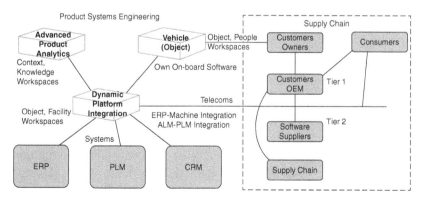

FIGURE 4.11 Enterprise and product lifecycle management integration strategies capabilities

enterprise software such as customer relationship management (CRM), supplier relationship management (SRM), product lifecycle management (PLM), and a plethora of other software system packages and productivity tools found in organizations today.

In the case of engineering and logistics organizations, the impact of planning and scheduling operations is critical to enable the flow of products and parts between suppliers and consumers. This is where the link between the product engineering systems of PLM and the enterprise ERP can be enhanced with a new kind of integration between the two major systems.

Rupert Fallows at KPIT explains: "We can develop new services that can link the supply chain with the vehicle data. This means, for example, we can capture an engineering CAD drawing and link through to a dynamic supply model to manage the product and spares." Rupert explains that the customer original equipment manufacturers (OEMs) – described as tier one suppliers – can be linked with tier two component suppliers using the software, which integrates ERP and PLM together: "This is a major competitive advantage when vehicles and supply chains may have 40 million to 300 million small components. With OEMs seeking to manage the profit margins on the end vehicle, and costs of after-sales warranty service, any help in managing complexity is a major benefit."

ALM + PLM and ERP integration

It is clear that the roles of product suppliers and software suppliers can potentially change in these new digital business models. Central to this is the role of application lifecycle management (ALM) that controls how the software code is distributed and maintained behind the scenes in the embedded systems, and the integration with the enterprise planning and control systems. The difference is that the ALM manages the software, whereas the PLM area manages the product and component content and specifications.

As we have seen in this case study, the increasing connection of software code into the actual products means that digital content is increasingly intertwined and becoming part of the product itself. This is the effect of "digitization" that is driving new capabilities and value in the way that enterprises and consumers can deliver and consume products and services.

Rupert of KPIT explains: "As we move into the future, the biggest costs that customers and providers will potentially have to cope with will be in requirements and software management to maintain these kinds of integrated systems. The management of software updates and patches is already becoming more frequent and a necessity to operating these types of technologies. The role of ALM will be a key capability in being able to bring products to market faster, with some estimates up to 50% faster by automating product and software integration with ALM."

The growth of product-technology enhanced business

The convergence of digital data into products and services is a key emerging theme: "Ten years ago we had mechanical engineering at the heart of the engine. Today it is fully computer controlled," says Rupert.[27] The challenges for practitioners in engineering and logistics are in managing complexity in product data management and parts data management. With a typical engineering organization seeing a 25% growth per annum in product data and a 27% annual change in the data already, it is little wonder that up to 40% of an engineer's time may be spent in searching for information and analyzing the part specifications.[28] Systems that can help automate product and parts management across the supply chain will make a real productivity difference. This is forecast to grow further as the enterprise becomes increasingly digital and connected and raises the following concerns:

- How to coordinate product specifications across multiple production, manufacturing, and distribution sites.
- How to compare and confirm if parts for the same product – sourced from alternative suppliers – meet the same engineering specification.
- How to introduce a change in the product specification so that the updated information is made available to all parts of the supply chain so that there is a consistent single version.

We have seen that new integrated embedded software systems in vehicles can be connected back into the product data management and logistics planning systems to address these challenges. By collecting data on different product specifications it is possible, for example, to use semantic data algorithms to automate the checking of different product specifications for consistency, in order to aid comparison of product alternatives.

The benefits of connecting embedded software with the physical assets across the supply chain opens up new frontiers for the machine and human experience. The potential is in the speed of better decision making, both in the real-time machine assistance in the traffic and vehicle movement in order to protect passengers and pedestrians, and to enhance the driver experience. However, it can also enable advance analytics insight to help design better products, improve energy efficiency, reduce emissions, and improve the total cost of the end-to-end product and service lifecycle (see Table 4.4).

TABLE 4.4 **Examples of strategic and analytics benefits of embedded software and product engineering**

Strategic Enterprise Benefits	Analytical Benefits
Improved enterprise operational strategy: • Reduce part costs (cost reduction) • Understand the supply network • Complexity reduction (part rationalization) • Part reuse across platform Improved supplier and parts management: • Source your parts from the right supplier • Discover the cost-effectiveness of your current suppliers • Leverage ways to negotiate with suppliers • Find the right parts suppliers for your organization • Provide a better portfolio of parts to your top suppliers	Improved in-regional management: • Eliminate significant financial penalties • Reduce regional sourcing tariffs/taxes • Improve import/export compliance • Target and track logistics/shipping impact Improved product design analysis: • Product design tools for cost and sourcing options • Rationalization tools to eliminate similar parts or low-use materials • Part search and reuse tools Improved regulation: • Improved data collection and reporting methods for regulatory compliance • Restricted materials and chemicals, RoHS, REACh • Regional sourcing requirements • Carbon footprints

4. Digital Hospitality Business Model – Enhancing Hospitality with Digital

Introduction

The modern hospitality industry has grown from its early beginnings in the 19th century when the rich and famous had free time to spend as they chose. As industrialization began to emerge, this gave rise to mass employment, workplace automation, and, in the 20th century, the eventual legal statutory employment rights for workers to be given a set amount of paid vacation and to have free time outside of working hours. The hospitality industry has, therefore, very much been a barometer of economic activity, creating jobs and a whole industry: from private lodgings to professional hotels, restaurants, public houses, wine bars, guest rooms, and the many related services such as catering, building maintenance, and cleaning.

The hospitality industry is not restricted to leisure time, and today is also integrated into the commercial industry activity of commuters and travel as the "glue" to a mobile workforce. This emerging role of the hospitality services has also grown wider, to often represent the cultural expression of cities and countries as they seek to promote tourism and their "brand" to a local, regional, and global audience. Indeed in the 21st century, with national sports events, festivals, arts, music as well as historical attractions and environmental sightseeing, hospitality services have become part of a wider ecosystem of the national identity and social, cultural expression of quality of life.

Hence, in looking at the hospitality sector it is also necessary to consider its relationship to other industries such as the tourism industry, which was recently reported by the World Travel and Tourism Council as representing 3% of global GDP.[29] But in reality, if taken as a whole encompassing the many industries that hospitality supports across distribution, transport, and other industry activities, it is more correctly described as driving direct and indirect effects toward 9% of GDP globally, generating one in ten jobs.

Today, hospitality has grown into a multi-service phenomenon that has moved beyond the basic concept of a room and a place to sleep to include many integrated services such as travel, tourism, and corporate events. Private and public automobile travel, road systems, buses, rail, and air travel connect to town and city hubs that are supported by hotels and other service industry facilities, enabling the local economies of those regions. Tourism has increasingly segmented to support many different customer lifestyles from families to specialist explorer vacations, which in turn have driven different types of hotel and hospitality services. The development of corporate hospitality has become a significant sector in its own right, with business events and trade shows becoming a significant growth area for hospitality services. As a result, the perception of the customer as a visitor has radically changed from the early days of leisure to the way people may use hospitality in their employment, free time, and lifestyle as a whole.

The nature of the hospitality service is very much associated with the psychology of human experience. Indeed the design and management of modern hospitality services seek to create a fundamental connection to human aspirations and lifestyles in what is termed the "needs and wants of the customer guest." The "customer experience" is consequently at the very core of hospitality, defined in the *Oxford English Dictionary* as "the friendly and generous reception and entertainment of guests, visitors, or strangers." This experience involves empathy and a personalization that reaches many different aspects of the customer journey to and from a hotel or restaurant, the experience during the visit, and the many associated services that can accompany the location and its context, the reason for the visit by the customer (see Table 4.5).

TABLE 4.5   Hospitality operational versus customer outcomes

Hospitality Operational Outcomes	Customer Outcomes
• Volume of tourists and visitor traffic	• Lifestyle aspirations
• Visitor spend	• Enjoyment
• Service efficiency	• Convenience
• Personalization and guest privacy	• Employment
• Return visits	• Cultural identity

Geraldine Calpin, senior vice president and global head of digital at Hilton Worldwide, described this as: "Start with the dream, people have dreams and how can we enable this as a reality with our hospitality." This is a wonderful aspirational take on the whole concept of the customer touchpoints, and a good example of the hospitality role in making the customer at the core of service excellence. Not surprisingly, this is also reflected in the stated Hilton corporate vision: "To fill the earth with the light and warmth of hospitality."

Hilton International is a US global hospitality company with a turnover of $9.735 billion in 2013, encompassing 4200 hotels with over 690,000 rooms in 93 countries. Hilton own, manage, and franchise 11 brands with 168,000 employees and 162,000 franchise employees.[30] Hilton continues to expand its hospitality assets with a further development pipeline of 1230 hotels, consisting of approximately 210,000 rooms reported in the second quarter SEC filing in 2014.[31] As reported in the second quarter of 2014, Hilton have a successful loyalty card service with over 40 million HHonors[TM] members worldwide.[32]

Digital hospitality leadership

Given the evolving connection of customer service and the extended definition of hospitality into adjacent industries, how have digital technologies been used to enable better hospitality?

Geraldine Calpin explains that Hilton International has already established digital solutions to enhance the hospitality experience and is currently working on new areas as well as future plans: "We see digital as essential to enabling hospitality. In developing our digital strategy we look at it through every stage of the customer journey. Our start point is the customer guest journey, this is where people start to dream, then they plan, they shop, then they book. Then they get ready to fly, to travel, then they arrive, then they leave, they depart by a check-out. The last part is what they share, which may include social media and other forms to describe their experiences." Indeed this idea of sharing to drive brand and service is in the Hilton loyalty scheme HHonors™ messaging "Experiences worth sharing." Geraldine comments: "What Hilton is seeking to do with digital is to understand how it can enable, improve, and enhance the guest experience and support the revenues at every point in that guest journey. Traditionally this has been through websites, mobile sites, and apps that create the booking capability and seeing it as the booking channel. The reality is that mobile and digital has changed how things work. I describe it as *the mobile phone is people's remote control to the world*. The digital solutions need to be designed around mobile and how it can be used to turn the customer experience into the journey with this in mind." Geraldine illustrates this point with an example of a customer who looks at the video of one of the Hilton hotels in Hawaii, and then goes online to book into the Hilton where they want to stay. Then, the check-in by the guest may be enabled remotely online the day before, providing added convenience and saving time. This may also be linked to the airline travel and provide facilities, again online, to give guests the choice of which room they want to stay in. Geraldine says that Hilton International have now mapped 300,000 of their 650,000+ rooms in the same way that airlines have seat maps for their aircraft cabins. Hilton now have floor plans available for most of their hotels, a level of guest choice in the location and room that is extended into guests being able to use their cell phone to open the hotel door itself: Hilton recently announced in 2014 a new service called Hilton Straight-to-room™, which enables the use of the cell phone as a remote key.

Geraldine explains that in their market research with guests they found that 84% would like the option to quickly check in and to go to their room on arrival. This gives business travelers, for example, more options than waiting to check in to get their room key, or having to wait in the restaurant or bar area.

The use of digital services available in mobile devices and apps is enhancing the way that Hilton meets their customers' needs and wants (Figure 4.12). These digital technologies enable a superior hospitality experience, empowering guests to select rooms, room types, and room numbers, subject to availability, using cell phones. Geraldine says that in some of the Hilton brands such as the Conrad brand service, the Hilton mobile apps allow guests to use their phone to order room service, or request a car rental from on-property services. In some hotel locations the same mobile app can act as a room environmental control enabling the guest to remotely open and close the window blinds, and control the room temperature. Geraldine says: "It is about 'digital hospitality' and also about 'digital revenue' but striking the right balance. Our

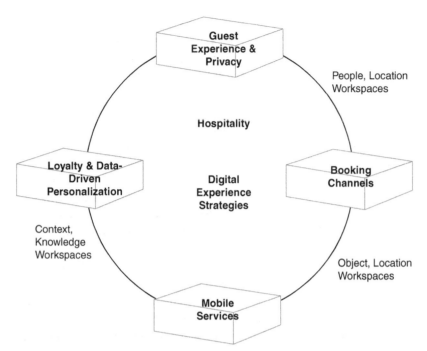

FIGURE 4.12 Smart hospitality – digital experience strategies capabilities

business is all about hospitality so it is primarily about making the stay more hospitable through enabling what the guest wants in order to achieve these outcomes."

This is just the beginning of what digital technologies might enable in the future of hospitality. Mobile is clearly a key strategy that is a central part in delivering an enhanced customer experience for guests at Hilton International (Figure 4.13). The hotel and room location, and even the features within the room such as the doors, the windows, and heating as well as the in-room services and entertainment, can all be accessed and enabled through innovative digital technology. Geraldine explains that Hilton has already been a leader in many of these areas and is planning for the future to create even more hospitality enhancements through digital technologies: "I can envision a situation where you are brushing your teeth in one of the Hilton hotels in the morning and the mirror will light up with a call from your partner; your schedule will be displayed underneath it. You are asked to pick up something on the way home and you can add it dynamically into your schedule there and then and automatically synchronize it back to your mobile phone and personal electronic diary."

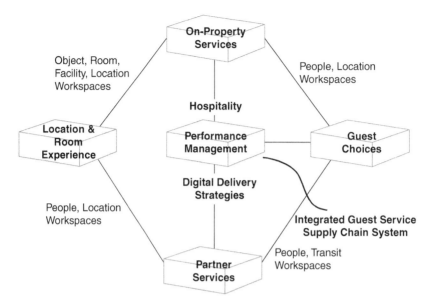

FIGURE 4.13 Smart hospitality – digital delivery strategies capabilities

These possibilities are not quite there yet, but Hilton is planning for the future and the ability to create a more immersive environment that is the great promise of the digital enterprise. This can be seen repeatedly in other case studies for leading companies such as Hilton that are pushing the boundaries of what is possible with digital technology. The connection between how to engage customers and Hilton's lifecycle of digital hospitality strategies have several lessons.

In the area of data analytics, large amounts of information is generated in many industries. Geraldine described this as an opportunity to enhance service personalization: "The issue today is being able to measure everything and having too much data. The challenge is often identifying which of the metrics are important to measure performance of the business and the impact of digital."

Big-data analytics can support the commercial side as well as the supply chain area for the operations and delivery of services. Geraldine explains that there are many metrics that can be used today in measuring guest service usage, the number of times they visit Hilton and partner websites, and the number of bookings. All these information points enable better insight and potential service opportunities.

"The other thing digital will enable apart from make guests lives easier is personalization with digital technologies. In the past we would use segmentation to classify customers, but now with digital you can treat every customer uniquely," Geraldine explains. "When a guest arrives at a hotel, the service could be enabled to provide enhanced services through already knowing what the guest's likes and preferences are. The concierge service at the front desk in the hotel can better anticipate what the guest might need, ask about past stays, and provide a more tailored service and advice to support the guest's needs. Personalization enables better hospitality and is a core aspect of the business strategy for Hilton." Geraldine also underpins this with the need for privacy of personal data preferences across all channels that touch the customer guest. This forms part of the Hilton International Global Privacy Policy covering how personal information is collected and managed. This includes all aspects of the operation, including mobile and location-based services in the digital and operational strategy.[33]

In the area of digital innovation Hilton have used crowdsourcing such as crowd marketplace service provider companies. For example, *Communispace* and *IdeaConnection* develop new ideas for business development, feedback on product launches, websites, and other areas that can engage.[34] Geraldine explains that there are also public community spaces that can provide ideas and opinion. An example is *FlyerTalk,* which is a social network website forum for frequent flyers in the airline industry.[35] These sites provide real-time social network chat and opinions from a range of potential and current customers that can offer very useful insight in reaction to current and future products and service ideas.

Performance management

Understanding how the hospitality industry works and its differences to other industries is a key point that Geraldine reiterates: "Competitive differentiation is different in the hospitality business to other industries such as manufacturing or pharmaceuticals because in those industries it is more about managing the right process and supply chain distribution and maintaining it once it is in place. In hospitality, no part of your business is factorized, we have to constantly monitor and deliver at every point because it is a service. We rely on people to smile and create that excellent customer experience every time they meet the guest. While it is not a low-margin business, it is nevertheless a complex business to re-create this experience every time the guest arrives and in every moment they use our services. Digital technology does not cut people out of this, it provides technology to employees to enhance the service to be more efficient and effective for our guests. It helps us to know who you are, to know your HHonours[TM] membership level and benefits, in order to give a personalized service to make the total visitor experience better end to end." Hilton has set this concept to work up and down their supply chain of operations in order to establish a connected hospitality experience.

Digital system capabilities are essential in managing the quality and performance at scale across a diverse range of locations and the mix of own premises and franchise businesses. These proficiencies also provide a useful lesson in best practice provided by Hilton International that underpins its business model and global brand operation built on people and the hospitality they deliver.

The hospitality industry in the 21st century has become part of the global economy and represents an integral part of the integrated services ecosystem. The use of digital technologies has and will continue to create significant opportunities for the new digital enterprise.

5. Digital Government and Cities – Toward a Digital Society and Smart Cities

A challenge is seen around the world from China, France, the Scandinavian countries, Germany, the Netherlands, the UK, South Korea, the United States, Brazil, Dubai, India, Africa, and to everywhere seeking a better way to develop better society and nationhood wealth and prosperity. The digitization of society is a global phenomenon that is found in developed and developing economies as they become connected by the web of mobile and telecoms services and content.

The classical separation of the types of economic markets to be found in an economy is usually given in three categories: primary, secondary, and tertiary sectors.[36] The primary and secondary sectors are differentiated by the extraction and creation of raw materials such as minerals and farming, compared with the manufacturing and processing of these materials into finished products. The tertiary sector refers to the services industries that are involved in supplying a range of services from medical health services, legal, education, to accounting and entertainment. In a modern economy, the delivery of GDP contribution by enterprises in these sectors can vary from country to county based on the country distribution of natural resources, availability of workforce skills, age, and income generation and competitiveness of these industries in local, regional, and global markets. However, the government public and federal ownership of industries tends to be the largest sector in most global economies, representing typically the largest percentage of GDP contribution.[37] This means that the public sector, as it is typically termed, is often the largest single employing sector in a country economy, and a source of domestic and national revenue generation through supply chains, national spending, infrastructure investment, and employment.

The impact of digital technologies in society will therefore be partly driven by its penetration within the public sector. This can range from relatively shallow digitization such as mapping and user reporting of environmental issues, through to much deeper applications such as in complex systems in healthcare and defense. We saw this in Chapter 3 in the case study examples such as Amsterdam city, digital health, the emergency recovery services, and connect car transportation – these sectors all demonstrate how digital technologies can play a real significant role in all aspects of the e-citizen of the future. Many governments around the world have initiatives to build a digital society as they recognize the connected economy, including the North American digital government initiative,[38] the European Union Commission's digital agenda for Europe,[39] and the Chinese government's adoption of social media and internet services development.[40] The United Nations e-government survey ranking from 2014 illustrates that this phenomena is both worldwide and of major strategic importance, yet for many areas it is still early days in terms of progress and investment.[41]

When considering the public sector and the impact of digitization, there are perhaps three areas that directly affect practitioner policy in the broader sense:

• The economic contribution of digital enterprise.
• The impact on employment and jobs from digitization.
• The cost of cyber security, effective counterterrorism policies, and the value of a human life.

Economics of digital

Ironically, the economists still refer to the digital economy as only representing 3% to 5% of total GDP.[42] Yet the ability of "digital" to pervade almost every aspect of physical services suggests that traditional physical accounting of goods and services is "missing a trick." Indeed a question has been raised by the Organisation for Economic Co-operation and Development (OECD) as to whether there is in fact a difference between the physical economy and the digital enterprise. This disconnection between the accounting for physical trading and online trading has presented challenges for governments to introduce taxation for online activity when often the digital enterprise may physically reside in a different country and tax jurisdiction. The OECD report on base erosion and profit shift (BEPS) in January 2014 raised this very question.

> OECD report on base erosion and profit shift (BEPS) in January 2014
>
> "The findings are that there is no such thing as *digital companies*, rather than digitization of the economy. There may not be therefore a solution for the digital economy but we will need to draw on features of the digital economy when we revise the system."

This appears to be a contradiction, but the fact is that the digital elements of the economy are clearly identifiable. The features of the digital economy include such things as virtual online marketplaces, digital currency payments, and intellectual property that can exist in virtual spaces and have no domicile in the consumer country, yet can be measured in terms of economy transactions and trade movements. The digital enterprise and the digital economy are in fact like the "glue" between the physical resources and activities.

Impact of digitized jobs

For practitioners, the digital enterprise is still real and a legal entity in terms of its ownership and trading of physical and virtual goods and services. It is just that the business operating models are different. The digital impact on jobs and employment is also tangible, often changing the basis of skills, automating parts or all of some existing manual jobs and creating new kind of jobs from web designers and data analysts to online marketing and digital media. The impact on jobs is unclear and in some reports and views may have a profound potential impact on society. Eric Schmidt, CEO of Google, raised this at Davos 2014, warning that the jobs "problem" will be the defining one for the next two to three decades.[43] By this he was referring to the impending perceived or otherwise real threat of human jobs involving mainly administrative skills and processes that could be computerized with current advances such as statistical processing, automated driving, and speech and image recognition services. An Oxford academic study predicted that 47% of today's job skills would be replaced within two decades by computer automation.[44]

Cyber security and progress

From an economic perspective the value of digitization benefits has been weighed against the costs and impact of increasing prevalence of cyber security threats. We explore this in the security and privacy section of this book in Chapter 6, but the underlying evidence is that the development of public services using digital technologies is moving ahead at a pace. These include: sustainability and energy management; open data initiatives; transport and capacity management for future distribution and travel; research and development with local and central governments and academic and business partnerships; health and citizen wellbeing; security and protection of citizen human rights and emergency services. No area is perhaps untouched by the potential to leverage digital information and digital services to create new forms of public amenity, connecting mobile devices, sensors, and data to empower individuals, social groups, and enterprises.

Practitioner perspectives of building smart government and smart city

Let us explore this further with a practitioner's perspective. From an outcome-based approach there are some overall goals that can be commonly seen in many government, societal, and city enterprise developments. Some key performance outcomes are show in Table 4.6.

A good life and a connected life

The development and delivery of public services for the benefit of the social and economic wellbeing of citizens has a set of unique choices beyond the pure financial return on investment. It must manage and represent the benefits and choices that may affect individuals, the society, and the ethical choices in decision-making processes.

In that sense it is therefore not just about the delivery of public services but the experience and outcomes they generate for citizens and society. In a more

TABLE 4.6 Smart government, smart city outcomes examples

"Enterprise" City Outcomes	Customer Experience Outcomes
Increased inward investment	Faster transit time
Higher energy efficiencies	Healthier environment
Primary and secondary demand creation	More employment
Improved geospatial policies – use of land	Better education
Higher connectivity and monetization of city culture and services	Better visitor experience

connected life that we see in digital technology in society today we may be able to create a more efficient life but we also have to question if it is a good life. What are the constituents of a good life versus a connected life?

This can be summarized as public programs that drive one or more outcomes:

- A good life
- A good community
- A good place to live

In the investment planning for public services such as welfare, education, environment, and healthcare, many different stakeholders can be involved: central government, federal government, local government, and industry partners represent the different key stakeholders that can influence these outcomes.

The aim here is not to define the specifics of governmental policy and decision making, but to demonstrate the contextual issues that the connected life has to address in driving a local and country-level economic development. Public value will need to address different concerns that consider the vision, community, and feasibility both in terms of social impact, organization skills to delivery and to support the public service, as well as the technical viability.

This presents priorities for politicians, public servants, and industry providers that has an impact on citizens' value from their government services as well as on overall social living standards. The search for public value is a key issue, as confirmed in the appraisal of public value and the choices between private value and public value by the UK Government Cabinet Office in 2011,[45] and research by the Institute of Governance and Public Management (IGPM) at Warwick Business School in 2007.[46]

The dilemma of choice

In the public sector the economic income is derived from a combination of central and local taxation, together with income from commercial activity as well as support for not-for-profit operations and charity organizations. The funds available from these sources represent a budget that has to be prioritized and measured in the way it is used to invest in community assets and infrastructure, improvement projects, and the running of community services.

A dilemma exists in being able to use a limited budget to meet all competing priorities that may have equal value in community service and citizenship.

For example, decisions to invest in a premature baby care unit in the health service versus investing in education facilities or in community law enforcement all have different personal and social outcomes:

- The value of a life saved versus the cost of healthcare.
- The value of a skilled workforce versus the cost of education.
- The value of a secure society versus the cost of law enforcement.

The underlying issue is expressed more significantly in a 2014 counterterrorism policy report form the CATO institute.[47] The report estimates the cost to human life from various events, the probability of these events occurring, and the acceptable risks involved in such judgments. Examples include improvement in car seat belts and airbags having a cost per life saved of US$140,000; and well over several million US dollars for investing in better industry hazard protection such as asbestos and other poisonous materials. Officials serving the public are tasked at the most fundamental level of spend funds in a manner that most effectively and efficiently keeps people safe. Yet the report suggests that regulators and administrators tend to be unwilling to spend more than $1 million to save a life, and they are very reluctant to spend more than $10 million, preferring instead to expend funds on measures to save lives at a lower cost. The root question this raises is what is the value of a human life? How much should governments and society spend in the prevention of attacks or malpractice to protect citizens from threats as compared with the cost of responding after the problem has occurred? Whether these predictions or the complexity of defining the digital economy are true remains a central question in government policy making and service delivery.

These translate into trade-off decisions that can have difficult ethical issues in comparing, for example, value for life saved and citizen safety. All have equal merit of importance yet with scarce budget resources that cannot support all outcomes. The use of innovative solutions such as digital can be one way to mitigate such dilemmas to maximize the use of funds and return on investment.

In a connected life, the use of digital technologies can potentially alter how the response to these competing priorities can be met. Digital health, access to digital libraries, and online education, as well as new ways to monitor local and regional security with cyber tools, represent both an opportunity and a challenge to public sector practitioners seeking innovations such as these for better outcomes.

Developing a public digital strategy

With so many possible priorities and opportunities for digitization, as we have seen for example in the concept of "smart city," the challenge for practitioners is to define digital value and to execute this into the organizational culture of the public sector. A recent study on enabling government digital leadership, citing the New York City Digital Roadmap, for example,[48] stated that coordinating investment through a clear point of leadership is vital to ensuring joint commissioning of digital products. *Joint* is referring to the partnership between government and industry technologists who enable these. Central to this are three aspects of practical activity:

- Executive understanding of the potential of digital technologies and how they are different to traditional IT investment projects, involving dependencies on social networks, telecommunications infrastructure, increased cyber security controls, and new charging mechanisms for hosted cloud and mobile app services – to name a few.
- Establishing clear demonstration of digital value outcomes. Many digital technologies create new user experiences for online access to self-service, to digital e-commerce services for booking, and using public services. These change the potential time and method for interacting online to create a "digital brand" for government services.
- Sector-wide leadership and community engagement across different government departments that can support local economic development needs versus central strategic plans. This is essential in leveraging return on investment from limited government budgets representing public money, and to commercial partnerships seeking viable business models for digital products.

Daniel Goodwin, an accomplished and experienced CEO of local government and government policy explains: "Digital strategy is useful, digital should be mainstreamed in government and enterprise strategy. In general, strategy requires a conscious extraction of the digital elements to make them happen, this is where it should be." Digital is not a separate strategy as a "two-speed" approach, but should be part of one and the same enterprise strategy.

An economist's perspective of the digital economy

The relationship between the public sector role of developing economic prosperity for citizens and the wider economy are closely related to economic planning. The distribution of wealth and assets across an economic region involves how work is created and delivered through employment, regional investment and regeneration, and the industrial base of commercial and manufacturing companies; the power utilities and sustainability; and the infrastructure of rail, road, airports, and telecommunications to support movement of information, people, goods, and raw materials.

This can all be viewed from a city and living spaces perspective and the network of connections both physical and digital.

Primary demand and secondary demand

How cites enable employment across industrial sectors by the demand for economic activity in the local region and the local communities matters in how the geography of the land is physically used.

Primary demand can be described as the *aggregate demand* for an entire class of products such as retail, manufacturing, school services, and hospital medical care. From the real-estate planning perspective of geographical land use this has a direct impact on manufacturing, distribution and transport facilities, and infrastructure that are built on available physical land.[49] This of course enables physical products and services production from these assets, as well as sales, employment, and economic wealth creation.

Secondary demand relates to specific interests in discrete demand for selected products and services. From an economic perspective this creates what economists describe as *addition employment multipliers* that are created from this type of demand, and economic wealth creation resulting from demand for industrial space.[50]

These two distinctions are important when understanding the physical economy value and efficiency of the region geographically.[51] It has a direct impact on the economic development of a city and region by the way demand is created and enables employment that, in turn, creates economic wealth and ultimately its share of GDP contribution. These activities help drive economic growth and highlight a number of concerns:

- How to develop inward investment to the city and region to attract high-value industries and global brands that can create more wealth and local employment – **industry economy.**
- How to create attractive employment and living environments in order to generate movement of workforce to the city and region to grow the available employee pool to industry enterprises in that region – **employment and skills economy.**

- How to drive more visitors to a city and region in order to promote tourism economic growth and leverage the culture and heritage for a vibrant **visitor economy**.
- How to drive innovation research and development in the local and wider economy through attracting and developing new industries, new technologies, and assets to grow competitive strengths – **knowledge economy**.
- How to develop the transportation infrastructure to improve rail, road, air, and shipping access to the city and region and its connectivity to other cities and regions. This impacts on import and export effectiveness and logistics capabilities to move transport, people, products, and services to customers to drive economic trading – **a connected transport economy**.
- How to develop sustainability for lower carbon emissions, improved energy efficiencies, and ethical use of materials and services – **a low carbon economy.**
- How to develop health services safety, diversity, and citizen quality of life in living spaces and services value for money – a **healthy life economy**.

Public and private finance equity models

Many local city and central government economic planning organizations seek to develop the objectives listed above. Often there are decisions in how the public sector equity-led model is used versus the private sector-led model in seeking sources of finance to invest in public strategic infrastructure and services. In public–industry partnerships there may be a blend of these or to seek a private solution to level more finance or retain a public-only ownership.

When considering digital technologies these issues become questions of how investment is used to direct traffic and e-commerce to the region. What effect may this have on creating new employment or, through job automation, reducing employment? What new skills may this require for the local workforce to be able to leverage mobile apps, big data analytics, or build cloud-hosted products and services, for example? Digital technologies can play a role in lowering barriers to entry for new skills and services. Open data, a concept of publicly published online data, is an example that is often cited in the public sector to drive opportunities for new digital services from the use of such data. While digital technologies enable new business models, they also potentially open up markets and disrupt old ones, changing the competition. Digital can play a role in "clustering" together resources and services in a more accessible way for public and private partnership and use.[52]

Expanding the knowledge economy

In attracting visitors, inward industry investment, or skilled workers, competition is increasingly fierce between physical destinations both inside and across many country borders, as international trade and movement of goods and services are enabled through global value chains (GVCs) and digital communications.[53]

When we then translate this into the digital economy and the use of digital technologies in concepts such as smart city, digital health, online education, and optimized transport, we can start to see that understanding the physical and online digital brand matters in marketing the region's knowledge assets.

Economies of scale and clustering

From an economic perspective, clustering matters in physical spaces in the way that assets can be leveraged for economies of scale. As described by Professor Henry Overman, a pioneer in economic geography at London School of Economics Centre for Economic Performance, clustering relates to two other concepts: *agglomeration model* and *spatial policies*.[54]

Clustering is in the grouping of similar resources into the same geographical area. For example, the movement of research and development laboratories in pharmaceuticals to be near universities and employment pools of high-quality graduates is a typical case of clustering. Another may be the movement of a well-known global computer brand's manufacturing and service facilities into new geographical locations for access to local markets, to gain tax advantages, and again, access to a high-quality skilled workforce.

Agglomeration is how the knock-on benefits of enterprises locating physically near to each other ("agglomerating") can create network effects that can stimulate economic activity and drive economies of scale from shared resources and attracting more employment into the region.

Spatial policies matter in promoting the clusters and agglomeration efficiencies to drive economic planning and improvement.[55]

Adding digital technology to this list potentially changes how clusters work as it no longer is just how physical spaces come together. Virtual businesses and online presence can also drive new digital ecosystems that are in effect "digital clusters." Virtual branding of local and regional enterprises and workforce skills potentially broadens the physical economy to include new digital economy benefits of economies of scale. These can extend to digital markets that may not be constrained by physical location or physical capacity, but open up new legal, security, and commercial challenges.

The "death of distance" and the digital counterintuitive effect

Digital technologies have in effect created the "death of distance." People and enterprises are no longer constrained by their own physical and spatial limitations. Social media and smartphones are enabling more connections between people locally and virtually. Digital technologies such as cloud and broadband are accelerating these network effects. This would give the impression that connecting across distances people and location no longer matters.

Yet the opposite seems to be taking place – with consumers now becoming more concentrated in cities where cluster effects enable the population to physically take advantage of local services and access to clusters of employers for more employment opportunities. A 2007 study by Professor Alan Harding at the Institute for Political and Economic Governance, University of Manchester, confirmed that clusters to cities had increased over the previous ten years across Europe.[56]

It perhaps can be attributed to access to the skilled labor market with acceptable community distances, the key issue being that digital technologies are accelerating this phenomena of access to local and global resources. There may also be other necessities that enable this such as local resources seeking to sell and deliver globally, and conversely, global companies seeking localization of their products and services. This "digital entanglement" of physical and virtual employment and resources is one of the foundations when exploring the issues in building the digital economy and the ramifications for the workforce and the economy.

From a digital city brand to digital workspaces

Major examples are emerging in today's cities that are forging ahead with initiatives to make real the potential of digital enablement (Figure 4.14).

The goal is to create virtual reinforcing cycles of scalable growth that connect different city workspaces that support enterprises and citizen wealth creation. We will explore this concept in Chapter 5, but for our purposes here, practitioners need to understand the new digital paradigm and how this reinforces physical and virtual economy wealth creation and wellbeing.

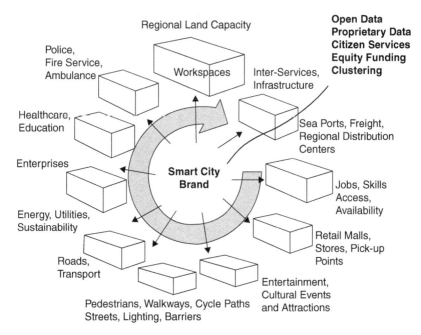

FIGURE 4.14 **Growing the smart city brand with digital workspaces**

Many examples can be found in the digital initiatives of governments and city planning. For example, Stokab is a city-wide municipal fiber-optical network in Stockholm, Sweden.[57] It is notable for the fact that it is not private-sector funded and, founded in 1994 and completed around 2004, it is an early pioneer of a municipal network that has enabled extensive broadband coverage across the city. This enables several benefits of better telecommunications and information systems services. The use of public government funding requires a coordinated set of goals and leadership that enables many governments and enterprises to work collaboratively. In the case of the Stockholm fiber network, Stokab leases fiber-optic networks that telecom operators, businesses, local authorities, and organizations use for digital communications. Leasing agreements are structured on favorable terms to encourage IT development and strong growth in the Stockholm region. Another example is the Sharp Project in Manchester, UK,[58] an investment in facilities to provide a home for digital entrepreneurs and production companies. It is a place where space, power, connectivity, and people converge. Occupants at the Sharp Project make, manipulate, or move digital content around the world.

A common theme is in getting together facilities and infrastructure to enable different clusters to exist and collaborate using digital workspaces that enable the smart city. This requires practitioner leadership to bring it together; several examples such as the world famous Silicon Valley in California have had enormous government investment as well as strong focus on venture capital and innovation investment.

Effectiveness and fairness

From a practitioner perspective there are different ways to get government or private industry investment, but these must have an outcomes focus to drive toward the overall goals for the society and industry. Using different funding models can drive different paths to digitization but also trade-offs in cost and price of the investment, using competitive market tendering compared to public subsidies-funded investment. The "Haldane principle" is a UK research policy idea which sets out that decisions about what to spend research funds on should be made by researchers rather than politicians.[59] Whether this concept works to the betterment of outcomes may be driven by several factors, but the overall aim is the same in how to make effective outcomes.

The quality of life of citizens, a good life versus a connected life, matters when seeking to help all sections of society, including reducing unemployment and providing better healthcare. The digital technology agenda has become a key lever for the smart government, smart society, and smart city of the future.

6. Digital Logistics Business Model – Smart Logistics

The practitioners in logistics are at the center of how physical goods and services are moved between geographical locations. They intrinsically understand the value of space and time in the movement of capacity between the demand and supply of materials between suppliers and customers. They understand that the performance metrics of service levels and customer experience is directly affected by how workspaces function.

Digitization of logistics has probably the most directly obvious connection as a concept, since it is occupying the spaces that people, objects, rooms, vehicles, and locations have to navigate. The use of information technology in logistics has grown, as network infrastructure coverage and the growth of lower-cost mobile devices and sensors has changed how planning to local operations can be coordinated in a distribution process.

Unipart is a multinational logistics, supply chain, manufacturing, and consultancy with global operations in Europe, North America, Australia, and Japan. Unipart Logistics specialize in a range of logistical services and expertise across several engineering and consumer industry sectors.

The "Unipart Way" is described in their "lean" philosophy, a proven industry practice sometimes also described as lean manufacturing, lean enterprise, or lean production. It is a systemic method for elimination of waste through a business process working from the perspective of the customer who consumes the product or service.[60]

Key outcomes of this approach are shown in Table 4.7:

TABLE 4.7   Lean outcomes

"Lean" Outcomes	Client Process Design Areas
• Streamline key work processes	• Supply chain network design
• Eliminate duplication	• Supply chain operations
• Eliminate reworking	• Supply chain systems
• Improve accuracy	• Centre of coordination
• Increase productivity	• Warehouse logistics and design
• Reduce lead times in processing cases	• Operational outsourcing
	• Expert advisory

Bringing lean principles to life

The use of information technologies has been a key part of "bringing lean principles to life." In a typical global supply chain there are many "nodes" in the total operating model represented by warehouses, assets, employees, products, and parts that are owned by the enterprise or owned by third-party client enterprises. Often these are in a "multi-tier" arrangement where each performs a step in the supply chain process, from the suppliers to the end customers. There is a fast pace of change in the way that these supply chains operate, frequently involving thousands of physical transactions of products and service exchanges across hundreds of business processes in many enterprises. The coordination and management of this using manual processes becomes an increasingly challenging task for all involved and has a direct impact on the overall supply performance and customer service levels.

A key question is how to use technology and information in a way to drive the right performance. How can the supply chain be managed in order to minimize the impact of industrial failure? Where can data be collected about business operations so there is a single "version of the truth" that represents the actual situation of the supply chain?

Global–local

Developing lean principles with technology involves taking a global–local perspective that enables remote operations to be connected and then coordinated in a consistent and measured way.

Collecting the right data

Collecting information at the point of activity is a key principle. The use of touch-screen technology can help to enter data more accurately and efficiently; another is the use of radio frequency scanners: for example, to collect parts and pallet information in the warehouses that can be more easily transmitted and collected. Collection of data enables actions to then be taken based on information of the event: for example, customer back orders that need to be processed to achieve targets for service performance.

Single set of measures

Establishing a consistent and relevant set of metrics across parts of the supply chain is key to enabling a "high level number" that management and ultimately the customers can gain as an overall picture of what is happening in the supply chain. With a set of structured data metrics it is possible to take the high-level number and drill down individual teams and part numbers in specific operational areas of the supply chain to improve supply transparency. This is very powerful in driving behaviors to improve metrics performance in, for example, product availability, customer back order reductions, warehouse capacity utilization, and in reducing freight costs and lowering carbon emissions.

Visualization and visibility

Digital technology enables data and information with measures that can empower all parts of the supply chain to "see" what is going on either in planned cycle times or often in real time. Technology again can assist in this by providing "dashboards" that, for example, can be viewed easily on smartphones and tablets.

Supply chain systems coordination

Unipart Logistics has developed systems that combine these global–local features with lean principles to drive supply chain performance. In 2011 they launched Unipart GLAS, a global logistics application suite (see Figure 4.15).[61]

FIGURE 4.15 **GLAS (global logistics application suite) capabilities**

Source: Public website – Unipart Logistics.

The system enables universal policies to be established across parts of the connected supply chain. The system collects data and transforms this into information that can enable enterprises to understand their supply chain better in order to gain competitive advantage. GLAS features include:

- Diagnostic assessment to understand your supply chain.
- Creating a global control centre to expose supply chain improvements.
- Implementation and adoption of creative problem solving to drive continuous improvement.

Supply chain and e-coaching

These systems are part of the supply chain management practices to gain end-to-end visibility and to gain a clear presentation of performance and areas requiring corrective action. It is important to be able to establish responsibilities and actions for both systems and employees inside the supply chain and for collaborating with operations locally and globally.

The supply chain is not a completely automated environment – often complex engineering products and systems require a blend of human and machine control in a connected supply chain. Information about a process has to be turned into information in context that requires a combination of human and system interventions.

In the lean approach, the technology can be used to help coach and develop the human performance in the supply chain. Everyone involved in the operations can use smart screen displays in warehouses and many other locations to gain visibility of the current supply chain status. Supervisors can use technology to assist in coaching, supporting health and safety at work, driving efficiencies and productivity in picking, and other critical activities that are the practitioner perspective of the real supply chain in action. The combination of environment and technology to measure and track activities can be used to affect the operational and outcome performance of the logistics operation.

The use of visualization technologies such as screens displaying metrics and status of operations, combined with data collection and tracking, enables new levels of visibility and control.

"Track and trace" – managing risk in the supply chain

The ability to visualize and take action on supply chains is advancing with digital technologies, which can introduce faster rates of data collection and new innovation in all parts of operations.

Another logistics enterprise leader, Deutsche Post DHL, an international sea- and air-mail logistics carrier, has developed technologies to track delivery of packages around the world. They have recently launched DHL Resilience360™, a supply chain risk-management solution that provides continuous risk assessment and software-based incident monitoring.[62]

With over 275,000 employees around the world, DHL Resilience360™ used web-based technology to create geospatial tracking visualization of regions around the world where the company manages half a billion shipments globally, representing thousands of packages across mixed transport routes every hour in more than 220 countries and territories served with approximately 500 airports and many regional logistics hubs.[63]

With so many employees, countries, and regions, a key issue for the global operation is to manage risks to delivery and employees from local natural disasters and socio-political events that can affect employee safety, operational efficiency, and profitability.

The benefits of these track and trace systems include helping to protect sales, maintain service levels, reduce emergency costs, enable fast post-disruption recovery, and protect client brand and market share. To deliver DHL Resilience360™, DHL leverage existing core capabilities – an extensive logistics expertise and supply chain, integrating information from many transport management systems (TMSs) and a global network. The system also uses third-party sourced risk data about current weather, local social and political, and other information. DHL partner with the world's leading risk-management data providers and risk intelligence experts.

The digital-platform integrated information from all these are sourced into a cohesive whole to provide short and longer visibility and planning support.

The system is also primarily to help protect employee safety and to manage risks from natural disasters and other operational risks to social and political factors.

Flying drones and augmented reality

Another area driven by DHL Innovation Lab in Bonn, Germany, has be in research areas that include flying drones to automate the shipping of packages, as well as examples in the use of virtual reality technology that scans a package QR code tag and creates a virtual image of "what is inside the box" to the handler but without having to open the package.

DHL announced the world's first regular drone flights starting in December 2014 from their "parcelcopter" research project that originated just a year earlier. The service will use an autonomous quadcopter to deliver small parcels to the German island of Juist, a sandbar island 12km into the North Sea from the German coast, inhabited by 2000 people. Deliveries will include medication and other goods that may be "urgently needed."[64]

DHL research also explores how virtual reality and augmented reality can be developed for advanced business and social processes and immersive experience.[65]

Virtual reality (VR) and augmented reality (AR) are two related approaches that combine physical and digital techniques. VR is a completely computer-generated, immersive, and three-dimensional environment that is displayed either on a computer screen or through special stereoscopic displays, such as the Oculus Rift. In contrast, AR (or mixed reality as it is also sometimes called) combines both the virtual and the real. Users of AR are still able to sense the real world around them; this is not possible when people are immersed in VR.

DHL examples include using wearable technology such as smart glasses and smart watches to project images and data in the viewer's eyeline. These can be used to send instructions for work tasks or information on products or work activities. Another example is QR codes that can be scanned by mobile smartphone cameras and processed by a mobile app to generate information about the object and location where the QR code is displayed.

These types of innovations help in expanding the possibilities of logistics and in compliance in tracking and tracing goods required by national laws, for example.

Digital technologies are changing the concept of logistics in many new ways, connecting the physical and virtual workspaces into an end-to-end digital supply chain. Given that local and global economies work in increasingly connected global networks of supply chains, the role of logistics is central to this journey.

7. Digital Health Business Model – e-health and m-health

Introduction

The development of e-health is an area of close interest for medical product and healthcare companies, medical practitioners, as well as government health and private agencies seeking to solve the double challenge of affordable healthcare and innovative new treatment. These seemingly different goals still both share common national healthcare and individual patient care outcomes, as set out in Table 4.8.

We have already spoken of a contradiction, sometimes called the health paradox, where corporations in particular are caught between on the one hand increasing lead times for investment in new innovation that may take increasing budget – and, on the other, achieving incremental or step-change patient care outcomes. Yet the rise of digitization has also introduced the possibility of lower-cost technology as the cost and speed of adoption of commercial smartphones, mobile apps, and hardware computation, memory, and network costs have become increasingly mass produced and commoditized. New e-health business models are emerging that present opportunities for both new affordable and reliable remote patient monitoring as well as new data analytics and networked services from "bench to bedside."

While the term e-health is often associated with electronic health and the use of technology, it is also perhaps more accurately described as understanding

TABLE 4.8   Healthcare enterprise and patient outcomes

Healthcare Operational and National Outcomes	Patient Outcomes
• Lower cost-per-patient care outcome • Increased productivity of clinicians • Higher patient attention time • Reduced GDP burden from state health costs • Reduced waiting times • Higher visit throughput and patient service contact time	• Longer lifespan • Improved recovery time • Survivability from major trauma • Speed of health call-out and service • Better independent living in the community • Increased personal safety inside and outside your home

how health works by connecting translation research, clinic, or health informatics and monitoring into a continuous loop. It is also the development of an integrated medical care strategy that combines all these aspects into a unified approach from the patient to the clinician and tiers of services, through to industrial applied research into drug and treatment and pure primary fundamental research.

Translation research is the facilitation of the practical application of scientific discoveries to the development and implementation of new ways to prevent, diagnose, and treat disease.[66] Health informatics is a range of information technology and information analysis skills[67] required in which medical data is analyzed and disseminated through the application of technology.[68]

Monitoring is the connections to patients with remote devices that can sense and collect information and transmit these to local or remote collection. This is fed back into the health analytics and to the translation research to provide patient data for immediate near-term support or ongoing future research into treatments. The immediate benefits are patient monitoring that is a real-time status of wellbeing; insight into information trends and patient conditions by front-line clinicians; and biomedical research. Being able to collect information from many patients, and to "crowdsource" this data, becomes an increasing benefit as a wider population of sample data becomes available under controlled patient data conditions that may anonymize the data or specific profiles. It is clear that with digital technologies these e-health strategies have the potential to transform both front-line patient care and new treatments developed from medical research (Figure 4.16).

Telecare in the community

Sybo Dijkstra, senior director and head of Philips Research UK, sees digitization as not to do with the enterprise but about innovation. Sybo explains, "It is about the creation of new services innovation by doing things differently to achieve better results for patient care overall." The connection of patients and health is being enabled by technologies that are empowering people to live better lives in the community. Sybo describes health monitoring as a 1990s concept but that this has greatly expanded with technology innovation over the past decades to be able to collect data fast and to link this with the clinicians and services for enhanced patient care. Sybo explains with an example of, "I do it my way, Mi (more independent)," a strategic community health initiative of which Philips Research UK is one of the partners.[69] Mi (more independent) is a UK government-funded initiative that is being

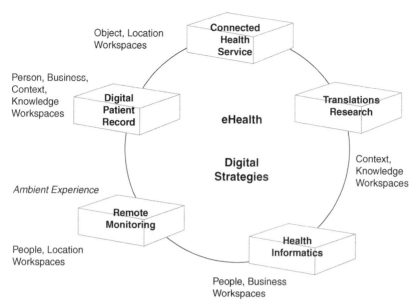

FIGURE 4.16 e-health digital strategies capabilities

piloted across four UK regions; Liverpool has been chosen as one of the pilot areas. The Mi partnership is funded by the Technology Strategy Board, the UK's innovation agency, which finds ways to boost the UK economy through technological innovations.[70] The initiative aims to provide life-enhancing services using technologies that can enable care in the community, and support for the elderly and patients, with cost-effective and more responsive services. The services make people's lives easier, keeping them healthier, and helping them feel more secure and less isolated in their own home. Simple activities – such as turning on the television, opening the fridge door to find what you are looking for, opening the curtains, or checking that the gas fire is switched off – are taken account of as being important lifestyle and wellbeing issues.

The Mi initiative includes life-enhancing technologies that use low-cost digital technologies to augment living spaces in the home. Examples include wearable technologies such as fall detectors and panic alarms, to many types of room and object sensors including a talking photo album, keysafe, an epilepsy detector, bed occupancy sensors, wireless smoke detectors, and medication dispensers. The Mi initiative also provides examples of the "smart house" that brings together some of the technologies to the outside and inside of the house – lounge, kitchen, bathroom, bedroom, and the garden and surrounding area of the house.[71]

Mi services connect community volunteer "champions" in partnership with the NHS home healthcare, health trainers, and call-center support to patients and community. Services such as these provide integrated healthcare that considers the whole lifestyle and living spaces. These technologies, apart from providing valuable public services, can also collect data about services and activities performance. Sybo illustrates this with a Philips innovation called "EncoreAnywhere™," a web-based patient compliance management system that makes treating sleep-disordered patients easier and more efficient. It is powerful, accurate, and compliant with the Health Insurance Portability and Accountability Act (HIPAA) of 1996.[72] This is the next generation of digital patient platforms that enables patient record data to be accessible and usable in a secure and effective way.

Systems such as these are becoming an imperative due to increases in the number of people who are living longer and, in general, require more longer-term healthcare services. In an article published in 2014 Sybo explained that technology can support efforts to provide better healthcare for patients in their own homes rather than in hospital. Clinicians can be in contact home and away, monitoring patients with chronic conditions in their homes with new technology improves patient survival and quality of care outcomes.[73]

As of 2015 it is still early days, however, and a wider scale of adoption across all communities and services will take time as new technology and infrastructure requires new practitioner skills and enterprise processes.

Activity monitoring and an emerging new model of healthcare

Professor Christopher James, head of biomedicine and technology at Warwick University, UK, has extensive experience in these technology roadmaps: "Novel sensor technologies, both wearable and in the home, can be combined with intelligent analysis techniques to infer much about the wearer and their interaction with their environment. This information can be used to monitor health trajectories in mental health problems such as bipolar disorder, as well as quality of life for independent living in the aging population."

Chris explains: "Activity monitoring can have many applications in managing health, illness, and in monitoring behavior impacting the quality of life and enabling augmented health intervention. While there is a new kind of emerging model of healthcare this also has a number of challenges."

The development of low-cost mobile apps that can use commercially available smartphones that are affordable to the general public can be put to work in the new model of care. The effect of connecting "ambient sensors" such as basic movement and body heat detectors, pressure mats, and low-cost webcams enables the digitization of living spaces.

Connecting personal monitors as a concept to smartphones, tablets, and mobile apps is already well under way in the lifestyle wearables marketplace. Sports bracelets and sensors attached directly to the body or clothing can now provide insights into fitness, heart rate, and blood pressure.

In the healthcare field, connecting this to ambient technology and medical wearables moves this to a new level that empowers individuals and healthcare professionals. It is promoting a phenomenon of moving away from illness management to promoting wellness (see Table 4.9).

This can support a range of conditions that are not just physiological and age-related, but can encompass chronic disease and mental illness. In these conditions, the ability to understand and monitor the physical and mental state of a person is essential to protecting the patient from self-harm and supporting their continuous health improvement needs.

Chris explains with an example of "personal ambient monitoring" (PAM), a self-help system that can use algorithms and sensors to monitor a person's behavior patterns and provide an indication of their mental state. Such systems use a variety of sensors indoors and outdoors, including:

- Mechanical detection (door switches)
- Passive infrared (PIR)
- Optics/motion capture (video/camera systems)
- Light, temperature, sound

TABLE 4.9 Emerging model of healthcare

Old Model of Care	New Model of Care
• Focus on acute conditions; reactive management	• Focus on long-term conditions, prevention, and continuing care
• Hospital-centered, disjoined episodes	• Integrated with people's lives in homes and communities
• Doctor-dependent	
• Patient as passive recipient; self-care infrequent	• Team-based, shared record
• Use of IT rare	• Patient as partner; self-care encouraged and supported
	• Dependent on IT and devices

Source: Professor Christopher James.

- Gait analysis/Kinect
- Radio frequency energy (radar, microwave, and tomographic motion detection)

Body-worn wearable sensors can include:

- Smartphone
- GPS
- Wearable kinematic sensors:
  - 3-axis accelerometers
  - Actigraphy
  - Data-logger
  - Pedometers

By combining these sensors and devices indoors and outdoors it is possible to provide a better level of care and condition-monitoring for patients. The term "geofencing" involves the ability to check the location of people in a vicinity that helps the individual or clinician services to ensure they are secure and safe. "Plot Projects," an initiative in geofencing services for commercial retail and telecoms, describes this as a virtual perimeter around a location that is a digital workspace with a physical range from 50 to 50,000m radius. The service provides easy-to-implement multiple operating system mobile apps, data analytics, and supports geofencing notifications and iBeacon™ notifications.[74] In the healthcare sector, Chris illustrates geofencing indoors with an example of the USEFIL EU FP7 initiative, unobtrusive smart environments for independent living that provides practical services for the elderly.[75] The aim is to develop affordable in-home unobtrusive monitoring and web communications using low-cost, off-the-shelf technology. The system can use video monitoring and open-source software and platforms to support software-driven wearable and ambient room monitoring.

USEFIL also considers geofencing outdoors, using GPS via cell phone to track locations of relevance in order to confirm the proximity of the wearable to the medical services, assistive living services, or emergency services.

Developing automated algorithms that can interpret image recognition and GPS signals into rules that trigger an alert if the person or their behavior is anomalous. This needs to be fit for purpose, and unobtrusive to the wearer or living space so that users can "get on with their lives."

A quantified self

The medium- to longer-term impact of digital health points toward many new innovations that will encompass both medical health and lifestyle into a broader scope of wellness. Digital technologies will be able to augment the person in their physical workspace, at home, or outdoors through the connectivity of mobile devices, wearable sensors, and telecommunications networks to software-virtualized services.

These services will need to have the telecoms network coverage to a reliable, fine-grained level in location accuracy and proximity if people's lives are to be safe – a service that is moving from illness management to preventative care and wellbeing. But with these sensors, devices, and connections, a new "quantified self" will be possible that captures every movement and behavioral element. Issues of personal privacy, and ethical use of data by companies and services, will become increasingly part of this landscape. But we can also see the possibilities of a new relationship with technology in which healthcare can enable new life-enhancing services.

Virtual workspaces can be created so that, in the future, remote intervention services can mean that a person, for example, calls up a center and they will be able to prescribe remotely a program that the person could join for a time period. The person will self-monitor their progress. Chris explains that enabling these types of services from teleworkers to telehealth will need more than "robotic answer-phone voices" on the end of a telephone, requiring instead new emerging "empathy systems" that combine human awareness and healthcare attention specificity for each individual's medical needs.

Conclusion

In this closer examination of the digital enterprise we have seen several business models enabled by digital technologies. A collection of capabilities can evolve over time driven internally and externally by processes, competitors, products, and services as well as technological change.

Customer experience and digital workspace experience

A key aspect of change that we have seen in the case studies has been the evolution of the customer experience journey as we travel through digitized environments. These connected spaces have the potential to create more immersive experiences that can transform how the digital enterprise will work in the future.

The customer touchpoints along the supply chain, or in a retail store – both physically and online – have become further connected by the digital workspaces that can join up different time frames of experience. User experience

Customer Touchpoint Journey

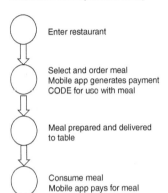

Digital Enterprise – Digital Workspaces

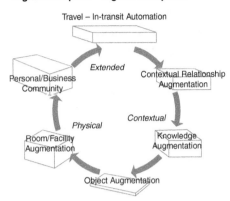

FIGURE 4.17 Connected digital enterprise architecture example

(UX) to customer experience (CX) has further developed into digital workspace experience that together represents the digital enterprise journey (Figure 4.17).

Toward building digital ecosystems

While digital workspaces are constructed environments, the net effect of objects, connections, and experiences is the evolution of digital ecosystems that transcend how we might think of a modern enterprise. The earlier discussion on value chains, including double- and multi-sided marketplace platforms, is clearly evident in the case studies.

There is a further journey beyond the digital workspaces that is one of ecosystems and how the digital enterprise will build out their digital platforms and experiences.

We have seen the early evolution of Web 2.0 with web apps and the internet now becoming more connected with mobile devices and sensors. Our case studies point toward these digital technologies combining together into digital workspaces that are forming two-sided marketplaces, multi-sided marketplaces, and ultimately establishing their value network ecosystems in the digital enterprise (see Figure 4.18).

Driving outcome-based thinking with digital enterprise

In the e-hotel example case study we saw the hospitality operational outcomes of the hotel enterprise seeking to meet their guest and partner outcomes.

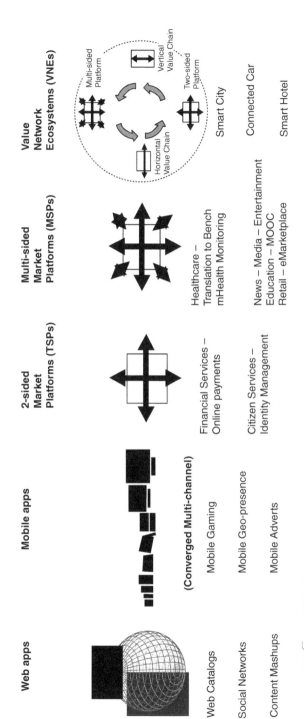

Web apps

Web Catalogs

Social Networks

Content Mashups

Mobile apps

(Converged Multi-channel)

Mobile Gaming

Mobile Geo-presence

Mobile Adverts

2-sided Market Platforms (TSPs)

Financial Services – Online payments

Citizen Services – Identity Management

Multi-sided Market Platforms (MSPs)

Healthcare – Translation to Bench mHealth Monitoring

News – Media – Entertainment Education – MOOC Retail – eMarketplace

Value Network Ecosystems (VNEs)

Multi-sided Platform

Vertical Value Chain

Two-sided Platform

Horizontal Value Chain

Smart City

Connected Car

Smart Hotel

FIGURE 4.18 Toward digital ecosystems

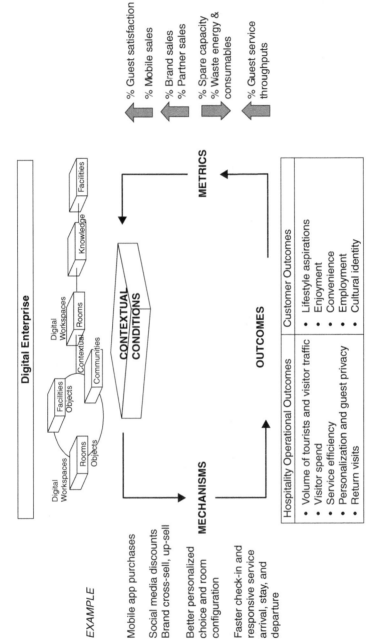

FIGURE 4.19 Designing digital workspaces that drive digital value

In the case of the digital technologies, the practitioners can select and implement smart doors and room sensors, and connect these to mobile apps and front desk and onward partner services. As we saw in the Hilton International case study, as with other case studies, they have successfully used these in the locations and spaces in which guests and service providers come together – in order to deliver an enhanced customer experience. We can draw examples from the case studies of how the outcomes of the service are driven by the design and performance of the digital enterprise. The digital workspaces can be thought of as methods to manage the contextual conditions of the enterprise and its wider ecosystems (see Figure 4.19 adapted from Henfridsson et al 2013):[76]

A useful way to consider this is to view the impact of contextual design on the overall performance of the enterprise. This can be described by a number of key practical digital design issues including:[77]

- **Contextual conditions** – how can the enterprise be supported by digital workspaces to enable contextual conditions? How can the specific conditions enable customers, employees, partners, or other outcomes to be contextually relevant to the situation?
- **Mechanisms –** what specific design features do we have in order to drive contextual conditions and outcomes? (We explore the concept of value and mechanisms in Chapter 5.)
- **Metrics** – what and how do we measure effective outcomes to assess the feedback and direction of the experience?
- **Outcomes** – what are the overall desired outcomes of the enterprise, the customer, and the wider environment that we seek to support?

In the e-hotel example case study each digital technology plays a part in the total digital workspace experience that together seeks to increase guest satisfaction and brand loyalty, which then helps to drive value in hotel capacity and partner services. This workspace experience is visible in the objects, rooms and facilities, the employees, partners, and customers, and the transport and travel that define the e-hotel digital-enterprise business model. Measurement of economic and social value outcomes then become the key goals to measuring true digital enterprise and digital economy value.

Chapter Summary

Business and information technology practitioners are facing a new kind of reality that requires thinking not just in terms of technological vision but an awareness of how the very definition of a business enterprise is changed by the impact of these technologies. In the next chapter we will see how these new digital business models are creating new monetization mechanisms for payoff and value. We explore the mechanisms of generating value in the digital ecosystem and how digital enterprises can leverage these models to create value.

5

How to Build the Right Digital Enterprise for Payoff and Monetization

Chapter Introduction

From the previous case studies we can begin to draw some conclusions on the types of digital practices that are evident in and across these cases. In this chapter we address the practical characteristics of digital technologies and their potential for value creation through three perspectives:

- Capabilities
- Operating-model practices
- Monetization strategies

Capabilities

A central theme running through this book has been how digital technologies actually work in practice and how they affect the wider business context. This includes concepts of customer experience (CX) design and user experience (UX) design, or the development of customer relationship management (CRM) and vendor relationship management (VRM) that develop collaborative social media and content design. Even when using this in what may be termed "digital transformation" of a company operating model, this is part of the rich design possible when taking business, data, social, and technological and other perspectives together in what is defined as "capabilities."

Capabilities can be simply described as the personal and organizational competencies to perform an activity in order to achieve an outcome. In the digital world these capabilities have been radically transformed by new digital content, networks, and devices that change many traditional supply chains and business processes that represent the enterprise capabilities. A well-known example is the digitization of books, which has been significantly altered both in terms of the marketplace structure and how the actual print and words are created and delivered.

A digital enterprise capability may be to *deliver an e-book*. This is an electronic book that is made up of many capability increments that include the creation of the content by authors, the design and management of the publication by publishers, the manufacture and delivery of the product, and the digital content that the customer consumes while reading on an e-reader device. The key to all of this is the *capability* – building the digital enterprise capabilities.[1]

The following definition of capabilities is a useful categorization that we will use in describing the features of the case study lessons:

> *Capability*
> *Definition: an ability that an organization, person, or system possesses. Capabilities are typically expressed in general and high-level terms and to achieve them typically requires a combination of organization, people, processes, and technology. For example, marketing, customer contact, or outbound telemarketing.*
>
> *Capability increment*
> *Definition: a discrete portion of a capability architecture that delivers specific value. When all increments have been completed, the capability has been realized.*

Operating Model Practices

We have seen in the case studies across industry market sectors that the multitude of different combinations of digital technologies has had a potential radical change to those markets and to the enterprises operating within them. We can explore this in two ways. First in the way that the market and the enterprise are unbundled and rebundled in new operating model practices. Second, the nature of the products and services are changed by digital technologies through making the physical components and functional utility into new virtual or digital forms. This changes the *agency* of the product and service such that it can be seen as a modular layered architecture that can support a distributed value network of connections.

> *Utility*
> *Definition: in the context of computing, utility refers to software, hardware, and devices that are used in a commodity- or consumer-driven context rather than a special customized asset of service. Their utilitarian nature has a state of usefulness that is practical for a specific use.*
>
> *Agency*
> *Definition: the effect created in a person, group, or place from the action of an intervention producing a particular effect.*

From a practitioner perspective, digitization can change the utility and agency characteristics of products and services in the design of digital capabilities. Let us explore these two statements further.

Market Unbundling and Rebundling

How a company defines its "portfolio of capabilities" can be described as the set of operating capabilities that collectively represent its operating model and the way it performs activities to compete and deliver products and services in a marketplace. These include the stages of production and distribution that can be modified, as well as the functions and features of the product and service.[2]

Digital technologies can potentially change the products and services, business processes, and social and working practices that define an organization. This disruption can be minor in the sense of commodity capabilities, but in other situations can – and often does – have the potential to transform the core of a business. This is what is described as *disruption* to the very business model of the enterprise and which affects the capabilities that define the enterprise. For both small and radical change impact, this is the journey of building the digital enterprise to *unbundle* and *rebundle* capabilities in the organization and potentially its relationship with other organizations, its customers, and suppliers in the marketplace – deconstruction and reconstruction of

TABLE 5.1   Unbundling and rebundling by digital – industry example

Industry Market Sector	Unbundling the Publishing Market and the Digital Enterprise	Rebundling the Publishing Market and the Digital Enterprise
Electronic Publishing	• Authors can create own content and publish in open crowdsource marketplaces. • Book content can be copied, extracted, and reused in multiple digital formats and resold digitally with no physical creation. • This enables additional monetization mechanisms. • This creates new cyber security and IP control challenges.	• Publishers can be digital content intermediaries offering multi-channel global access direct to customers. • Online marketplaces such as Amazon can create and mediate customer experience, and offer customized content promotions for specific customer preferences using gamification.

the organization. It can work in both directions in the construction of new capabilities, aggregating some and disintermediating others.

In the case of e-books, the unbundling and rebundling of this market can be summarized as shown in the examples set out in Table 5.1.

Restructuring Capabilities

This aspect of digitization in the industry example shown in Table 5.1 creates new enterprise capabilities that are enabled through digital technologies. The structural changes include connectivity across the physical geography of telecommunications and the capabilities that become intermediated in new ways through the separation of digital content, digital platforms that represent software and hardware, and devices that can read and display this content for other intermediaries and customers.

Digitization restructures capabilities, creating different ways to define a set of capabilities and the marketplace industry in which it operates. This is summarized in the following key examples of digital restructure effects on enterprise and market economies:

• Unbundling physical products and services into separate capabilities that can be sold and reused.
• From bundling digital content into new products and services, rebundling digital products and services into new types of personalized services.

- Creating digital platforms for two-sided and multi-sided marketplaces, making these digital services that can both service individual one-to-one needs and reach multiple customers and groups, building communities online and new marketplaces.
- Creating new types of business processes and data-enabled analytical services that form new performance opportunities for rapid delivery, online commerce payments, and incentives to drive new business cross-selling and up-selling.
- Restructuring the touchpoints for an organization and its employees with the marketplace and its supply chain.
- Digitization changes and lowers the barriers to monetization in the microeconomy, altering how suppliers, customers, and intermediaries may interact and service each other. The macroeconomy can restructure through cross-cutting digitization links between primary, secondary, and tertiary sectors.

From the perspective of practitioners designing and implementing digital capabilities, we can illustrate this restructuring with many examples in the case studies we have examined so far. Table 5.2 provides just some of the examples of the digital unbundling and rebundling of the digital enterprise.

TABLE 5.2 Unbundling and rebundling capability examples of industry markets and enterprise

Industry Market Sector	Unbundling the Market and the Digital Enterprise Examples	Rebundling the Market and the Digital Enterprise Examples
Government-funded innovation	• Public–private partnerships • Municipal self-services	• Open-data services • Smart building services
Consumer home-products industry	• Online marketplace purchases • Self-service purchases	• Social media marketing • Crowdsourcing
Consumer energy industry	• Mixed-energy selling • Alternative switching resellers	• Alternative energy sourcing • Smart energy meters
Metropolitan industry	• Community-sourced services • Start-up incubation	• Smart amenity • Community innovation
Consumer electronics industry	• Mobile-device services • Cloud hosting	• Smart home appliances • Cloud brokering
Global package logistics industry	• Self-service shipping • Shipping e-commerce	• Crowd shipping • GPS package tracking
Consumer goods industry	• Consumer co-branding	• Online order and home delivery

Continued

Table 5.2 *Continued*

Industry Market Sector	Unbundling the Market and the Digital Enterprise Examples	Rebundling the Market and the Digital Enterprise Examples
Automotive industry	• Co-design with partners and customers • Vehicle automation	• Embedded software feedback • Product data management mediation
Fast-moving consumer foods industry	• Local online services • Pro-sumer product-marketing collaboration	• Co-branding • Crowd marketing
Software gaming industry	• Open source software • Collaborative software testing	• Integrated gaming online community • Hybrid cloud design to run marketplace
Hospitality industry	• Crowdsourcing • Self-service	• Automated arrival services • Mobile apps
Sportswear industry	• Apparel sub-segments • Wearables self-service	• Lifestyle services • Embedded added-value services
Financial services consumer industry	• Payments start-ups • Digital currency alternatives	• Context-based product-payment links • Digital wallets
Healthcare services industry	• Private partner services • Self-service medical appointments	• e-health monitoring • m-health tracking and personalized feedback
Agriculture industry	• Community land management • Alternative sourcing	• GPS farm-asset tracking • Online market selling
Security assurance industry	• Self-service backups • Service and product assurance complexity	• Cloud capacity management • Rapid response and recovery
Open government	• Open source • Online marketplace sourcing	• Open-data services • Response management
Healthcare travel industry	• Personal medical records access • Medical data controls	• Inter-country medical data management • Mobile health response
Medical research industry	• Data collection and testing • Community collaboration	• Big-data new medical research • Patient–clinician and research integration
Emergency services industry	• Responder-led data collection • Response distribution	• Cloud-based recovery and persistent connectivity • Integrated service response
Automotive power industry	• Driver-community branding • Self-service electric charging	• Integrated car services platform • Embedded sensor automation
Automotive design industry	• Embedded product performance data feedback • Engineering collaboration	• Product data management • Application lifecycle management

Continued

Table 5.2   *Continued*

Industry Market Sector	Unbundling the Market and the Digital Enterprise Examples	Rebundling the Market and the Digital Enterprise Examples
Aerospace engineering industry	• Crowd collaboration • Mediation of engineering field data	• Embedded software telemetry • Big-data analytics integration
Financial investment services industry	• Machine learning automation • Self-service investment decision support	• Automated investment management • Multi-investment products management
Security industry	• Multi-device security issues • Own IP and identity mediation	• Zero-days crowd testing • Privacy assurance

Unbundling of Markets

The key issue is that digitization and digital technologies are pervasive and potentially intrusive. As we have seen in the case studies, the considerations of how the architecture changes with digital technology is paramount to enabling outcomes.

What is happening from the examples of digitization in industries is that a fundamental unbundling of the market is occurring (see Figure 5.1). Academics describe a socio-technical dynamic of digital infrastructures that they see as new patterns of connections between social and technical systems.[3]

As shown in Figure 5.1, the idea of a product with functions and feature characteristics can be deconstructed using digitization into new types of products and services. Furthermore, the idea of an enterprise as an entity breaks down as parts of the product and service may be unbundled and rebundled into new forms.

E-book unbundling and rebundling

Consider the example of an e-book, which has fundamentally changed the notion of physical books. The traditional book in the marketplace can be digitally unbundled into its constituent parts:

- The **content** of the book.
- The **services** to write, publish, sell, and distribute the book.
- The **devices** that you use to read the book.
- The **network** that delivered the book to the markets and the end consumer.

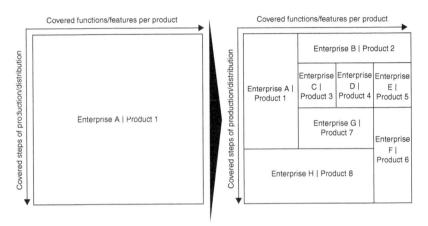

FIGURE 5.1 Unbundling of markets

Figure 5.2 illustrates that unbundling a book into an e-book form means that the content, delivery, and other aspects might be also *disintermediated*. The book content can be syndicated to many channel outlets digitally. The book could be read on many devices from mobiles to tablets to web browsers. The functions and features of the e-book can also be *rebundled* to create a new book not originally envisioned in the first publication. Digital content can be copied, edited, and merged to develop new content that can be syndicated and reused – a constraint of the physical paper book.

Modularity

Another key feature of digitization that enables unbundling and rebundling is *modularity*, a concept enabled by the ability to use digital services and digital content abstracted from the physical devices and infrastructure by various degrees.

To explain these phenomena we can look at the four layers again and define these as, first, constituent capabilities that are modular in that they represent separate parts of the whole yet can be individually used independently or in other new combinations.

Content can be digitized and moved, replicated or modified, inside and outside an enterprise. A digital-content ecosystem can be described in relation to a specific industry or marketplace and can be to specific enterprise requirements.

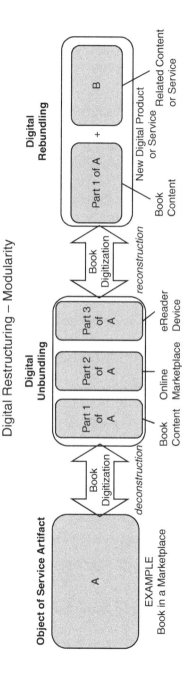

FIGURE 5.2 Modularity, unbundling, and rebundling

Second, products and services can be digitized to enable these modular capabilities to be able to move and transmit their capability from one to many consumers. The intermediation and disintermediation of digital content and these modular capabilities, together with the medium through which digitization exists and is built, is itself part of the digitization.

New Modular-layered Architectures

Traditional technology platforms have an application, platform, and communications infrastructure, yet in restructuring this with digital technologies a different kind of general pattern in services becomes apparent. In the case of the example of an e-book, the unbundling and rebundling of capabilities can be clearly seen in how the content, services, networking, and end devices come together in different ways.

The creation of an enterprise capability using digital technologies can be described in four loosely coupled levels: contents, services, network, and device (see Figure 5.2).[4] We can illustrate this model with an example of an e-book:

- **Device layer** – the mobile device or fixed device used to consume the e-book.
- **Network layer** – the telecommunications networks that are used to connect to the service.
- **Services layer** – the marketplace online to purchase the e-book to download.
- **Content layer** – the e-book content written by the author.

The *degree of coupling* of each layer is something we introduced earlier in the idea of vertical and horizontal integration and the creation of two-sided and multi-sided marketplaces. These layers represent a logical abstraction of the digital technologies, but also how they can cluster into different types of mediation brought on by the characteristics of digitization to create virtual resources services and device ecosystems (see Figure 5.3).

Market unbundling is reflected in the digital products and services.

Modularity and Layered Modular Architecture

In the effects of modularity on the marketplace in our example of the e-book we have what is described as clusters of modular capabilities that can be further described:

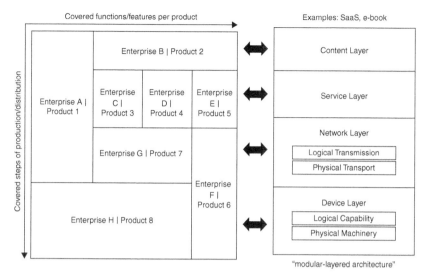

FIGURE 5.3 / **Modular-layered architecture**

Source: Adapted from Yoo, Henfridsson, and Lyytinen, "The new organizing logic of digital innovation: an agenda for information systems research," *Information Systems Research*, Vol. 21, No. 4, December 2010, 724–735. Copyright © 2010, used with permission.

- **Device ecosystems layer** – the clusters of mobile devices, sensors, and other forms of devices that enable the consumption and user experience, and interaction with digital content.
- **Network ecosystems layer** – the clusters of internet, NSP, and ISP networks and local networks, the server as internetworking between the wider area internet and local wireless or other connectivity medium to transport the digital content.
- **Services ecosystems layer** – the range of digital services that manage and intermediate the digital content from its inception, development, and delivery to consumption.
- **Content ecosystems layer** – the original, replicated, or modified content or related service metadata that define the digital artifact.

Professor Youngjin Yoo, a pioneer in digital design thinking, describes this as "competition moving to the ecosystem level, not just products at the product level."[5] Yoo describes how digital technologies can bring changes to a company and further defines this as a "multi-ecosystem in constant change."

This is a fundamental difference between just modular physical or digital products and the idea that digitization creates clusters than can form layers across physical markets to enable the creation of digital ecosystems, digital markets, and the digital economic activity. Figure 5.4 illustrates this by considering the many ecosystems in our e-book example. In the case of the illustration in Figure 5.4, two books – Book A and Book B – may have several combinations of different devices, networks, and sources of the same content.

In the devices ecosystem, Android, iOS, Blackberry, and many others for example, can compete as devices for end users to access content through their smartphone, tablet, or other device. Then, the networks used to access content on the device can have competing telecoms provider networks, Wi-Fi hotspots, and other forms of access to networks, including mobile, wireless, and satellite.

The services ecosystem is the manifold network of websites, social networks, and other myriad places that may search, offer content streaming or download, or associated commentary or e-commerce of other services associated with the content, connection, and device mediums. Content ecosystems are the many digital content choices that exist, from digital books, music, film, and conversation to many other variations of static or interactive content that exist today.

The "customer experience path" can connect between many ecosystems across these layers. Digital enterprises can be formed to make a vertical ecosystem (such as a branded tablet with pre-installed apps for access to specific content), horizontal ecosystems in one layer (such as online B2B or B2C trading platforms to service many customers), or telecom network platforms for connectivity and content services. By recognizing the modularity and layers of an industry, in so doing practitioners are building the digital enterprise platforms and services that define their capabilities.

The consequences of these digital clusters are the formation of ecosystems that drive new kinds of scaling and monetization strategies. In the next section we explore the mechanisms that drive digital monetization.

The Rise of the Hyperscale Digital Enterprise

It is an inescapable fact that at one extreme of digital technologies is the phenomenon of the "hypercloud" investment – notably in public cloud computing by Google, Amazon, Microsoft, and a few others who are investing billions of US dollars in data centers and associated infrastructure.[6] The characteristics of these investments are specific to those companies who offer typically global-scale scalable computing, storage, and access to software applications

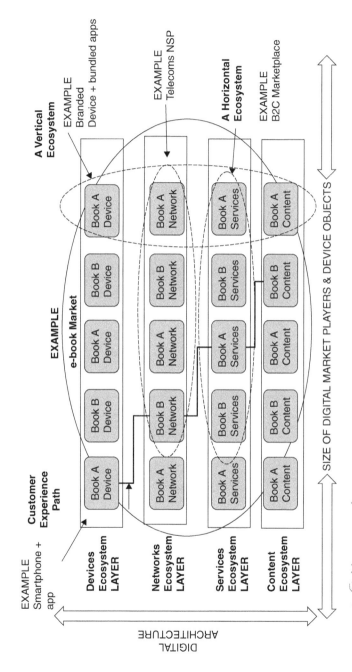

FIGURE 5.4 Multi-ecosystem layers

and services in many layers of ecosystems. To some extent this is, at its most extreme, a Pareto principle of a few hyperscale digital enterprises that create a distorted yet very real potential for new digital business models. These are the outliers and the exceptions to enterprise models that are otherwise represented by the vast majority of existing and smaller enterprises that may have started as physical business or virtual organizations "on the net." Nevertheless, this scaling effect of digital is the first key principle in how investment in digital technologies can create a self-reinforcing cycle of larger and larger user adoption that can, in the right circumstances, potentially grow exponentially.

Mechanisms for Scaling Digital Enterprise Adoption

In the case of hypercloud investment, the methods in which these digital enterprises became the worldwide phenomena they are today is down to a number of key personality traits and skills of their founders, as well as investment decisions and timing, but, more precisely, how the digital architecture was created to enable such massive growth (see Figure 5.5).

Professor Ola Henfridsson, a pioneer in digital platforming strategies, describes this as "generative mechanisms of digital infrastructure evolution." In a research paper by Henfridsson and Bygstad, they argue that the

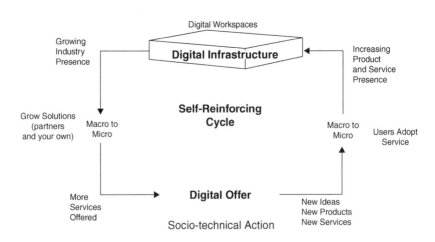

FIGURE 5.5 Self-reinforcing socio-technical mechanism

Source: Adapted from Figure 1 in O. Henfridsson and B. Bygstad, "The generative mechanisms of digital infrastructure evolution," *IS Quarterly*, Vol. 37, No. 3, September 2014, 912. Copyright © 2014, Regents of the University of Minnesota, used with permission.

consequences of digitization change the nature of how products and services are created and expanded – using several key mechanisms that involve innovation, adoption, and scaling methods that drive self-reinforcing feedback to scale digital products and service offers.[7]

The mechanism for generating digital value is defined as a socio-technical system (STS), a theory that is concerned with organizational development as an approach to complex organizational work design that recognizes the interaction between people and technology in workplaces. The term also refers to the interaction between society's complex infrastructures and human behavior. In this sense, society itself, and most of its substructures, are complex socio-technical systems.[8] The digital infrastructure represents the content, services, networks, and devices that define the existence of the digital offer. It is the mechanisms that drive the digital infrastructure to generate value from the digital offers.

Comparison of Physical Object and Digital Object Characteristics

For practitioners in the field working with digital technologies, the identifying mechanism to charge for digital products and services is often different from the trading exchange of physical goods and services.

Examples of physical products and services characteristics

1. Physical products and services are at the speed of transaction in the human perception of time period of seconds and minutes, and limited to the number of human-to-human or human-to-machine requests that can be processed cognitively.
2. Physical products and services are located in geospatial position of their existence.
3. Physical products and services can be replicated by additional manufacturing and production processes.
4. Physical products and services can be modified by physical redesign or physical modification.
5. Physical product and services are exchanged, rented, or leased to generate monetary value.
6. Physical products and services can be used by community-based asset sharing. They can also be developed by collaborative resources in and across a supply chain network.

The methods of digital monetization are not constrained by many of these physical characteristics. Digital data by its very essence exists as electrons or equivalent in physical artifacts such as software, hardware, and embedded storage mediums. In a sense it has no physical reality other than its action on the external world.

Examples of digital products and services characteristics

1. Digital products and services can scale extremely rapidly from tens to several thousands of transactions per second or minute at peak. This leads to massive scalable revenue potential.
2. Digital products and services have no physical existence, they only exist in a virtual sense but must reside in some form of physical host. They are not limited by geospatial distances and can be simultaneously in multiple physical or virtual locations at the same time.
3. Digital products and services have technical malleability in that they can be replicated but also recoded and recombined into new products and services. Their original digital specification can be altered.
4. Digital products and services can be reflexive, being able to be self-referential back to itself. This property can be illustrated by data that has attributes that syntactically describe itself.
5. Digital products and services can be copied and exchanged by uploading a replication of itself or through remote streaming or access. This supports rapid scaling of virtual services that can be monetized through renting – leasing of time-limited access: for example, digital music subscription.
6. Digital products and services can be created and owned simultaneously by many people or enterprise entities, for example – activities and open source code.

These properties of digital products and services enable new capabilities in the design of digital enterprise, which in turn enables new forms of capabilities inside the enterprise and in the wider economy.

Building Innovation Mechanisms in the Digital Enterprise

In the case studies, we saw a number of examples of disruptive innovation that were creating new products and services, supported by new business operating models (Figure 5.6). Examples of digital innovation mechanisms in the case studies include:

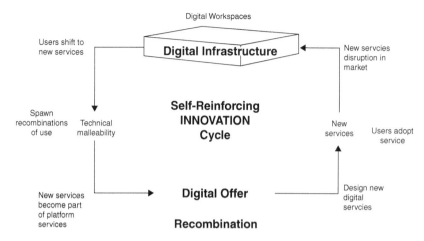

FIGURE 5.6 Self-reinforcing innovation mechanism

Source: Adapted from Figure 4 in O. Henfridsson and B. Bygstad, "The generative mechanisms of digital infrastructure evolution." *IS Quarterly*, Vol. 37, No. 3, September 2014, 919. Copyright © 2014, Regents of the University of Minnesota, used with permission.

Innovation mechanisms to drive self-reinforcing scaling cycles:

- Digital innovation to drive *self-reinforcing feedback* about personal health and lifestyle is *creating new markets* in, for example, the sportswear industry. A new category of wearable lifestyle and activity health products such as wristbands, shoe sensors, and other clothes enhancements collect activity and general health data.

- Digital innovation to drive *self-reinforcing higher product performance choice* can *disrupt existing markets* with substitution products such as, for example, the electric car: a new proposition of greener, fuel efficient, and new automated features to enable a new kind of driving experience.

- Digital innovation can drive *self-reinforcing up-selling and cross-selling* by *creating extensions into new forms of marketplace delivery* in, for example, the home appliances industry. Connected fridges and televisions enable existing objects and appliances to act in a new way as a platform of digital services to connect to supply chain networks of services and products.

- Digital innovation can drive *self-reinforcing medical advances and higher patient care service using integrated data analytics* and, in the field, practitioner-led engagement in the medical-health research industry. Translation research in the medical lab can be collected from medical trials and practitioners and passed back for analysis that in turn can be field tested with the practitioners to provide an integrated assessment and research model.

Building Adoption Mechanisms in the Digital Enterprise

The challenges in moving from existing technology and ways of working to new technological solutions is the roadmap of adoption. In a number of case studies we have seen examples of mechanisms that either accelerated digital technology adoption or lowered barriers to technology adoption through ease of use and agency of services for customers (Figure 5.7). Examples of digital adoption mechanisms that we saw in the case studies include:

Adoption mechanisms to drive self-reinforcing scaling cycles:

- Digital adoption mechanism can drive *self-reinforcing higher consumer purchasing rates* by use of seamless *user experience integration* of digital services to provide easy convenience of access to online payments in, for example, the financial services industry through digital wallets and contactless payments.
- Digital adoption mechanism can drive *self-reinforcing energy and emissions reduction* by use of *embedded digital technology* to create enhanced user interaction and experience in the energy utility industry. Smart energy

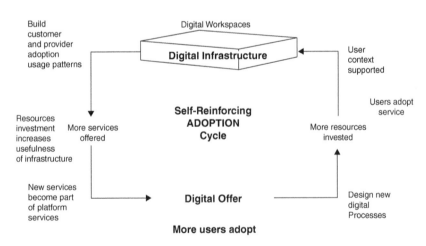

FIGURE 5.7 Self-reinforcing adoption mechanism

Source: Adapted from Figure 5 in O. Henfridsson and B. Bygstad, "The generative mechanisms of digital infrastructure evolution," *IS Quarterly*, Vol. 37, No. 3, September 2014, 919. Copyright © 2014, Regents of the University of Minnesota, used with permission.

sensors can manage room temperature and energy consumption, optimizing building-energy demand management. Adoption grows as efficiencies in automated systems drive metrics in savings and performance of assets and consumer behavior.

• Digital adoption mechanism can drive *self-reinforcing higher customer satisfaction rates and cross-selling and upselling* by development of *new services on existing digital devices* such as smartphones to act as new service devices in, for example, the hospitality industry. Smartphones can be the remote control to open hotel doors, order room services, and other facilities to increase the adoption of new hotel services.

• Digital adoption mechanism can drive *self-reinforcing data accuracy quality and decision coordination* by the establishment of *common data standards* for coordination and interoperability of product management and supply chain logistics in, for example, the engineering design industry. Product data management systems improve information management and design engineering efficiencies across different suppliers and sourcing standards, in which many use different product identity and naming standards. By using semantic data, standards adoption could be driven across a supplier ecosystem that uses commonality of parts and product standards, enabling efficiencies in design, logistics, spares, and service management.

Building Scaling Mechanisms in the Digital Enterprise

From the perspective of initiating new digital technology solutions into a market there may be early success in pilots and the creation of a number of communities of early adoption, yet the critical issue is in scaling this early activity to a *critical mass* that shifts to a mass appeal for the solution (Figure 5.8). Some venture capitalist practitioners describe this as a start-up business threshold that can pass through a series of scalable barriers defined by potential levels of investment, size of the enterprise, the number of customers, and size of market. Venture capital funding stages depend significantly on the type of products and service characteristics in the digital enterprise. The rapid scaling of successful adoption means that the 1 million user threshold can be reached well before three years. In an extreme example, Facebook scaled to 500 million users in seven years, achieved through a combination of strategies including, horizontal scaling investing in computing that could handle large expansion of traffic; strong organization management to handle the

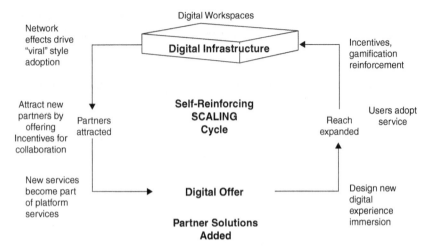

FIGURE 5.8 Self-reinforcing scaling mechanism

Source: Adapted from Figure 5 in O. Henfridsson and B. Bygstad, "The generative mechanisms of digital infrastructure evolution," *IS Quarterly*, Vol. 37, No. 3, September 2014, 919. Copyright © 2014, Regents of the University of Minnesota, used with permission.

day-to-day pressures of technical operations; and investment backing to grow the business.[9] A key feature was also innovation in the way that the Facebook "product" adapted to meet the customer experience, creating features that enabled customers to post and share pictures, and develop communities of interest and social interests.[10] Finding funding to scale up as the digital technology increases the size of the customer base can present challenges. While the Facebook example is well documented in the media, the vast majority of digital businesses are not scaled to this size and are typically aiming for an adoption for thousands or millions in the case of commercial enterprises. Some investment scaling examples from venture capital funding stages are shown in Table 5.3.

In the case studies looked at in earlier chapters, we examined end users using digital technologies to enable their enterprise to benefit from digital capabilities. The issue of scaling for digital technologies, from niche pilots to large-scale industrial solutions, is in fact similar when considering the range of small- to medium-size companies or large multinational enterprises. Whether the scope is a small local digital service involving a few employees and customers, a city-wide digital services implementation, or a multi-country implementation of digital services spanning many time zones, thousands of employees and millions of customers – several scaling mechanisms were illustrated in the case studies.

TABLE 5.3   Examples of scaling for investment

Customer Adoption Scale	Examples of Enterprise Activity	Example Venture Capital Funding Stages
1–10 users	Conceptual idea	Seed $250,000–$1 million VC capital
1000 users		Early stage – start-up
10,000 users	Typicall.y in business less than three years	Early stage – first stage
100,000 users		Formative stage – includes seed and early stage
500,000 users	Typically in business for more than three years	Later stage – commercialization, sales, manufacturing, distribution
1 million users		Later stage – third stage – major expansion
10 million users		Later stage – expansion stage – second and third stages
100 million users		Later stage – mezzanine (bridge) stage – going public and represents a bridge between expanding the company and the IPO
300 million users		
700 million users		
>1 billion users		

Scaling Mechanisms to Drive Self-Reinforcing Scaling Cycles

- Digital scaling mechanism can drive *self-reinforcing citizen "hearts and minds" engagement and self-service value by creation* of *digital platforms* in smart city initiatives to increase internet of things (IoT) services adoption. There are manifold areas including open data hosting, local services assisted living, community services, and online education and welfare access support.

- Digital scaling mechanism can drive *self-reinforcing consumer network effect leverage* by the use of *open innovation crowdsourcing* to engage existing and potentially new customers in the co-production of marketing and product feedback in the FMCG industry. Scaling to reach larger audiences of new products, as well as raising awareness of company and product brands, could be accelerated through engaging open dialogue with online crowd platforms.

- Digital scaling mechanism can drive *self-reinforcing consumer behavior influencing* by developing a *programmatic marketing* combining digital technologies of data analytics, social media, smartphone apps, and gamification to profile and target better customer influence and focused product and service engagement. In the FMCG industry, franchise vendors can be supported through mobile marketing services that enable self-service empowerment of the third-party franchises through access to web-based services on mobile apps and cloud computing. These services help smaller franchise operations to scale who otherwise would not have resources to market themselves.

• Digital scaling mechanism can drive *self-reinforcing automated transaction effectiveness* by the development of *machine learning algorithms* that can dynamically scale with the workload in the financial services industry.

Mechanisms for Monetizing Digital Enterprise Payback

While in the last section we considered the methods to scale digital technologies to build the digital enterprise, the means justifying the purpose of scaling is to seek better outcomes for the enterprise and the wider economy (Figure 5.9). The outcomes do not necessarily have to be just financial, as we can see in the case studies so far, the outcome benefits in driving higher customer service may result in higher market share and revenue but can also support lower greenhouse emissions, higher energy efficiencies, better customer lifestyle, improved patient life expectancy, and many others.

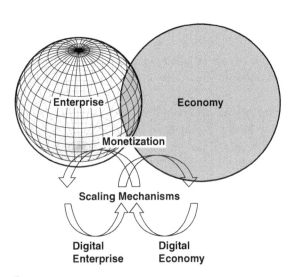

FIGURE 5.9 Monetization and scaling

The payback of digitization can, therefore, have many benefits both financially and in terms of social and societal benefits. This assertion is based on the pervasive nature of digitization that this book seeks to demonstrate through the rise of digital workspaces that touch all areas of industry and living styles.

Yet the payback has to consider the return on investment and the movement of cash flows that digital technology investment can bring. The scaling mechanisms that we discussed previously can be used to drive new ways to create income. These may often be incremental through many users, and use different remuneration and payment mechanisms such as advertising and pay-as-you-go subscription models.

The term *monetization* in its use here refers to the process of creating financial wealth from human and systems activities. Monetization in the financial banking industry is the process of converting or establishing something into legal tender. It usually refers to the coining of currency or the printing of banknotes by central banks. In our case, we are concerned with how physical and digital assets and activities can be used to generate financial wealth.

Professor Irene Ng, a leading innovator and entrepreneur in marketing and economics, describes the impact of digital on the creation of value and wealth in an economy. The issue is in the mechanisms of digital value creation in business models and the wider economy.[11] Value is created when something is experienced that may have some agreed financial numerical value. This does not necessarily equate to the *worth* of that experience, which is related to how a person perceived this experience. For example, a family photograph may have very little financial value in terms of cost of the picture and the picture frame, but have great worth to those family members as it has significance and meaning to them.

The monetization mechanisms to generate the photograph in the digital world are different to the old world of photochemical processing and the act of printing and then framing the image inside a physical frame. In the digital world, of course, it is possible to create many digital images in fractions of a second that can be copied, e-mailed, posted on a website, edited, or indeed printed and hung in a picture frame as a physical object. The monetization mechanisms of digital pictures, music, and other data can benefit from the scalable cycle of self-reinforcement of reuse and reselling of digital content. In the case of a family photograph this may be of small financial value and high worth, but in the case of commercial activity the monetization potential for syndicating digital content and services are considerable.

Digital Microeconomics and Digital Macroeconomics Mechanisms

From a practitioner perspective it is useful to link the methods of digital monetization to the general concepts of microeconomics and macroeconomics.

Microeconomics is a term that refers to the specific performance of the enterprise operating model, its organization structure, skills, and resources – and how these are arranged and the decisions made to generate economic activity.

Macroeconomics, on the other hand, is concerned with the wider structure of the markets, the industry players of multiple enterprises, the suppliers, customers, and intermediaries – and how they interconnect to generate economic value.

While microeconomics is a branch of economics concerned with the individual person and enterprise decisions around limited resources, it is often this effort to develop your own enterprise capabilities that needs to change to encompass the wider impact of digital and specific mechanisms on value creation that span beyond the individual and organization. In building a "digital enterprise" there is a need to focus on the monetization mechanisms that you can pull or push – capabilities to join the inside your own company with the external ecosystem of customers, partners, and channels as ways to generate revenue and profitability.

Macroeconomics is the consideration of how digitization can change the wider environment and ecosystems that you are operating in. These monetization strategies are more focused on macro behaviors and scale of monopolies between participants and geographic locations. These exist in physical and virtual spaces in digital networks that are inside and outside the enterprise operation, yet can change how the economy can function as a digital economy. In building the digital enterprise these monetization mechanisms seek to redefine and share the operating standards and connections with crowds and social networks, in particular, to create and make new digital markets.

We can examine monetization mechanisms that, using the distinction set out here, relate to the microeconomic and macroeconomic levels:

Microeconomic mechanisms to drive self-reinforcing monetization

- Operational monetization mechanisms:
  - Digital capabilities to accelerate operating demand and supply performance – the ability to bundle new digital products and services.

- Growth monetization mechanisms:
  - Digital capabilities to access and grow existing and new market segments – geographic regions with existing and new digital products and services.
- Terms and conditions monetization mechanisms:
  - Digital capabilities to source investment funding – leverage intellectual property and innovative contract pricing models.

Macroeconomic mechanisms to drive self-reinforcing monetization

- Community monetization mechanisms:
  - Digital capabilities for community building – community identity, feedback, and connection building.
- Channel monetization mechanisms:
  - Digital capabilities for working across multi-channels to market – channel mix incentives and ownership of the "gateway" to the market.
- Industry standards monetization mechanisms:
  - Digital capabilities for enabling shared access to products and services – supporting interoperability and consistency across homogeneous and heterogeneous market environments.

In the case studies, we saw many examples of these monetization mechanisms that were used to generate financial income from the scaling mechanisms of digital technologies.

Operating Model Monetization Mechanisms to Drive Self-Reinforcing Monetization

- Operating model monetization mechanism can drive *self-reinforcing online payments enabling improved yield in customer services* in the financial services industry. Using online payment systems can create faster payment mechanisms that enhance revenue volume through the payment issuer and the partner services.
- Operating model monetization mechanism can drive *self-reinforcing patient care cost reduction* through augmented patient care sensor-feedback technology. The cost of care can potentially be optimized through lower-cost wearable device monitoring for geospatial and behavioral monitoring that otherwise might only be available at a higher cost through manual monitoring, measurement, and intervention therapies.
- Operating model monetization can drive *self-reinforcing cash flow optimization through digitally supported vendor managed inventory (VMI)* in the

retail fast-moving consumer industry. Stock and transport costs can be optimized through geolocation tracking and digital tagging of assets.

Growth Monetization Mechanisms to Drive Self-Reinforcing Monetization

- Growth monetization mechanism can drive *self-reinforcing market share revenue growth* by using open innovation of crowdsourcing in marketing to open up existing market expansion. This creates efficiency in marketing spend and service creation of marketing brand and product promotions.
- Growth monetization mechanism can drive *self-reinforcing new horizontal market creation* using a digital platform to host open data for smart city services. Open data value can be created through targeted citizen community engagement and mobile applications that support easy access. Creating financial monetization may be through secondary effects of partner products and services activity that are driven off the back of open data.
- Growth monetization mechanism can drive *self-reinforcing vertical service market creation* using sports augmentation with wearables, for example, lifestyle activity wearable wrist bands connecting to a website to track and provide lifestyle and sports activity advice. This can create vertical integration with customers and the product brand, soliciting feedback and community building to potentially reduce customer churn – switching to alternative products.

Terms and Conditions (Ts & Cs) Monetization Mechanisms to Drive Self-Reinforcing Monetization

- Ts & Cs monetization mechanism can drive *self-reinforcing incentives pricing to*, for example, *reduce carrier costs based on contextual marketing* in the global package logistics industry. The cost of shipping and pricing can be modified to support service contracts that optimize carrier costs.
- Ts & Cs monetization mechanism can drive *self-reinforcing dynamic pricing to enhance incremental revenue and average revenue per user (ARPU)* in, for example, the hybrid cloud orchestration by ICT-hosting service providers.
- Ts & Cs monetization mechanism can drive *self-reinforcing sustainability and CSR regulation efficiency savings and emission target reductions* in, for example, the consumer goods industry, via the use of digital technologies to monitor social engagement and corporate buying, sourcing, and facilities management activity to meet sustainability targets.

The following monetization mechanisms aim at the wider structural issues of the economy and how building a digital enterprise can influence and create favorable digital economic conditions.

Community Monetization Mechanisms to Drive Self-Reinforcing Monetization

- Community monetization mechanism can drive *self-reinforcing market creation in crowdsourcing* in, for example, the FMCG industry. Crowdsourcing can be used to seek and generate community building of new products and services that in turn become a market segment.
- Community monetization mechanism can drive *self-reinforcing medical research investment return* in, for example, the healthcare industry. Digital technologies can be used to enhance translation research to improve efficiency of research investment.
- Community monetization mechanism can drive *self-reinforcing gamification to generate up-sell and cross-sell opportunities and reduce cart abandonment* in the retail industry. Social media networks can help drive crowd brand reinforcement and drive online and offline purchase behavior.

Multi-channel Monetization Mechanisms to Drive Self-Reinforcing Monetization

- Multi-channel monetization mechanism can drive *self-reinforcing multi-channel consumption* in, for example, the hospitality industry. The development of mobile apps can be used to help support guest services and visitor experience, and to support additional up-sell and cross-sell of guest services from restaurant and in-room services to travel and tourism planning.
- Multi-channel monetization mechanism can drive *self-reinforcing public services investment return efficiency from smart city platform services* in the government and city municipal services industry: the ability to support shared platform services for city planning and transport and emergency services, and enable economies of scale.
- Multi-channel monetization mechanism can drive *self-reinforcing gaming industry traffic generation* in, for example, the online gaming industry. Online communities and digital gaming environments can be used to create high levels of social interaction and online digital presence that can be leveraged with advertising and subscriptions that further build online communitization.

Industrial Standards and Interoperability Monetization Mechanisms to Drive Self-Reinforcing Monetization

- Industrial standards and interoperability monetization mechanism can drive *self-reinforcing product investment and utilization across a supply chain* in, for example, the aerospace industry – by establishing common product data management standards to improve efficiency in wastages in sourcing engineering parts and common standard parts.
- Industrial standards and interoperability monetization mechanism can drive *self-reinforcing new product introduction* in, for example, the smart electric car industry – use of electric charging standards to enable local and regional car-charging portals to spread the rate of electric car access and geographic adoption.
- Industrial standards and interoperability monetization mechanism can drive *self-reinforcing market creation through product interoperability in,* for example, *the smart home market* for the consumer home products industry – by supporting common home appliance APIs and data sharing, it is possible to enable a wider utility and agency of home IoT platform services connecting fridges, cookers, TVs, and other objects to support consumption patterns and lifestyle augmentation.

Specific Examples of Monetization Strategies

Table 5.4 summarizes examples of monetization mechanisms classified into the types of monetization strategies. These can be seen to be in two types of monetization strategies. Firstly, those that can be generated inside the enterprise, and, secondly, the monetization strategies that are driven outside and external to the enterprise but affect monetization for an enterprise in a digital ecosystem. This classification can also be described as microeconomic monetization mechanisms and macroeconomic monetization mechanisms because of their focus on the internal enterprise and the other on the external market.

- Microeconomic monetization strategies
  - Operating model monetization mechanisms
  - Business growth monetization mechanisms
  - Terms and conditions monetization mechanisms.
- Macroeconomic monetization strategies
  - Community monetization mechanisms
  - Multi-channel monetization mechanisms
  - Industry standardization monetization mechanisms.

TABLE 5.4 Examples of monetization strategies

	Monetization Mechanisms	Practitioner Methods to Implement Digital Payback Strategy
Operating Model Monetization Mechanisms		
1.	Fractionalization	Divide resources for optimal loading Maximize digital portfolio cost optimization/savings
2.	High productivity	Leverage resources at high-utilization loading Focus on higher operating margin for products and services
3.	High volume	Offer mass consumption and mass scalability Exploit price-demand curves to sell commodity products and services
4.	High yield	Enable complementary usage of resources Thin provisioning of capacity
5.	Niche	Scarce resources/skills/knowledge Knowledge leverage
6.	Crowdsourcing	User-sourced and developed resources, ideas, knowledge, skills Co-innovation, collaboration
7.	Auction	Use of auction market model to source and trade
Growth Monetization Mechanisms		
8.	Horizontal market expansion	Leverage geo, size, industry presence Exploit cross-selling, annuity selling
9.	Vertical market expansion	Supply chain, stakeholders Cross-selling, annuity selling
10.	Horizontal service expansion	Within one business process and IT stack Aggregation
11.	Vertical service expansion	Adjacent business processes with similar requirements Aggregation
Terms and Conditions Monetization		
12.	Innovative billing	Incentive pricing, advertising, and charging Financial engineering
13.	Dynamic pricing	Adjust pricing based on demand Modify pricing based on buying behavior and needs profiling Ramsey pricing to adjust marginal cost pricing based on scarcity of products and services
14.	Advertisement	Leverage assisted charging of traffic to advertising revenue
15.	Data debt	Leverage of personal data rights to monetize of value

Continued

Table 5.4   *Continued*

	Monetization Mechanisms	Practitioner Methods to Implement Digital Payback Strategy
16.	Financing	Capital/cash-flow sourcing Risk allocation
17.	Litigation	Patent leverage Trolling, market positioning of IP
Community Monetization Mechanisms		
18.	Community	Own or control boundary creation, management and containment Group behavior, membership, values, brand
19.	Gamification – reward/feedback	Incentives and feedback reinforcement experience Preference targeting
Multi-Channel Monetization Mechanisms		
21.	Channel mix	Resource/market awareness balance Portfolio mix
22.	Gateway ownership	Control access methods to products and services Addressable market
Industry Standardization Monetization Mechanisms		
23.	Standardization	Access specialization Product/service grouping consistency
24.	Interoperability	Market portability and interoperability Governance domain controls

Chapter Summary

We have established the nature of capabilities and the way these capabilities, through digital technologies, might be used to deconstruct and reconstruct markets and enterprise operation. This chapter has considered how these drive economic value for the enterprise. This includes the specific methods that digital technologies can introduce to create the ability to generate revenue from the use of digital technologies or the digitization of products and services.

In the next chapter we explore the case studies in the light of the practitioner lessons learned from the aspects of how digital technologies can transform capabilities, change operating model practices, and generate new forms of monetization for payback.

Reflections on Impact of Digital Practice

Chapter Introduction

To conclude our journey into the practices of building the digital enterprise we explore practitioner perspectives on the impact of digitization in their fields of expertise. From this we are able to draw conclusions that are evident from this path and the likely future ahead for the digital enterprise and the digital economy:

- The development of a quantified life and the digital self
- The meaning of good data and big data
- The digital supply chain
- The digital geotourist
- Toward a new kind of digital privacy.

A Quantified Life

Irene Ng

What is an enterprise? What is a digital enterprise? Is an enterprise a collection of entities and people? What is the impact of technology on society? How are businesses, how are people, how are markets changing?

It is about sense making and the role of information technology and its entanglement into human life.[1] Information technology built into products and services have become the key drivers for service innovation. How information technology-enabled services (ITESs) affect consumer wellbeing has become increasingly important in the design of services that are transformative through this technology. In particular, how consumer wellbeing is derived from the consumption of ITESs in consumers' daily lives.

Let me start with the micro aspects of human life and how digital is affecting this. My interests are grounded from my early days as a physicist and the use of computational thinking to always be solution-oriented and problem solving as a systemic applied discipline. I am a systems analyst and a systems thinker and my interest in digital was revived almost 11 years ago, particularly when I was living in many countries around the world. I found that digital technology was a great leveler in being able to be in contact with family members in different places. Skype™ would be on all day, even when there was no one there at times, so there was a virtual connection. When family members in one house ran up the stairs and called out "where are my socks!" I could see them and call out "have you tried the bottom drawer?" – or someone could hear chopping noises in the kitchen and call out to ask "what are you making for lunch?" even though we were both in different physical locations. This connection created across space – digital space, material space – is possible. It has transformed those spaces where we live and eat. It is something that is transcendental across digital space because it can enable functional connections. It is not a replace to a face-to-face relationship, it just creates a different dimension. To draw an analogy, an escalator does not "substitute the staircase" – there is co-presence that is enabled by the virtual space connections and that still enables empathy. Technology can make things happen – digital life creates new possibilities for interaction.

If I use my WhatsApp there is a "whole family" feature that enables a group of people who may be in physically different countries, doing completely different things, to share comments and experiences as if in the same virtual space together. It all takes place on the digital app and the digital platform, which enables conversations to be created. It does not replace physical contact, there is no substitution going on with the real world – there may be some cannibalization between digital channels being used, but only in your head is this channel different. People play with these digital channels using examples such as Facebook and Twitter. The difference is that these are digital platforms and digital services owned by those companies who are commercial entities, listed on the US Securities and Exchange Commission (SEC), and so the idea of privacy is different since you are a "user" of their service and as such there is no notion of personal privacy in a physical sense.

This does not stop certain things being made available through the site, and Facebook is a great curator of certain things. For example, through my newsfeed I can follow Bloomberg, Wired, the *Financial Times*, and others, to get a mix of business content, family, and other pieces that are specific to me. This makes the "ideal newspaper" for the morning read, rather than the traditional printed newspaper that is static and not contextual to my needs.

In a *digital life, curating* is important, as is the idea of a *sense of togetherness*. We live in a knowledge economy where the internet enables all kinds of connections to be made. Curation is the key to that, and we choose our curator. This could be a social media curator or a serious news feed organization as a curator. The sense of togetherness is a bond, a different kind of bond that requires both sides to understand how it works, the emphasis of how this works as well, such as the "viral" effect of social messages and the effects of crowd behavior online.

The other aspect in looking at digital spaces is "personas" that people can create online. It is the *association* between the self and the digital devices such as cell phone, tablet, and sensors that creates personas that represent a person's digital presence through the device. I see this as an existentialist view, a belief that philosophical thinking begins with the human subject, not merely the thinking subject, but the acting, feeling, living, human individual.[2] We do not live in a narrow existence walking a predefined path, we can choose what to do in our life. We may follow an "average life" but we also will oscillate between different extremes, or personas that may occur when we are doing different tasks or need different things during the day or life's events. These may be planned or unplanned such as going to the shops, driving a car, graduating from school, or a change in plans because of the weather or a serious sudden medical emergency. There is a range of possibilities that happen in real life, which may have limits that a person can cope with, or for which they may need help. Digital can help address the "unknown-unknown" because the generative effect of digital can stimulate creativity that can meet human needs that one individual alone may not be able to do. The possibilities of generative creativity is driven by humans seeking answers. There is still a future of the "digital unknown" but digital can enable a creative exploration of possibilities. Take the material graphene, for example: it is an incredibly thin, nearly transparent sheet, one atom thick and yet a hundred times stronger than steel – so what are its possibilities for industrial use? This is why the markets come about as they seek answers to opportunities.

Innovation and structuration

The digital enterprise seeks to create platforms and forums to enable closed and open innovation to play with the boundaries of possibilities and to have a mindset to think this way. We can be trapped by our own mindset and "boxes" that may be limited by existing physical environments. The digital medium enables new business models that can disrupt existing thinking. This can be incremental innovation or disruptive innovation, and at times beyond disruption, discontinuous innovation that completely changes the way an experience or product works. We have seen this evolving at a rapid pace in the digital world with the PC, the cell phone, the internet, and data expansions where first-mover advantage can create large opportunities and new "markets-makers" for consumers and providers.

What do enterprises need to do to leverage the creative ways of digital? There can be two extremes to stimulate the economy, for example: there is a tension between a completely open platform such as Linux and a completely closed platform such as Apple. A completely open platform lacks structure, which we see from structuration theory (ST).[3] This is a concept where human behavior is the interaction between meaning, standards, and values and the different dynamic relationships of society. The idea is that structures are needed to rule all societies. You can think of structure as a physical object such as a chair or a wall or column, or you can consider it as a social structure, the norms and values that govern an enterprise or social behavior. "How do IT structures work" is similar to an analogy in sociology of a "blank open grass field": if people want to cross this field, there is no structure, and so no one crosses to the other side, there is no path to follow. No one wants to make a path and no one knows where to make the path. Society can be paralyzed when there is no structure. Not all structures are all bad, but sometimes if someone makes a path this may be bad or good depending on the situation. If someone makes a path then people start to use it, but it may be the only path available and a slow method until new paths come along. Structures evolve and change with time, and structuration theory suggests that society needs structures. I am just using an example analogy to illustrate this concept using Linux and Apple and the development of Android and others that may be a middle ground between the two. There is a constant oscillation between too little structure and too much structure. If you have too much structure you can impede innovation and progress; too little structure and there are challenges to start innovation and for it to be adopted.

The rise of the platform

This is common across the world – in Europe, Asia, the US, and many other places we see similar huge opportunities and challenges in digital and smart cities, for example. A purely open platform may have difficulties to grow, some structure is needed to start to build adoption paths so that practitioners can address the sociological and economic barriers. In digital enterprise it is possible to build structure with digital workspaces in the physical and virtual world. The "death of distance" means that this can then be moved around to different locations and time zones.[4] The nature of digital is different because it changes the nature of relationships – its much more modular structures allow you to create structures much faster and to share information from the past, present, and future. But it is also hard to get digital content and digital services to be adopted and used effectively. This is why we see the *rise of the platform* such as Amazon, Google, and Facebook, because structure is good, but if it becomes overly structured it becomes legacy or barriers.

The economic model of digital platforms needs to include some structure such as UX and CX but at the same time needs to have an openness to help people and enterprise to adopt and maximize value. There is a tension between rigidity and openness in the design and strategic process. This can involve moral and ethical choices in decisions to use products and services or in market trading. In digitization it is again different because it can be possible to use computation to predict future outcomes from present-day decisions. For example, algorithms can be used to model future market trading in the stock exchange, or control the steering of a car to avoid an oncoming obstacle. This is the kind of possible future that a digital life may have, where the sense of now and the future can be combined with increasing foresight. Indeed the future of government, with the increase in digitization using automated algorithms, may drive more regulation of algorithms to check the data-based governance. Of course it is still "garbage in – garbage out" with base data, and enterprise and government policies may change to see better data resources and services. The key point is that the situations in life can change all the time, so decisions need to weight the *probabilities* of outcomes and constraints. This is the "probability of data quality" about the past, present, and future but also "probability of context" and the validity of resources and locations, the spaces we live in. The way we experience our digital life will be much more contextual, driven by the probabilities and needs in the moment, in the physical and digital spaces where we live our life.

The Meaning of Good Data and Big Data

Jacqui Taylor

How data works in the 21st century is very different from the 20th century and all others previously. The expansion of information on the internet has radically changed how data is collected, manipulated, and used for social, commercial, or other means. This has given rise to the advent of massive data analytics where it is commonplace today to think of "big data" in the context of industrial scale. Yet it also has profoundly changed in the way that "small" data is used, in the way people and machines can automate and transact services and communication. Where hitherto we would have treated databases and transactions as separate data types of "data as rest" and "data in motion." This is a fallacy in terms of what that data value represents.

This matters greatly from a practitioner perspective that has grown up with data sets and databases that were structured and defined. In the digital world the definition of data has evolved beyond the range of basic records and relationships into a wider and more diverse range of media including sound, video, and data streams. The rise of machine data from sensors has expanded this even further with all manner of telemetry, as explored in previous chapters. Data and metadata has also captured the relationships and sense of human and machine communication that we today now see as social analytics and behavioral science and machine automation. In short, data has grown a whole lot bigger both in quantity and in richness of information about the context of experience.

Indeed, data can be more properly defined as the representation of places, objects, and people that represent the social and economic environment and marketplace. This description is in the context of a kind of journey mapped out, with the digitization of the information in the physical world mapped into the virtual domain – a *digital fingerprint* of the products, services, and life experiences of consumers, enterprises, and economic and social activity.

Jacqui Taylor is a Founder and CEO of FlyingBinary Ltd, a specialist company in big data analytics and advisory services in cyber security and data. Jacqui defines her role as a web scientist and agrees that this is very much a journey that can be traced back to the origins of the internet: "Tim Berners-Lee sat in the research lab at CERN, Switzerland, connected two protocols and said 'Hello World', with this message in 1989 often cited as the birth of the World Wide Web."[5] It was not until 1991 that the first webpage was launched with the hypertext mark-up language enabling links to other pages and so was born the connected network of web pages. Jacqui explains, "I see this as three stages of evolution, this was the first stage that enabled a kind of web encyclopaedia for the economy online, this was Web 1.0. Yet even at that stage people were asking 'what do we need web pages for?' 'What can we do with this capability?' The next stage is what web scientists call Web 2.0. This was no longer about referencing and searching for information. The development of the internet was about the relevance of ranking in web pages and content through search engine technology. It was about learning to put yourself in context with the sphere of web content that was being searched. But now we are moving into a new era of Web 3.0 where it is no longer about relevance, but about *resonance*."

Web 3.0

Web 3.0 is variously described as a description of an evolution of the internet where the web pages and the content are semantically described to enable meaning to be inferred. This enables intelligent search to provide internet content as services that meet a specific need rather than just a list of relevant content. John Markoff of the *New York Times*, in a 2006 article suggested naming this third-generation of the web that took the notation "Web 3.0." He declared that computer scientists and many start-ups were adding a new layer of meaning on top of the existing web that would make it less of a catalog and more of a guide – and even provide the foundation for systems that can reason in a human fashion.[6]

Jacqui suggests that these connections are ways for humans to understand knowledge and make meaning from those connections. "Web 3.0 is about us, this is what we are seeking to develop in FlyingBinary Ltd – to establish better understanding of all the data around us. What this is about is you have to ask the question 'how relevant is my message?' – so when you are working out the customer journey that is personalized, this is about personalized data journeys, that is making it *resonate* with your consumer, or your client or your system." Jacqui explains that you have to define what is important in your data or society in order to create this resonance with communities. An example of how this is changing human experience is the emergence of a new kind of industry that Jacqui refers to as "data journalism."[7] "We see many people who specialize in all manner of subjects, can encode this knowledge onto the web, and create a generational impact of the human story – new kinds of journalism such as interpretive newsrooms. In work with the UK government around open data we have focused on how people understand data at a fundamental level asking 'what is their journey?,' 'what is their story?'"

Jacqui recommends that this is critical to understanding the human connection in data analytics, which is key to the philosophy of Web 3.0 where you can ask a person specific questions as to what they need and the meaning behind this. "We have evidenced that only 8% of people who interact with data will actually understand it."

Open data

Open data is not a new phenomenon; the need for public communication was in part the foundation of municipal libraries for the access and distribution of printed books for public consumption and education. The newspaper industries have grown into large-scale commercial entities but with the internet new forms of newsgathering have spawned in the form of personal online blogs, social media microblogging sites, and crowd bulletin boards. Whether this has been legitimate public information broadcasting, propaganda, or commercial interests, the distribution and access to data is now integrated into almost all areas of society and everyday life. Indeed, access to the internet has been unanimously backed as a fundamental human right by the United Nations Human Rights Council in 2012 resolution. The resolution says that all people should be allowed to connect to and express themselves freely on the internet. All 47 members of the Human Rights Council, including countries such as China and Cuba, signed the resolution. The resolution came with the stipulation that the "free flow of information on the Internet and the safe flow of information on the Internet are mutually dependent," to enable all member states including countries such as China to pass the resolution.[8] A BBC World Service poll in 2010 of 27,000 adults across 27 countries found a strong support for internet access on both sides of the digital divide,[9] a term used to describe those with and those without access to the internet. The survey conducted by GlobeScan found that 87% of people who used the internet felt that internet access should be "the fundamental right of all people." The survey indicated that seven out of ten non-internet users felt they should have the right to access the web. Dr Hamadoun Touré, secretary-general of the International Telecommunication Union (ITU) was cited by the BBC as saying, "The right to communication cannot be ignored," and as being a powerful potential source for enlightenment. He went further to suggest that governments must "regard the internet as basic infrastructure – just like roads, waste, and water."

Jacqui elaborates her corporate website message, "We are passionate about the benefits of public open data, free at point of use, and its ability to promote innovation and growth."[10] These issues are key to understanding the wider value creation that open information can enable. Several practices are evident in how to achieve open data value, as developed by the Open Data User Group, a UK government ministerial advisory group:

• Community engagement is needed to promote public interaction with the open data services.
• Creation of a transparent process to demonstrate the source and efficacy of the data.
• Creation of demand-led open data that is targeting at the needs of communities and users.
• Data curation and ownership to manage the quality and maintenance of the data sources.

These factors in demand creation speak of the context and outcomes necessary to drive the need for the data in the first place. Creating open access is clearly a first stage in the maturity of the data process. This works in both the collection of reliable and up-to-date data, but also its aggregation and management of its sourcing into storage platforms that can be maintained. The other side on citizen-centric engagement is in fact all about the definition of the digital workspaces that people and enterprises are able to access, and to populate and curate the data to enable the delivery of value from the open data.

Data marketplaces and demand-driven data

It is interesting that the development of data is closely aligned to the creation of data marketplaces. The UK government cloud services store has converged into a digital services for the public sector.[11] How this drives value outcomes in the context of the service and the location remains to be seen. It is clear that in the use of mobile services, for example, creating effective data platforms are central to placing the service usage in the control of the consumer at the point of contact in the location.[12]

The challenge is to understand the industry you are in and to develop services that meet the needs of people and organizations in those industries. But it is also about understanding the needs of individual people who have the actual local understanding of the sourced data, and importantly, the quality of that data and its efficacy in the first place. It is something we call "demand-driven data," where we need to look at ways to develop data services that meet the actual demands of the end user but also who will participate in developing the quality and usability of that data.

The Digital Supply Chain

Ben Waller

Over the course of a hundred years, the car sales and aftersales sector evolved from uncertain beginnings. Horse traders became a channel for the emergent and numerous small car makers, and so became car dealers, whilst carriage works began to offer car service and repair in addition to building bodies for early motor cars. By the end of the 20th century, the automotive distribution sector had become a global industry involving a complex and established network of specialist services.[13] The main channel to market for car manufacturers remains the franchised dealer through which independent business owners represent the brand in the market, selling new cars, replacement parts, and aftersales services.[14] Until very recently, the franchised dealer role, responsibilities, and operational business model has proved remarkably resistant to change.[15] However, new services emerging from the digitization of cars, sales channels, and changing customer expectations brought from other sectors is forcing change.

First, the car – the "machine that changed the world"[16] – is soon to become the third main platform for applications and connected services, after tablet computers and smartphones.[17] Mercedes-Benz already offer on-board up-to-date information on your car lease whilst you are driving the car, and the long-anticipated emergence of telematics capabilities unlock many new ways to offer services to car owners and users. General Motors have been offering OnStar for many years in North America, and this connectivity platform is about to become standard with all new cars sold by this brand in the United States. Google have been working with a number of car makers to project a "heads-up" display onto the inside of the driver's windscreen to provide interactive navigation that includes real-time enriched Google Maps content. Mobile network providers have established networks and interests, but want to access the connected car as a platform for engaging with their customers.[18] In the United States, AT&T offer an additional simcard service for on-board connectivity for only $10 if the customer already has a monthly cell phone contract.

Second, roads in megacities are expected to become highly interactive environments as the "internet of things" combines with on-board connectivity to bring innovations such as real-time traffic optimization, targeted in-car marketing, and enhanced safety through semi-autonomous driving. Volvo cars have been piloting "convoying," where cars communicate with each other and the urban environment to facilitate a virtual "road train," whilst Mercedes-Benz already offer an optional semi-autonomous "follow the car in front" feature that aims to make driving in dense traffic easier and make accidents less likely to happen. Google, urban authorities, and car manufacturers are all interested in managing the relationships and service channels.

Third, low-cost mobile connectivity through smartphones has brought old niche services into the mainstream, such as car-, ride-, and taxi-sharing. Smartphone-assisted mobility is developing in conjunction with changes in social attitudes toward car ownership and mobility, encouraged through incentives and government policies; car ownership is becoming both less attractive and less necessary to access on-demand mobility in urban areas. The sector remains turbulent and fragmented, and many established transport businesses are looking to extend their offer to include newer mobility solutions. The result is that public transport authorities are competing with car manufacturers and rental companies to provide on-demand, flexible, and short-term car use. Flinkster, the car-sharing service from Deutsche Bahn, offers rentals from one hour to one month of cars that are located at on-street locations in over 140 German towns and cities. BMW and Sixt car rental together offer DriveNow, a flexible and "free-floating" car-sharing service in several cities worldwide, whilst Daimler Mobility Services offer the similarly flexible and international Car2Go car-sharing service. Both car manufacturers offer these mobility services at a discount to customers who also conventionally buy or lease a car. In 2014 it was already possible to book a shared taxi, a multi-mode travel ticket, and access a car on demand for only a couple of hours – are all familiar and established smartphone-enabled services in many large cities. As a result, such services are democratizing car use in cities where car ownership has become increasingly expensive and exclusive.[19]

Fourth, new and used car customers, and increasingly, aftersales customers, are looking to do most of their information search and transactions online. Research in Europe conducted in 2014 by ICDP found that, on average, new car buyers now visit two to three dealers, down from seven dealer visits a decade earlier. The reason is that customers visit the dealership far later in the selection process, having narrowed their choices of brands, products, and services well in advance of contacting a dealer, who is then just an order facilitator for many customers. Whilst manufacturer websites remain the most important source of information on product, third parties have entered the space, bringing with them new retail methods. Brokers and resellers are nothing new in the automotive sector, but their role in connecting customers with cars has expanded rapidly in the online world. As a result, third-party platforms such as TrueCar and Cars.com in the United States have disrupted the traditional purchase process to the extent where dealers now have no choice but to cooperate with them.

Finally, new powertrains have enabled a much greater connectivity with the car maker or service provider and require new infrastructures. For example, the Nissan Leaf was designed to be able to communicate via charging points, allowing the manufacturer to extract useful usage and on-board diagnostics data, which also allows the owner to analyze the energy efficiency of their driving.[20] In parallel, the commercialization of electric vehicle drivetrain technology has created the need for new infrastructure, for example, charging points and management systems for information on charge point location and availability. But car manufacturers cannot build the new infrastructure without help from established energy and systems infrastructure providers. Renault-Nissan are building a differentiated range of partnerships, experimenting in markets with a number of potential partners, to enable innovation, reduce risk, and access the experience of established energy businesses. In France, Renault has partnered with EDF for the provision of electricity to electric vehicle customers, and Total and Schneider for the provision of charge points and systems.

The common thread that runs through the digitization within all these areas is that established sectors are finding their business space increasingly encroached upon by a combination of new entrants and giants from other established sectors of the economy. Each sector-dominant business has a natural interest in protecting what it sees as core business. So, for example, the energy company wants to make sure that supplying electric car customers is their business, and that they have the direct household or corporate relationship with the customer, rather than supplying energy indirectly as a white label service from a car manufacturer. The provision of mobility services may not remain the natural preserve of the car manufacturer and franchise channels, despite the clear interest of car manufacturers to expand their service offering to protect that core relationship with the customer. The account management relationship is key to maintaining the role of the key digital services integrator, and car manufacturers will not want to cede that relationship to others, be they Google, EDF, Deutsche Bahn, TrueCar, or AT&T.

However, offering a multi-channel, always-on relationship with the customer both online and offline over numerous devices, platforms, and channels will mean that car manufacturers will require many partnership specialist-service providers, and the car manufacturer network of franchise outlets will need to adapt to becoming just another part of the car manufacturer customer-focused service offering. The growth of private leasing in many mature markets also underlines a shift from ownership to use. Several car manufacturers, including BMW and Mercedes-Benz, are already putting the building blocks in place for a customer service model that allows for new services to be added and bundled into pay-monthly finance fees. The implication is that customers will be offered a convenient and simple single monthly mobility fee. This fee could include all servicing, data services, telematics, insurance, breakdown services, tolls, parking and energy or fuel fees, and include the flexibility of adding on further mobility services as required, such as car sharing. Moving from selling cars and aftersales as infrequent transactions, toward offering a monthly contract service as seen in the cell phone sector, will mean a big shift in the skills, roles, and responsibilities required of the car manufacturer and the established franchised networks. It represents a big shift – a long journey from horse dealing and carriage making.

The Digital Geotourist

Shaon Talukder

It is astonishing perhaps that in a recent survey on the use of social media by children in Finland, over three-quarters of the communication with their parents was to ask about their location.[21] "Where are you?," "What are you doing there?," "What time are you coming back?," "Where can we meet?" and so forth, are the normal everyday traffic of the digital life of conversation. Yet this activity with cell phones today would have been, a mere 10 or 20 years ago, conducted at a much slower pace over e-mail or pager, and before that a landline telephone call or paper correspondence. In the modern economy we take for granted this speed of communication, irrespective of where we live, who, and when we want to contact. We can pick up a cell phone, look up a social network, or access a web marketplace to search and get what we want, and connect instantly to whomever we want to in near real time, as if they were in the same physical geographical location (in most cases subject to network coverage). It would be like magic to people years ago who lived in a non-digital world.

This is just the start of endless possibilities with not just cell phones but the digitization of where we live and work. We can reimagine the digital enterprise as a series of building blocks that represent the physicality of places to visit and the things we do there. But it does not have to be just where you physically are but can potentially link anywhere in your network of virtual connections. This is like your personal value chains and the value networks of the space–time experiences enabled as physical and virtual spaces.

Part of realizing this is in mapping out the spaces of rooms, buildings, cars, and places. There are examples emerging today where physical objects are being digitized. From QR codes on works of art and public monuments and "talking statues," to industrial information boards, digitization enables a degree of information to be retrieved, viewed, or listened to on a mobile device.[22]

"Scan and record" is a crowdsourcing approach and something that has already been used extensively to digitize streets with images that are linked into geographical maps: we see Google Maps and StreetView,[23] and open crowdsourced digital maps such OpenStreetMap.[24] These sources of geographical data can be accessed by public APIs and today do so much more than just location visualization. Directions and route traffic planning, and location-attached information, are sourced from and often combined with public sources.

This can also change from being a passive experience to an active one, where information can also be recorded by visitors to a place. This approach, using crowdsourcing apps such as Mapbox,[25] make it possible to pin travel spots on Pinterest, find restaurants on Foursquare, and visualize data on GitHub, an open source development platform. Other mobile apps such as "Moves" enable personalized tracking of physical movements, capturing your location by the minutes and seconds. In addition, using the movement accelerator sensors in the mobile device it can predict the type of movement from running, walking, cycling, or traveling by vehicle. Similarly, the range of personal information through wearables is increasing as heart rate, blood pressure, and other information becomes a "recorded record of your life" in digital pictures, movement locations, activities, and wellbeing.[26] These are early stepping stones that are starting to map out the physical and digital world.

Shaon Talukder is a founder of GeoTourist, a company working on the delivery of compelling, geographically relevant content to consumers using their smartphones. An entrepreneur with a strong focus on the geospatial world of digital content services, Shaon sees the world of contextual services as the new frontier for digital technology. When you visit locations you can record and use the past experiences of tour guides with subject matter expertize. This can then be made available to the public visitors who can, whilst at the site, access these experiences on their cell phone in order to learn about the history or present day. This can also use the public as a crowdsource too, recording and sharing their photos, comments, and experiences in a similar way. A recent example is where a person found and heard an old radio broadcast from a deceased relative talking about their war experience from the local area where they lived. These things help people to make connections from many different perspectives:

- Authoritative connections from subject matter experts about a location past and present.
- Social connections shared between common experiences at a location.
- Personal connections to local inhabitants and visitors through sharing their life story and the life stories of other locals and visitors.
- Future connections of the potential of the location and foresight of future events.

Digital enrichment "jigsaw"

This enables a richer experience by design digital services that create better outcomes that perhaps a search engine alone may not be able to do. Most advertisers will talk about the relevance of a product in front of the consumer at a particular time, collecting cookies about the kind of preferences that people have. But when you are out and about in physical space this is a whole new opportunity for a new kind of advertising that is more engaging. For example, individuals or groups of tourists at an attraction can learn and share information that may be more in context of the moment and occasion. This also changes using a crowd approach because each visitor may have different experiences at the same location. If this is recorded, then at a later time a person may be seeking information that a previous visitor may have already found, or may have shared an alternative view. In a way it is building a "digital jigsaw" of experiences in which the power of the collective mind and experience has value.

The "digital geotourist" sees information as a social experience that can be a truly shared collective value to all. The idea of just collecting and presenting information in a place is only a small part of the total story and experience. Crowdsourcing has shown that collection of information can be a two-way process and that the collective experience can be shared.

To emphasize the business opportunity of tourists moving around a geographic location you only have to study some of the many surveys on buying behavior to see the comparison. For example a "shopping tourist" may spend on average £680 per visit compared to the average visiting tourist who spends £580.[27]

But the emergence of digital spaces that enable crowds to share experiences is more than communitization: it is a new kind of philosophy in thinking about digitally enabled experience. Rather than platforms directing the availability of community services through the web, it is a complete juxtaposition of this, saying that people living in a physical space have a say in the local information and experience as a kind of democratization of digital information. This means not receiving information passively about what to look at, but being able to change this by looking at things that matter to your community and making it matter to the way you want to live your life in the way of what the community can offer. Once a community decides what information is important to them and can surface this, suddenly a newcomer visiting that area can see more relevant information without having to go through the whole process of filtering out information to get to what they need. In that way, they can get the most relevant information, in the right place, in the right context, and can know that it is valuable based on a community approach. This helps speed up information in context search, avoiding extraneous searches in wikis or archives. Relevant community information can be accessed quickly and efficiently.

Given the explosion of data that is growing on the internet every second, this is an opportunity to put a human face to it, to make it a community. Using this philosophy, the digital geotourist can create "smart community geotourist information." This can be powerful in a city or enterprise location where citizens, visitors, and employees will be seeking only relevant information for their needs in those locations. The "map" has location-based tagged information that might include images, sound, text and be available in multi-languages so that a person may be physically in that location or can "visit" that place virtually. This crowd-driven information is different to social networking and crowdsourcing that provide instant social connections. Potentially any location, object, and event can be recorded and enhanced by this approach, using individuals and groups. Each person becomes a "micro-community" who can choose to share their experience with others or view others' community contributions and notifications. Similarly, cities, councils, and organizations can publish their own content to followers and communities of enthusiasts in order to create greater engagement and interests of relevance.

The digital geotourist can be about an object, a building, a place, a city, or even a country – or you may be on a particular journey through all of these. You may rent a car or use a hotel in this journey or simply want to experience living in the local community or to engage with the business marketplace. In a sense it brings this all together into a new kind of digital façade that is not about "going from A to B" but will tell you a story anywhere along and between those two points and the surrounding radius locations. This is an exciting new challenge and opportunity.

Digital Art, It's a Kind of Magic
Simon Bedford

A new kind of co-producer value

Exploring the ideas of physical space in the digital world has a different meaning when taken from a perspective of spectator crowds, the "viewing public" that occupy those spaces. Within this is the world of performance art and theater and the emerging use of digital technology that can augment and change the art form, the artist, and the audience perspectives.

There are many new lessons that can be learned and applied from this world of artistry and entertainment and how digital effects can conjure new experiences and senses.

There is a kind of co-producer relationship between the artist and the audience. A performance, whether physical or digital, is an act of communication and shared meaning. The artist without the audience, and an audience without the artist, is not a complete performance. There is a shared experience between the two that creates value for each participant.

In the digital space we have the opportunity to create this "shared performance" with artists and audience that may not be taking place in a physical space or time frame but connected across social network connections and recorded digital media that can be consumed and shared in different virtual spaces in real time of recorded playback.

There is a desire for collective consumption that we see many times in social media conversations or shared video clips on YouTube or Vine, for example. The online gaming world is replete with massive online experiences of gamers displaying their prowess with online virtual audiences "watching" the virtual world play out.

The audience can be used to co-create the show

Something new is happening between the physical and digital worlds. The audience is no longer a passive bystander looking on but can be a participant giving feedback in real time. In one form this can be social network traffic on a game media performance between like-minded viewing crowds. An online live streaming event of professional gamers on Twitch, for example, can get up to 20,000 consistent views in a single night from a crowd online from all over the world.[28] In other circumstance the virtual audience can actively give feedback in real time to affect the performance as it unfolds. In UK TV gameshows such as *The Million Pound Drop* and *The Bank Job*, there are mobile apps that enable these live interactive gameshows, where viewers compete with on-screen contestants.[29] In both cases, while the virtual audiences may be passively or activity involved in the performance, it is the digital medium that enables new kinds of social realities. This has not gone unnoticed by advertisers, who see the collecting of big data and social interaction as a way of persuading the Facebook generation (the millennials) to watch television. It is also potentially big business, where many existing and new digital strategies by companies realize the value of large digital crowds who can self-generate "noise" feedback about products and services. This in turn can directly drive physical and virtual commerce as brands and services can be promoted to these social crowds who share the experience.

Audience-generated content

Complex social structures and stories can emerge using the convergence of digital with physical performance art. Using digital technology such as cell phones and social media, live streaming networks with fast broadband infrastructures enable the start of dialogues with people who go through what performance artists call "narrative arcs." This varies by how much each person participates in the digital exchange. Many marketing efforts have parallel comparisons to theater producers using digital as it allows them to prepare the audience for the experience of the brand. This allows for a number of things to happen:

- It allows us to respond to audience reaction.
- It allows us to be more vacuous.
- It allows us to be expansive.
- It allows us to create themes.
- It allows us to get to know our audience.
- It allows and empowers the possibility to ask people to create their own "plots," to make audience-generated content

Digitization enables "live performance" and "live reaction" to coexist in the same moment by the use of clever digital imagery, digital sensors, and feedback that connect the artist or work of art with the audience as a collective crowd or for each individual.

Building asymmetry and engagement agency with digital

Digitization of content and communication in a "performance" enables us to create a "knowledge asymmetry" in our audience. In any drama there is an asymmetry in the story, which is the perception of the individual moment, or context, personal to each performance or event. As in real life, the audience is not living in a kind of cyclic, persistent "Truman show" – as in the 1998 film that depicted a personal life filmed unaware to a voyeuristic viewing public.[30] They coalesce and have "attention" for the three minutes, thirty minutes, or two hours that represent the duration of that performance moment. We can consider that this may yet be a possibility – to collect data on every conceivable event – but for our purposes here we are focusing on how the context of the event is exchanged. It is like an interactive book that can be constantly updated and written by a crowd collective, such as Wikipedia is a crowdsourced knowledge hub. Digitization enables content and experiences to be "collected" in a way not possible in physical experience – as seen on Facebook timelines that record a digital life history of events. But digitization is also creating a "live interactive show," a performance, but its very nature is as a medium of "agency" – physical, collaborative, and connected. In the design of digital spaces, how do these situations work? How do they relate to each other? What kind of agency do audiences find important?

- Agency in physical space: how we use sensors and devices to connect the "art" to the audience user.
- Agency in perspective: how we contextualize what the individual or crowd want or see from the performance. What does the artist or art want to convey to the audience?
- Agency for communication: the ability to collaborate and share the moment or knowledge.
- Agency over narrative: the ability to change and alter the flow of the performance.

In exploring these ideas with Simon Bedford, the concepts of "living art" and digital performance spaces can greatly enhance objects, rooms, buildings, and societal living spaces between the artist and audience experience.

There is a blurring of the lines between marketing and communications, experience and spaces, performance and engagement, and getting the audience and the artist engaging.

Simon says: "The life of the theater building during the day changes, in the morning, during the afternoon, and in the evening we have different visitors and 'audiences.' During the day the building is more a working space but in the evening it has a second life that has lots of people from outside the local area visiting to see a performance. There are also many other organizations outside the building, and organizations within the building space that all have different needs and uses of the space. Lots of people have no direct engagement with the artists in the theater or the works of art in the building. The magic of art is just there and it engages the senses and context. I see the use of digital as a way to bring out the magic of the art to engage in the public space."

There are three important aspects that involve thinking about designing digital spaces as magical, interactive places. First, that spaces are "living" and can change over a time period due to different visitors and usage needs. Second, the physical building and visitors have a sense of place that is local, but also of the area and region it belongs to. People and buildings can cluster local events but can also be a bridge to other places both physically and virtually. Third, it is about being able to bring the magic of the performance to the audience to help make new social and experiential connections using the power of digital.

Simon illustrated these points citing Watershed, a theater group based in Bristol, UK, which uses performance ideas that blend technology, interactive design, magic, and illusion.[31] They had recently done a "world first Magic Hack," much like a software hackathon but this time with magicians and technologists.[32]

Making the space playable

"The idea is to blend the basic objects, action, and performance with technology that can take ideas to make it more playable. The technology allows us as producers to create many variations of experience in a performance. We can create the 'wow factor,' we can 'charm' and make it more 'fun' to use and experience the living space."

Simon explains that the creativity of ideas can be incredibly varied. Some artists such as Sam Underwood, a musician and sound artist, can turn the very walls and fabric of a building into a musical instrument.[33] The building's metal support columns, wooden beams, tables, chairs, doors – anything can have a percussive feature. In effect you can "play the building" as you can a musical instrument by adding technology into these walls and objects to bring the building alive. It allows people to look at a building in a different way and to interact with it differently. For example, by adding body heat sensors in rooms that detect when a person walks into a specific area, this can be connected to color lighting and sound recordings that change the mood and ambience of the space. This means that objects, rooms, and the whole building and surrounding land become interactive spaces that work with humans and objects using visual, audio, haptic, and other feedback media to engage the sense and convey or share stories.

This idea of digital augmentation using art as a medium to engage people and audiences creates a special and unique opportunity to think about technology and art in new ways. Simon explains: "It is not limited to just the current timeline of today, we have developed for example a room that has historical recording from World War II. As a person enters the location, the signs, sounds, and content is 'played' in a choreographic way to tell a story of local history."

In this way, digital technology is not only the present and the future, but is also about the past. Another aspect is that it tells a story about not just the building and location, but the city and regional identity.

Simon says: "Small electronic devices can turn artworks into subtle or intrusive objects, for either passive or active engagement. By careful design and placement of sensors and art, it can be experience 'enhancing,' augmenting the human connection. It is important, however, that this is led by the connection more than the technology. That is, not to get overexcited with the technology and forget the human connection behind it."

These factors affect the quality of experience for individuals and crowds that make up formal and information audiences. Simon sees this as a longer-term trajectory of using technology: "Dynamic spaces need to be persistent to be able to create social value, aesthetic value, and brand commercial value. Digital technology helps understand the audience and to work closer with audiences. In the case of theater, this means matching the artistic program and spaces with the audience and the organizations that come together in the artistic spaces. It is helping to open up the whole environment, not just the objects, building, and performances, but also the walking pathways, roads, parks, and open spaces using art and technology. We can use data analytics to analyze how these spaces are used, of course, and improve things even further. But it is really about understanding that building (space) behaves in different ways depending on the people in the building. The context, sound, lighting, and imagery interact as a kind of intelligent workspace."

Toward a New Kind of Digital Privacy

Susan Wakenshaw

To define the subject of cyber security is itself a major undertaking but is a vitally important aspect of modern life that impacts physical and virtual living spaces, working relationships, and social and personal experience. The development of digital data that can record and track personal identity, images for facial recognition, and the voices and social behaviors of individuals and crowds have forever changed the physical world. The connectedness of the internet has become a paradox in being both a benefit as well as a bane of modern life, as the ecosystem of information in the internet can be used for good and bad activities. The linguist and political researcher Noam Chomsky described this phenomenon in "the internet could be a very positive step towards education, organization and participation in a meaningful society."[34] This suggests that the use of information and the internet should justify the means by which this information is obtained and used. Yet this may not always be for the good of individuals or for the digital enterprise, or wider society. High-profile examples that are cause for concern are such as the growth of online "trolls" in intellectual property, the use of social media in online bullying, the proliferation of distributed denial of service (DDOS) cyber attacks and cyber theft of industrial and national secrets. The World Economic Forum report in 2014 on risks and responsibilities in the hyperconnected world even described this as a potential "backlash to digitization" from the cyber threats.[35] While technological innovation is enabled, accelerating digitization and creating between US$9.6 trillion and US$21.6 trillion in global economic value of the remainder of the current decade represents 10% to 20% of global GDP. Cyber threats may remove an estimated US$3 trillion in potential value creation from these technologies unrealized. This may be just a reflection of the wider society and human behavior that is manifest in the digital ecosystem, yet the properties of digital mean that this is another important viewpoint that must be considered in the pursuit of building the digital enterprise.

The rise of digitization changes the meaning of privacy and how it may be defined to a person, as set out in Table 6.1.

The concept of privacy is elusive and ill-defined. The notion of privacy has been primarily discussed as the right to be left alone; limited access to the self; secrecy; control of personal information, personhood, and intimacy.[42] Due to the dominant notion of privacy as social withdrawal, information

TABLE 6.1 Definitions of privacy

Privacy	Definition
Privacy as rights	"The right[36] to be left alone."
Privacy as state	"A state of limited access to a person."[37]
Privacy as control	"Selective control of access to the self."[38]
Privacy as commodity	"Discrete package[39] ... that can be exchanged for something else."[40]
Privacy as property rights	"A right in individual to sell their personal data and capture some of the value their data has in the market."[41]

privacy has also centered on the individual's right or ability of control of information about oneself – from acquisition and disclosure to use. Indeed, the large majority of work on privacy has tended to focus on providing anonymity or on keeping personal information secret from hackers, governments, and faceless firms.

Personal data has become the new oil field in the 21st century. With the recognition of the value of personal data, the notion of privacy as commodity has also been suggested. Commodified personal data is a discrete package of personal information that can be exchanged for something else. Similarly, the property rights approach to privacy suggests giving individual property rights to personal data to promote information privacy in cyberspace. This approach would allow individuals to have rights to sell their personal data and capture some of the value of their data in the market. In the meantime, this approach would force company enterprises to internalize certain social costs of the widespread collection and use of personal data, and to make better decisions about what data to collect and what use to make of the data. In addition, in many situations in everyday life, people need and want to share information with others. Privacy work should focus on how to empower people with choice and informed consent so that they can share the right information, with the right people and services, in the right situations. Privacy, after all, entails much more than just control over a data trail, or even a set of data – privacy could be perceived as a dialectic and dynamic boundary regulation process between the individual (data subject/self), the others (firms and other individuals), and the data/information (premise).

As a dialectic process, a method for resolving disagreement through argument, privacy could be regulated by situations such as our own expectations and experiences, those of others with whom we interact, and social norms recognizing the need for both in a cultural and social context. As a dynamic process, privacy could be viewed as being under continuous negotiation and management of:

1. **Disclosure boundary:** what information might be disclosed under what circumstances, albeit with varying degrees of direct control.
2. **Identity boundary:** the display and maintenance of identity of parties on both sides of the information exchange.
3. **Temporality boundary:** boundaries associated with time – that is, where past, present, and future interpretations of, and actions upon, disclosed information are in tension. Privacy could be a fluid and malleable notion with a range of trust levels and needs.

Boundary regulations could enable privacy management between the self and others to be appropriate and fair by meeting the expectations, and following the norms and rules, to create zones of intimacy and inclusion that define and shape the relationships.

In the future we may have to define privacy in the digital world as a set of norms that are respectful of the boundaries in social, technological, and cultural norms that exist both in the physical and the virtual world. Regulators and practitioners seeking to establish legal and governmental controls will have to understand these new boundaries and norms: how the digital self as a person, their data – either direct or associated – and the separation to any other party access to this data will work together in the future.

Chapter Summary

We have explored some views of the digital era – how building a digital enterprise will change the way that physical and virtual spaces will interact and work with humans, objects, and devices. Some of these ideas are new in the sense that they are still emerging into the mainstream of commercial services, but like all the case studies, many are now a reality in many enterprises today.

Ahead is an unprecedented time of opportunity and growth ushered in by the internet. The challenges for practitioners with all new innovation will be to learn the new practice to make sense of the possible and to put into action the practical.

It is like Prospero in Shakespeare's *The Tempest* – looking on at the end of the Renaissance and the birth of the modern era. Prospero, the usurped Duke of Milan and sorcerer, finds himself gone from his kingdom where he is no longer needed. Cast away on an island he tries to manipulate the situation to get revenge but, after some acts of old magic, there is a realization of the merits of the new order for the benefit of the next generation – and the old magic is gone forever.

Today's practitioners are the purveyors of the new magic of the digital era.

Notes and References

/ Notes

Chapter 1 – Introduction – The Rise of Technological Ecosystems

1. Digital Economy: Innovate UK, Technology Strategy Board website, https://www.innovateuk.org/digital-economy.
2. Expert group on the taxation of the digital economy, "Digital Economy – Facts & Figures," Working Paper, Directorate General, Taxation and Customs Union. European Commission, March 2014, http://ec.europa.eu/taxation_customs/resources/documents/taxation/gen_info/good_governance_matters/digital/2014-03-13_fact_figures.pdf.
3. Compilation of comments received in response to request for input on tax challenges of the digital economy, "Base erosion and profit shift (BEPS) report," OECD. January 2014, http://www.oecd.org/ctp/comments-received-tax-challenges-digital-economy.pdf.
4. S. Vossoughi, "Today's Best Companies are Horizontally Integrated," Harvard Business Review Blogs, 14 December 2012, http://blogs.hbr.org/2012/12/todays-best-companies-are-hori/.
5. D. Robertson and K. Ulrich "Planning for product platforms," *Sloan Management Review*, 39 (1998), 19–31.
6. T. Sakao and M. Lindahl (Eds.), *Introduction to Product/Service-System Design* (London: Springer Publishing, 2009).
7. A. Hagiu and J. Wright, "Multi-sided platforms," Working Paper, Harvard Business School, 2011.
8. S. Ankaraju, "What is a multi-sided platform?," Get off the Drawing Board – Blog. 22 March 2010, http://www.getoffthedrawingboard.com/2010/03/22/what-is-a-multi-sided-platform/.
9. "Right to be forgotten" ruling (C-131/12), Fact Sheet, European Commission, http://ec.europa.eu/justice/data-protection/files/factsheets/factsheet_data_protection_en.pdf.
10. Open Internet, Federal Communications Commission FCC website, http://www.fcc.gov/openinternet; Internet live stats website, http://www.internetlivestats.

com/total-number-of-websites/; Frederic Lardinois, "Number of registered web-site domain names: Verisign Domain Name Industry Brief," *Techcrunch*, April 2013, http://techcrunch.com/2013/04/08/internet-passes-250m-registered-top-level-domain-names/; W3C Semantic Web activity, December 2013, website, http://www.w3.org/2001/sw/; Daniel Nations, "What is Web 2.0? How Web 2.0 Is defining society, about technology," about tech, http://webtrends.about.com/od/web20/a/what-is-web20.htm; T. Berners-Lee, J. Hendler, and O. Lassila, "The semantic web," *Scientific American Magazine*, 17 May 2001; J. Fowler and E. Rodd, "Web 4.0: The ultra-intelligent electronic agent is coming," big think, 28 March 2013, http://bigthink.com/big-think-tv/web-40-the-ultra-intelligent-electronic-agent-is-coming.

Chapter 2 – From Physical Workplaces to Digital Workspaces

1. J. Gaskin, N. Berente, K. Lyytinen, and Y. Yoo, "Towards generalizable socio-mateiral inquiry: A computational approach for zooming in and out of sociomaterial routines," *MIS Quarterly* 38(3) (September 2014), 849–871.
2. S. C. Levinso, *Pragmatics*. Cambridge: Cambridge University Press, 1983.
3. M. H. Kennedy and S. Mahapatra, "Information analysis for effective planning and control," *Sloan Management Review* (Winter 1975), 71–83; G. M. Marakas and J. J. Elam, "Semantic structuring in analyst acquisition and representation of facts in requirements analysis," *Information Systems Research* Vol. 9, No. 1 (1998), 37–63; P. Bera, A. Burton-Jones, and Y. Wand, "Research note: How semantics and pragmatics interact in understanding," *Information Systems Research*, Vol. 25, No. 2 (2014), 401–419.

Chapter 3 – The Business Impact of Digital Technologies

1. "Elliot Project – experimental living lab for the internet of things," EU FP7 STREP 258666, website, June 2013, http://www.elliot-project.eu/node/67.
2. Bosch und Siemens Hausgeräte (BSH) website, http://en.wikipedia.org/wiki/BSH_Bosch_und_Siemens_Hausger%C3%A4te.
3. BSH Homeconnect™ website, http://www.pocket-lint.com/news/128600-bosch-homeconnect-platform-will-offer-one-app-to-control-your-home-appliances-regardless-of-brand.
4. Charles Whitworth, "Smart appliances given a boost as Nest thermostat hits the shelves in the UK," loveenergysavings blog, April 2014, https://www.loveenergysavings.com/blog/2014/april/smart-appliances-given-a-boost-as-nest-thermostat-hits-the-shelves-in-the-uk/.
5. Lance Whitney, "Google closes $3.2 billion purchase of Nest," CNET, February 2014, http://www.cnet.com/uk/news/google-closes-3-2-billion-purchase-of-nest/.
6. "Alertme case study," UK Technology Fast 50, Deloitte website, http://www.deloitte.co.uk/fast50/winners/2013-case-studies/alertme.cfm.

7. Amsterdam Smart City website, http://amsterdamsmartcity.com/.
8. METRO Group, Wikipedia website, http://en.wikipedia.org/wiki/Metro_AG.
9. METRO Group website, http://www.metrogroup.de/internet/site/metrogroup/node/158350/Len/index.html.
10. United Parcel Service website, http://en.wikipedia.org/wiki/United_Parcel_Service.
11. Dave Barnes, "The Logistics Cloud," media interview for ConnectShip Technology Conference, UPS Press room 2011, http://www.pressroom.ups.com/About+UPS/UPS+Leadership/Speeches/David+Barnes/The+Logistics+Cloud.
12. Laura Stevens, "For UPS, e-commerce brings big business and big problems," *Wall Street Journal*, 11 September 2014, http://www.wsj.com/articles/for-ups-e-commerce-brings-big-business-and-big-problems-1410489642.
13. Marks & Spencer website, http://en.wikipedia.org/wiki/Marks_%26_Spencer.
14. M&S Plan A Sustainable Retail website, http://corporate.marksandspencer.com/plan-a.
15. Volvo Corporation, Wikipedia website, http://en.wikipedia.org/wiki/Volvo.
16. Volvo Cars, Wikipedia website, http://en.wikipedia.org/wiki/Volvo_Cars.
17. "Volvo case study" Exact target Marketing cloud, Salesforce.com website, http://www.salesforcemarketingcloud.com/resources/case-studies/volvo/.
18. The McDonald's Corporation, Wikipedia website, http://en.wikipedia.org/wiki/McDonald%27s.
19. Rosie Baker, "McDonald's preps crowdsourced Olympic ads," Marketingweek, 3 August 2012, http://www.marketingweek.com/2012/08/03/mcdonalds-preps-crowdsourced-olympic-ads/.
20. Russell Parsons, "McDonald's Preps 'Biggest' Games Campaign," Marketingweek, 27 June 2012, http://www.marketingweek.com/2012/06/27/mcdonalds-preps-biggest-games-campaign/.
21. SEGA, wikipedia website, http://en.wikipedia.org/wiki/Sega.
22. "SEGA game testing using colt and vmware hybrid cloud hosting environment," Vmware blog, 24 April 2012, http://blogs.vmware.com/vcloud/2012/04/another-vmware-cloud-sega-europe-runs-their-hybrid-cloud-on-vmware.html.
23. "Hilton revolutionizes hotel experience with digital check-in, room selection and customization, and check-out across 650,000-plus rooms at more than 4,000 properties worldwide," Hilton International Corporate News, 28 July 2014, http://news.hiltonworldwide.com/index.cfm/newsroom/detail/27192.
24. Lucas Mearian, "Hilton and Starwood hotel guests can soon unlock rooms with smartphones," Computerworld, November 2014, http://www.computerworld.com/article/2842645/hilton-and-starwood-hotel-guests-can-soon-unlock-rooms-with-smartphones.html.
25. Nike Inc wikipedia website, http://en.wikipedia.org/wiki/Nike,_Inc.

26. K. Valentine, "Ice, Lycra and Nike Plus – getting gamification and engagement right," Huffington Post, 20 February 2013, http://www.huffingtonpost.co.uk/kent-valentine/ice-lycra-and-nike-plus-g_b_2344144.html.

27. "MasterCard Introduces MasterPass – the future of digital payments.," MasterCard newsroom, 25 February 2013, http://newsroom.mastercard.com/press-releases/mastercard-introduces-masterpass-the-future-of-digital-payments/.

28. https://www.telushealth.co/health-solutions/patient-and-consumer-health-platforms/products/home-health-monitoring/.

29. Claire Swedberg, "Farmers develop RFID system to protect children, animals," *RFID Journal*, August 2011, http://www.rfidjournal.com/articles/view?8691.

30. R. Beneito-Montagut, D. Shaw, and C. Brewster, "Disaster 2.0, emergency management agencies use and adoption of Web 2.0," Aston University, UK, University of Warwick, UK, EU Commission funded, 2013, http://www.disaster20.eu/wordpress/wp-content/uploads/2014/03/D2_SM_Report-170314.pdf.

31. "West Yorkshire fire and rescue service is using satellite broadband and wireless video to transform the way it manages communications at incidents," Excelerate website, http://www.excelerate-group.com/case-studies/west-yorkshire-fire-and-rescue-service/.

32. Open Data , Wikipedia website, http://en.wikipedia.org/wiki/Open_data.

33. US Government Open Data website, https://www.data.gov/.

34. EU Open Data Portal website, http://open-data.europa.eu/en/data/.

35. Ghana Open Data Initiative website, http://data.gov.gh/.

36. Open Data Portal Government of Canada website, http://open.canada.ca/en.

37. Data.go.jp Japanese Government Open Data Portal website, http://www.data.go.jp/.

38. UK Government Open Data Portal – Beta website, http://data.gov.uk/.

39. "UK GEMINI v2.2 Specification for discovery metadata for geospatial data resources," AGI Association for geographical information website, http://www.agi.org.uk/storage/standards/uk-gemini/GEMINI2.2.pdf.

40. "Maccabi Healthcare Services – our Healthcare system," Maccabi website, http://www.maccabi4u.co.il/1781-he/Maccabi.aspx.

41. Christopher James, Director of Digital Health, University of Warwick, UK, October 2014.

42. "Maccabi Healthcare Services delivers coordinated care to over 1.9 million members," Intel Digital health coordinated care white paper, http://www.intel.co.uk/content/dam/www/public/us/en/documents/white-papers/coordinated-healthcare-from-maccabi-and-intel-paper.pdf.

43. U-BIOPRED website, http://www.europeanlung.org/en/projects-and-research/projects/u-biopred/home.

44. Anna Laura van der Laan and Marienne Boenink, "Beyond bench and bedside: Disentangling the concept of translational research," Abstract, Springer link December 2012, http://link.springer.com/article/10.1007/s10728-012-0236-x.

45. Panos Panagiotopoulos, "Twitter has been important for emergency management in the UK local government, especially during the 2011 riots," LSE blog http://blogs.lse.ac.uk/politicsandpolicy/twitter-has-been-important-for-emergency-management-in-the-uk-local-government-especially-during-the-2011-riots/.
46. "P&G Connect + Develop" website, http://www.pgconnectdevelop.com/home/pg_open_innovation.html.
47. "P&G and CircleUp partnership crowdfunding" website, http://www.pgconnectdevelop.com/home/stories/cd-stories/20130125-pg-and-circleup-partnership.html.
48. Chargepoint website, http://www.chargepoint.com/.
49. "RFID Integrated Solutions System optimizes maintenance efficiency," Boeing, Aero QTR_01.12, http://www.boeing.com/commercial/aeromagazine/articles/2012_q1/2/.
50. Statpro website, http://www.statpro.com/.
51. "Data breach Investigations report," Verizon, 2014, http://www.verizonenterprise.com/DBIR/2014/.
52. Elizabeth Palermo, "What is a Zero-Day Exploit?," Tom's Guide, November 2013, http://www.tomsguide.com/us/zero-day-exploit-definition,news-17903.html.
53. Zero Day Initiative website,http://www.zerodayinitiative.com/.

Chapter 4 – Techniques for Building Effective Digital Business Models

1. "Accelerating the growth of ecommerce in FMCG," Kantar Global FMCG ecommerce Survey, 16 June 2014, http://www.kantarworldpanel.com/global/News/Accelerating-the-Growth-of-Ecommerce-in-FMCG.
2. Cooper Smith, "Shopping cart abandonment: online retailers' biggest headache is actually a huge opportunity," business insider, 4 March 2015, http://www.businessinsider.com/heres-how-retailers-can-reduce-shopping-cart-abandonment-and-recoup-billions-of-dollars-in-lost-sales-2014-4#ixzz3Jiib4pCc.
3. "£91 billion spent online in 2013," IMRG Capgemini e-Retail Sales Index, Press release, Capgemini website, January 2014, http://www.uk.capgemini.com/news/uk-news/ps91-billion-spent-online-in-2013-imrg-capgemini-e-retail-sales-index.
4. David Sheldon, "How retailers will deliver the omni-channel experience," *Business Reporter*, 22 February 2015,http://business-reporter.co.uk/2015/02/22/how-retailers-will-deliver-the-omni-channel-experience/.
5. Brian Burke, "Gartner redefines gamification," 4 April 2014, http://blogs.gartner.com/brian_burke/2014/04/04/gartner-redefines-gamification/.
6. Mark Elkins, "Coca-Cola accelerates online sales growth with digital shopper marketing," *Retail Times*, 19 October 2012, http://www.retailtimes.co.uk/coca-cola-accelerates-online-sales-growth-with-digital-shopper-marketing/.

7. Vouchercloud website, http://www.vouchercloud.com/.

8. CCE PRO avec vous website, https://cokecce.secure.force.com/ProAvecVous/.

9. CCE PRO mobile app, Apple app store website, https://itunes.apple.com/fr/app/pro-avec-vous/id622307337?mt=8.

10. "CCE Combining Profit and purpose survey" Coke CCE website, October 2014, http://www.cokecce.com/news-and-events/news/new-study-finds-the-future-of-successful-business-is-a-combination-of-profit-and-purpose

11. Financial Sector statistics, the World Bank website, http://data.worldbank.org/about/world-development-indicators-data/financial-sector.

12. Stijn Claessens, "Competition in the financial sector: overview of competition policies," IMF Working Paper, IMF, 2009, http://www.imf.org/external/pubs/ft/wp/2009/wp0945.pdf.

13. Mark Rennie Davis, Jeff Stroud, and Steven Paese, "MasterCard advisor US insights. EMV: The catalyst for a new US payment ecosystem." MasterCard website, http://www.mastercard.us/mchip-emv.html.

14. "How secure are RFID contactless payments?," Feature, infosecurity, 20 November 2012, https://www.infosecurity-magazine.com/magazine-features/how-secure-are-contactless-payments/.

15. "Retailers seek alternatives to EMV to avoid fraud liability, let's talk payments," LTP Team, 17 October 2014, http://letstalkpayments.com/retailers-seek-alternatives-emv-avoid-fraud-liability/.

16. Gramm–Leach–Bliley Act, FTC Government website, http://business.ftc.gov/privacy-and-security/gramm-leach-bliley-act.

17. Stripe website, https://stripe.com/about/press.

18. James Anderson, "MasterCard Digital Enablement Service (MDES): making digital payments happen," MasterCard website, September 2014, http://newsroom.mastercard.com/2014/09/10/mastercard-digital-enablement-service-mdes-making-digital-payments-happen/.

19. EMV website, http://www.emvco.com/.

20. Sydney Ember, "New York regulator outlines changes to Bitcoin rules," *New York Times*, 18 December 2014, http://dealbook.nytimes.com/2014/12/18/new-york-regulator-outlines-changes-to-bitcoin-rules/?_r=0.

21. "Internet of things IoT," Cisco website, http://www.cisco.com/web/solutions/trends/iot/overview.html.

22. KPIT corporate website, http://www.kpit.com/.

23. "KPIT ReVolo^{TM} plug-in hybrid car management system," KPIT website, http://revolo.kpit.com/about.html.

24. "Tesla Motors – Premium Electric Cars," tesla website, http://www.teslamotors.com/.

25. Damon Lavrinc, "The Tesla model S raises the suspension based on location," Jalopnik, 19 September 2014, http://jalopnik.com/the-tesla-model-s-raises-the-suspension-based-on-locati-1636877061.

26. "Software 6.0 update," Tesla blog website, 19 September 2014, http://www. teslamotors.com/blog/software-v60.

27. "utonomous Vehicles ," KPIT Report, TechnTalk@KPIT, Vol. 6. No. 4 (October–December 2013), Business Models http://www.kpit.com/downloads/tech-talk/tech-talk-oct-dec-2013.pdf.

28. KPIT Product Data Management Seminar Oct 2014,Jaguar Land Rover Muscum, UK.

29. "Global travel & tourism industry defies economic uncertainty by outperforming the global economy in 2012 – and predicted to do it again in 2013," Hospitalitynet, World Travel and Tourism Council (WTTC), http://www.hospitalitynet.org/news/4059643.html.

30. Hilton International global website,http://www.hiltonworldwide.com/about/.

31. "Second Quarter business results" – Hilton International," businesswire, 30 June 2014, http://www.businesswire.com/news/home/20140801005062/en/Hilton-Worldwide-Reports-Strong-Quarter-2014-Results#.VDFA-_ldWSo.

32. "Hilton revolutionizes hotel experience with digital check-in, room selection and customization, and check-out across 650,000-plus rooms at more than 4,000 properties worldwide," Hilton International Press Release, 28 July 2014, http://news.hiltonworldwide.com/index.cfm/newsroom/detail/27192.

33. "Hilton International Global Privacy Policy – Code of Practice," Hilton website http://hhonors3.hilton.com/en/promotions/privacy-policy/english.html.

34. "Partnership development for Hilton Hotels: An open innovation solution to help Hilton Hotels develop its business," case study, ideaconnection, http://www.ideaconnection.com/open-innovation-success/Partnership-Development-for-Hilton-Hotels-00140.html.

35. FlyerTalk website, http://www.flyertalk.com/.

36. "Economic sectors," Wikipedia website, http://en.wikipedia.org/wiki/Economic_sector.

37. "World Economic Outlook Database analysis," IMF report, April 2012, IMF, http://www.imf.org/external/pubs/ft/weo/2012/01/weodata/index.aspx.

38. "Digital Government, North America,"Whitehouse Government website, http://www.whitehouse.gov/sites/default/files/omb/egov/digital-government/digital-government.html.

39. "EU Commission digital agenda for Europe," European commission website, http://ec.europa.eu/digital-agenda/en/news/gunther-h-oettinger-commissioner-digital-economy-and-society-portfolio.

40. Carl Rubinstein, "China's government goes digital," *The Atlantic*, 29 November 2014, http://www.theatlantic.com/international/archive/2012/11/chinas-government-goes-digital/265493/.

41. "UN e-Government Survey 2014," UNPACS website, http://unpan3.un.org/egovkb/en-us/Reports/UN-E-Government-Survey-2014.

42. "Base erosion and profit shift (BEPS) report" OECD, January 2014, http://www.oecd.org/ctp/comments-received-tax-challenges-digital-economy.pdf.

43. Emily Young, "Davos 2014: Google's Schmidt warning on jobs," BBC online 23 January 2014, http://www.bbc.co.uk/news/business-25872006.

44. Carl Frey and Michael Osborne, "The future of employment: How susceptible are jobs to computerization," Oxford Martin Institute, UK, September 2013, http://www.oxfordmartin.ox.ac.uk/downloads/academic/The_Future_of_Employment.pdf.

45. Iestyn Williams and Heather Shearer, "Appraising public value: past, present and futures," public administration, doi: 10.1111/j.1467-9299.201.01942.x 2011 http://www.birmingham.ac.uk/Documents/college-social-sciences/social-policy/HSMC/publications/2011/appraising-public-value.pdf.

46. John Benington, "From private choice to public value?" Institute of Governance & Public Management (IGPM) Warwick Business School, UK, http://www.cihm.leeds.ac.uk/document_downloads/John_BeningtonPrivate_Choice_to_Public_Value.pdf.

47. John Mueller and Mark Stewart, "Responsible counterterrorism policy," Policy Analysis, CATO Institute, September 2014, http://object.cato.org/sites/cato.org/files/pubs/pdf/pa755.pdf.

48. Maia Beresford, "Smart people, smart places, realizing digital local government," NLGN New local government network, UK, March 2014.

49. "Market analysis, land and property," Local Enterprise Partnership LEP, Liverpool city region UK, SuperPort, NAI Global Commercial real estate services, Worldwide, March 2014.

50. Hariskesh Nair, Jean-Pierre Dubé, and Pradeep Chintagunta, "Accounting for primary and secondary demand effects with aggregate data," *Marketing Science*, Vol. 24, No. 3 (Summer 2005), 440–460.

51. "Primary and discrete demand definitions," Business Dictionary website, http://www.businessdictionary.com/definition/primary-demand.html.

52. "Connected cities – the link to growth," City growth Commission, UK Government, 16 July 2014, http://www.citygrowthcommission.com/publication/connected-cities-the-link-to-growth/.

53. "Liverpool city region visitor economy strategy to 2020," October 2009, figures updated February 2011. VisitLiverpool, UK, http://www.knowsley.gov.uk/pdf/LC09_LiverpoolCityRegion-VisitorEconomyStrategy2020.pdf.

54. Gibbons, Steve, Henry G. Overman, and Max Nathan, "Evaluating spatial policies," SERC Policy Papers, SERCPP012. Spatial Economics Research Centre, London School of Economics and Political Science, 2014.

55. Max Nathan and Henry G. Overman, "Agglomeration, clusters, and industrial policy," *Oxford Review of Economic Policy*, Vol. 29, No. 2 (2013), 383–404.

56. Alan Harding, "What polices for globalising cities," Club De Madrid, OECD March, 2007 http://www1.oecd.org/gov/regional-policy/49680222.pdf.

57. "Stockab, Municipal wide fibre optical network for the city of Stockholm," Stockholm city website, http://www.stokab.se/In-english/.

58. "The sharp project," Manchester, UK, website, http://www.thesharpproject.co.uk/.

59. "The Haldane principle", www.parliment.uk website, http://www.publications. parliament.uk/pa/cm200809/cmselect/cmdius/168/16807.htm.

60. "Lean", Wikipedia website,http://en.wikipedia.org/wiki/Lean_manufacturing.

61. "Unipart Logistics GLAS – Global Logistics Application Suite," Unipart Logistics website, http://unipartlogistics.com/services/supply-chain-systems/global-logistics-application-suite/.

62. "DHL Resilience360™," DHL website, http://www.dhl.com/content/dam/downloads/g0/logistics/resilience360/dhl_resilience_360_flyer_en.pdf.

63. DHL Global website, http://www.dhl.com/en.html.

64. Alex Hern, "German DHL launches first commercial drone delivery service," *Guardian*, 25 September 2014, http://www.theguardian.com/technology/2014/sep/25/german-dhl-launches-first-commercial-drone-delivery-service.

65. "Augmented reality in logistics – Changing the way we see logistics – a DHL perspective," DHL website 2014, http://www.dhl.com/content/dam/downloads/g0/about_us/logistics_insights/csi_augmented_reality_report_290414.pdf.

66. "Translation research," Webster dictionary website, http://www.merriam-webster.com/dictionary/translational%20research.

67. "Health Informatics," ehow website, http://www.ehow.com/facts_5672206_definition-health-informatics.html.

68. "Medical Informatics," medical dictionary the free dictionary website, http://medical-dictionary.thefreedictionary.com/Medical+informatics.

69. "Mi More Independent," website, NHS Liverpool Clinical Commissioning Group, UK, http://www.moreindependent.co.uk/.

70. "Technology Strategy Board, the UK's Innovation Agency," website, https://connect.innovateuk.org/web/dallas.

71. "The SmartHouse demonstrator – Mi," website, NHS Liverpool Clinical Commissioning Group, UK, http://www.moreindependent.co.uk/life-enhancements/smarthouse/.

72. "Philips EncoreAnywhere™," Philips Healthcare website, http://www.healthcare.philips.com/main/homehealth/sleep/encoreanywhere/default.wpd.

73. Sybo Dijkstra, "Clinicians in contact home and away," *Health Care Journal* Philips, 3 June 2014, http://www.hsj.co.uk/Journals/2014/06/03/z/o/s/Telehealth-special-report.pdf.

74. Plot Projects website, http://www.plotprojects.com/?utm_expid=66248451-11. Cw6ggXUqTpukf9MyY0eJLw.0&utm_referrer=http%3A%2F%2Fwww.plot-projects.com%2Fgeofencing-product%2F%3Fgclid%3DCj0KEQiA8MSkBRCP 5LaRlcOAusMBEiQAiqldktKFDzxtCLi-113szWCYNQvz5t-1zcuJIJMNmkPB TMYaAlLD8P8HAQ.

75. "USEFIL, unobtrusive smart environments for independent living," FP7-ICT-2011-7 EU, https://www.usefil.eu/.

76. Henfridsson and Bygstad, "The Generative Mechanisms of Digital Infrastructure Evolution,"*MISQ*, Vol. 37, No. 3 (2013), 907–931, http://misq.org/the-generative-

mechanisms-of-digital-infrastructure-evolution.html?SID=7ntdq5gqhaegskupgq omh3l9j4.

77. Youngjin Yoo, "Digitization and unbounded innovation," slideshare website, http://www.slideshare.net/yxy23yoo.

Chapter 5 – How to Build the Right Digital Enterprise for Payoff and Monetization

1. "TOGAF® 9.1 › Part I: Introduction › Definitions," website, The Open Group http://pubs.opengroup.org/architecture/togaf9-doc/arch/chap03.html.

2. John Hagel III and Marc Singer, "Unbundling the corporation," *Harvard Business Review*, March 1999, https://hbr.org/1999/03/unbundling-the-corporation/ar/1.

3. Tilson, Lyytinen, and Sorensen, "Research commentary: digital infrastructures: the missing is research agenda," *Information Systems Research*, Vol. 21, No. 4 (2010), 748–759, http://www.uio.no/studier/emner/matnat/ifi/INF5210/h14/pensumliste/articles/tilson-et-al-2010.pdf.

4. Yoo, Henfridsson, and Lyytinen, "The new organizing logic of digital innovation: an agenda for information systems research," Journal Information Systems Research, Vol. 21, No. 4 (December 2010), 724–735, http://dl.acm.org/citation.cfm?id=1923786.

5. Youngjin Yoo, "How companies innovate and evolve with digital technology?," Fox Idea Marketplace Community blog, 15 November 2013, http://www.fox.temple.edu/posts/2013/11/companies-innovate-evolve-digital-technology/.

6. Brandon Butler, "Microsoft goes all-in on hybrid cloud with Azure-in-a-box. CEO Satya Nadella says Microsoft is in cloud computing game for the long haul," Networkworld, 20 October 2014, http://www.networkworld.com/article/2836373/cloud-computing/microsoft-goes-all-in-on-hybrid-cloud-with-azure-in-a-box.html.

7. Henfridsson and Bygstad, "The generative mechanisms of digital infrastructure evolution," *MISQ*, Vol. 37, No. 3 (2013), 907–931, http://misq.org/the-generative-mechanisms-of-digital-infrastructure-evolution.html?SID=7ntdq5gqh aegskupgqomh3l9j4.

8. "Sociotechnical system definition," Wikipedia website, http://en.wikipedia.org/wiki/Sociotechnical_system.

9. "Venture capital investing stages," Investopedia website, http://www.investopedia.com/exam-guide/cfa-level-1/alternative-investments/venture-capital-investing-stages.asp.

10. "7 scaling strategies Facebook used to grow to 500 million users, high scalability," highscalability blog, 7 August 2010, http://highscalability.com/blog/2010/8/2/7-scaling-strategies-facebook-used-to-grow-to-500-million-us.html

11. Irene Ng, "Value & worth: creating new markets in the digital economy", 20 August 2012, InnovorsaPress.

Chapter 6 – Reflections on Impact of Digital Practice

1. Susan Y. L. Wakenshaw, Will Venters, Irene Ng, C. L. Lloyd, and D. Ashley, "Sense-making of consumer wellbeing in information technology-enabled services from a relational ontology position," WMG Service Systems Research Group Working Paper Series, 2013, http://wrap.warwick.ac.uk/55454/1/WRAP_Wakenshaw 1073733-wmg-090713-wp-13_sensemaking_of_consumer_wellbeing.pdf.
2. "Existentialism," Wikipedia website http://en.wikipedia.org/wiki/Existentialism.
3. Anthony Giddens "The theory of structuration," theory website http://www.theory.org.uk/giddens2.htm.
4. Evgeny Morozov, "The rise of data and the death of politics," *Guardian*, 20 July 2014, http://www.theguardian.com/technology/2014/jul/20/rise-of-data-death-of-politics-evgeny-morozov-algorithmic-regulation.
5. "The birth of the Web," CERN Web site http://home.web.cern.ch/topics/birth-web.
6. John Markoff, "Entrepreneurs See a Web Guided by Common Sense," *New York Times,* 12 November 2006, http://www.nytimes.com/2006/11/12/business/12web.html?pagewanted=all&_r=0.
7. John Mair, Richard Lance Keeble, with Paul Bradshaw and Teodora Beleaga (Eds.), "Data Journalism: Mapping the future," Arima Publishing, 10 January 2014.
8. "The Promotion, protection and enjoyment of human rights on the internet." A/HRC/20/L.13, Human Rights Council United Nationals 20th Session. 29/06/2012 http://daccess-dds-ny.un.org/doc/UNDOC/LTD/G12/147/10/PDF/G1214710.pdf?OpenElement.
9. "BBC World survey in 2010 on the right to Internet Access," BBC News 2010 http://news.bbc.co.uk/1/shared/bsp/hi/pdfs/08_03_10_BBC_internet_poll.pdf.
10. FlyingBinary website, http://www.flyingbinary.com/#aboutus.
11. "UK Government Open Data Sets," UK Government website http://data.gov.uk/data-request.
12. "Digital Marketplace," UK Government website https://www.digitalmarketplace.service.gov.uk/.
13. Paul Nieuwenhuis, "An ecosystem approach to the transition to new business models – an automotive industry case study," in *Proceedings: Sustainable Consumption and Production: Framework for Action*, ch. 8, 10–11 March 2008, Brussels, Belgium, Conference of the Sustainable Consumption Research Exchange, (SCORE!) network, supported by the EU's 6th Framework Programme.
14. Thomas Dicke, "Franchising in America, the development of a business method 1840 – 1980," in *Agent to Dealer* (Durham, NC: University of North Caroline Press, 1992), ch.2.
15. Dan T. Jones, "Maturity and crisis in the European car industry: structural change and public policy," Sussex European Papers 8, Sussex European Research Centre, University of Sussex, 1981.

16. J. Womack, D. Jones, and D. Roos (Eds.), *The Machine that Changed the World* (New York: Rawson Associates, 2007).

17. Ian Murphy, "Cars are the next big developer platform," *Future Insights*, 13 February 2014, http://www.futureinsights.com/home/cars-are-the-next-big-developer-platform.html.

18. Payl Taylor, "AT&T leads the charge into 'connected' cars," *Financial Times*, 17 January 2014, http://www.ft.com/cms/s/0/5d1ea1c6-7b75-11e3-a2da-00144feabdc0.html#axzz3JLRNcQvY.

19. Tony Dutzik and Travis Madsen, "A new way to go, the transportation apps and vehicle-sharign; tools that are giving more americans the freedom to drive less," Frontier Group; U.S. PIRG Education Fund Frontier Group, Fall 2013.

20. Nissan Leaf website, http://www.nissan.co.uk/leaf-reservation/get-it/closed.htm.

21. "IoT towards ecosystems," University of Helsinki National IoT Program Finland website, http://www.internetofthings.fi/.

22. Dipesh Gadher "It's Queen Vic, talking statue, on the line," *Sunday Times*, 6 July 2014, http://www.thesundaytimes.co.uk/sto/news/uk_news/article1431008.ece?shareToken=a2f72c0837e8c9da0b7b948b058cb24e.

23. Google streetview website, https://www.google.com/maps/views/?gl=gb.

24. OpenStreetMap website, https://www.openstreetmap.org/#map=5/51.500/-0.100.

25. Mapbox – build a custom map website, https://www.mapbox.com/.

26. Moves app – activity diary of your life – website, https://www.moves-app.com/.

27. "Visit Britain – Marketing Britain overseas and developing the visitor economy," Visit Britain website, UK National Tourist Board, http://www.visitbritain.org/mediaroom/pressreleases/shoppingisgreat.aspx.

28. Cameron Keng, "Online streaming and professional gaming is a $300,000 career choice," *Forbes*, 21 April 2014, http://www.forbes.com/sites/cameronkeng/2014/04/21/online-streaming-professional-gaming-is-a-300000-career-choice/.

29. Maggie Brown, "TV looks to new era of interactive game shows to lure the Facebook generation," *Guardian*, 5 February 2012, http://www.theguardian.com/tv-and-radio/2012/feb/05/interactive-quizzes-tv-online.

30. "The Truman Show," IMDb website, http://www.imdb.com/title/tt0120382/.

31. "Magicians in residence," Watershed, iSHED, website, http://www.watershed.co.uk/ished/magic.

32. "What happened at the world's first magic Hack," Watershed, iSHED, website http://www.watershed.co.uk/ished/projects/2013/magicians-in-residence/journal/what-happened-at-the-worlds-first-magic-hack.

33. Sam Underwood, musician, sound artist, and artist-in-residence at THSH Birmingham, UK, www.mrunderwood.co.uk.

34. The Noam Chomsky website, http://www.chomsky.info/.

35. "Risk and responsibility in a hyperconnected world," Insight Report, World Economic Forum WEF in collaboration with McKinsey & Company January 2014, http://www3.weforum.org/docs/WEF_RiskResponsibility_Hyperconnected World_Report_2014.pdf.

36. Warren and Brandeis, "The right to privacy," *Harvard Law Review*, Vol. 193, No. 4 (1890).

37. For a discussion of the dynamics resulting from online media on reputation, see Daniel Solove, *The Future of Reputation* (New Haven, CT and London: Yale University Press, 2007).

38. Ferdinand D. Schoeman (Ed.), *Philosophical Dimensions of Privacy: An Anthology* (Cambridge: Cambridge University Press, 1984).

39. Leysia Palen and Paul Doursih, CHI, "Unpacking 'privacy' for a networked world," 5–10 April 2003, Fort Lauderdale, Florida, https://www.cs.colorado.edu/~palen/Papers/palen-dourish.pdf.

40. Paul M. Schwartz, "Property, privacy, and personal data," Berkley Law Scholarship Repository, 1 January 2003, http://scholarship.law.berkeley.edu/cgi/viewcontent.cgi?article=1068&context=facpubs.

41. Pamela Samuelson, "Privacy as intellectual property?," Working Paper, Information Management and of Law, University of California at Berkeley, http://people.ischool.berkeley.edu/~pam/papers/doc/privasip_draft.doc.

42. Daniel J. Solove, "Conceptualizing privacy," *California Law Review*, Vol. 90, No. 4 (2002); Scott Lederer, Jason I. Hong, Anind K. Dey, and James A. Landay, "Personal privacy through understanding and action: five pitfalls for designers," Carnegie Mellon University, Research Showcase @ CMU, 2004, http://repository.cmu.edu/cgi/viewcontent.cgi?article=1077&context=hcii.

International Technical and Business Standards Bodies and Suggested Further Reading

The following link provides a selection of active standards bodies in the field of digital enterprise and digital ecosystems development. You can find details of the key themes at http://building-the-digital-enterprise.com/international-technical-and-business-standards-bodies-and-suggested-futher-reading.

Index

Printed and bound by CPI Group (UK) Ltd, Croydon, CR0 4YY